BIRDS
of BRITISH COLUMBIA

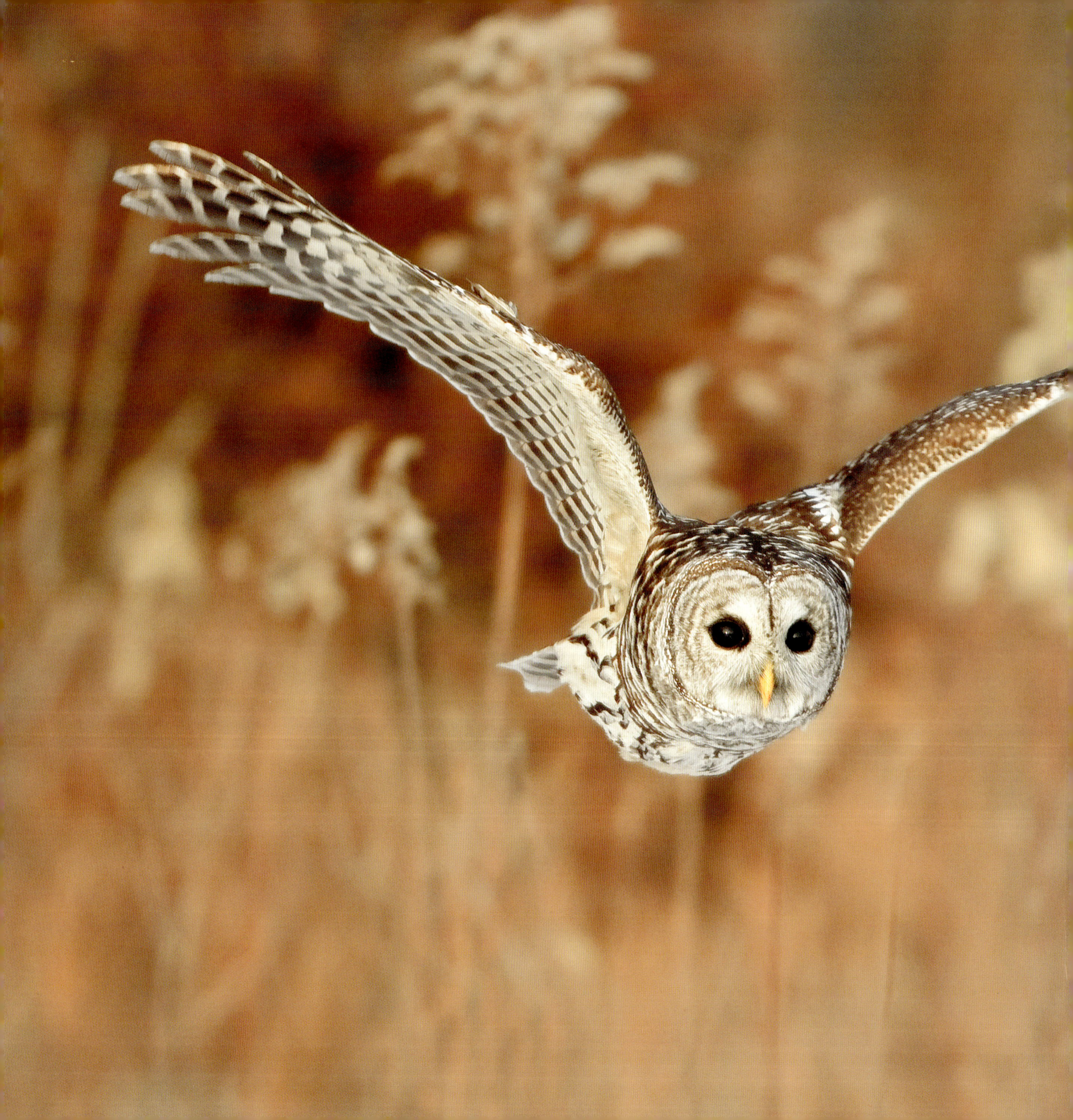

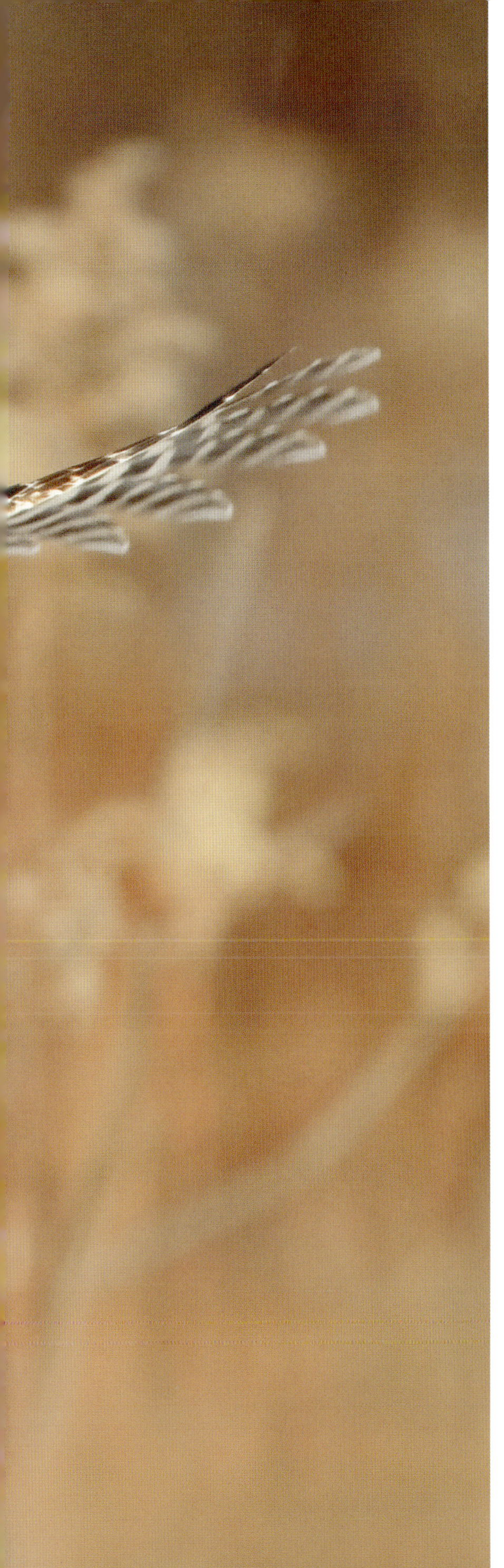

BIRDS

of BRITISH COLUMBIA

A Photographic Journey

Glenn Bartley

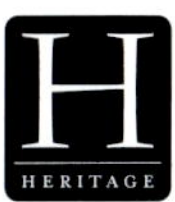

VICTORIA · VANCOUVER · CALGARY

Heritage House Publishing Company Ltd.
heritagehouse.ca

LIBRARY AND ARCHIVES CANADA CATALOGUING IN PUBLICATION

Bartley, Glenn
Birds of British Columbia: a photographic journey / Glenn Bartley.
Also issued in electronic format.
ISBN 978-1-927051-69-6
1. Birds—British Columbia—Pictorial works. 2. Birds—British Columbia—Identification. I. Title.

QL685.5.B7B37 2013 598.09711 C2012-906245-6

Edited by Kate Scallion
Proofread by Karla Decker
Cover and book design by Jacqui Thomas
Cover photos: Peregrine Falcon (front), Steller's Jay (back) and Common Yellowthroat (front flap) by Glenn Bartley
Frontispiece photo: Barred Owl by Glenn Bartley
All photos by Glenn Bartley except where noted.

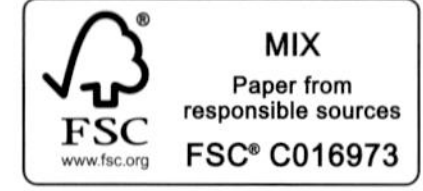

This book was produced using FSC®-certified, acid-free paper, processed chlorine free and printed with vegetable-based inks.

Heritage House acknowledges the financial support for its publishing program from the Government of Canada through the Canada Book Fund (CBF), Canada Council for the Arts and the province of British Columbia through the British Columbia Arts Council and the Book Publishing Tax Credit.

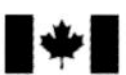
Canadian Heritage Patrimoine canadien

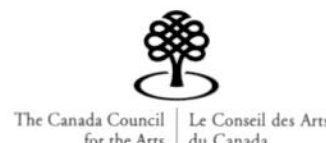

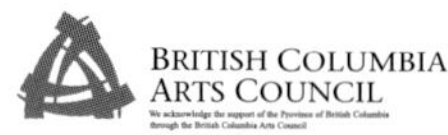

17 16 15 14 13 1 2 3 4 5

Printed in China

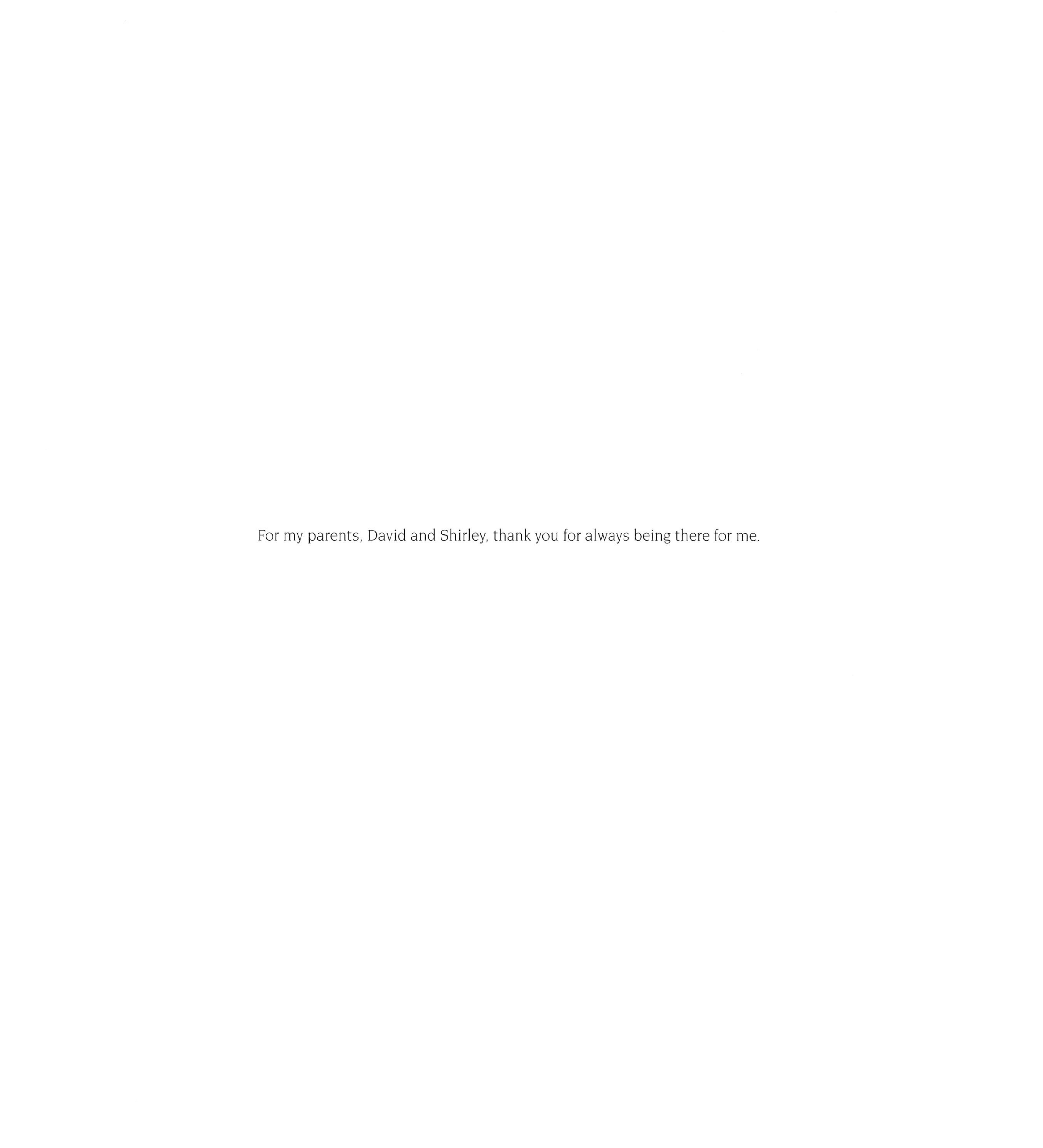

For my parents, David and Shirley, thank you for always being there for me.

BIRD HABITATS OF BRITISH COLUMBIA

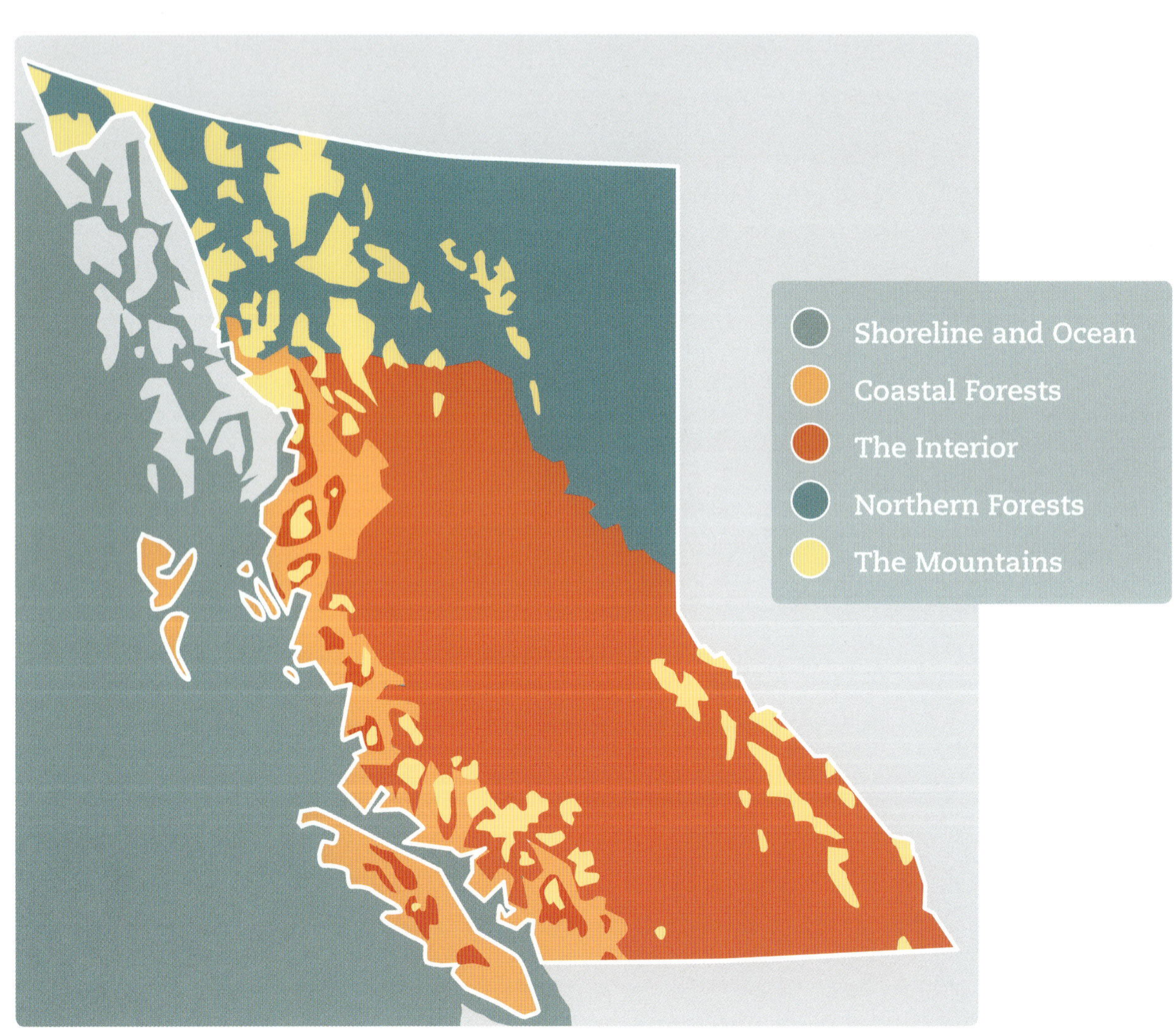

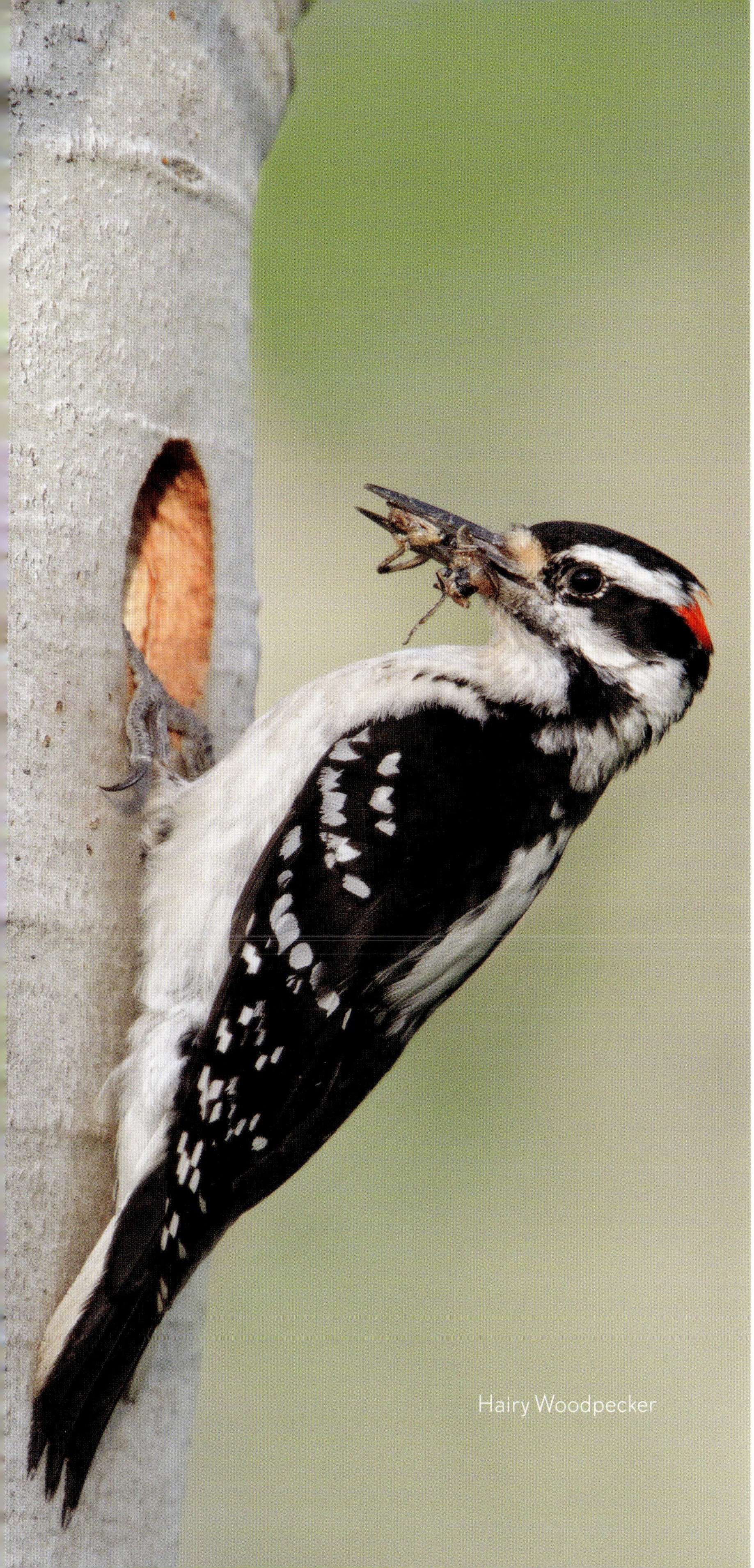

Hairy Woodpecker

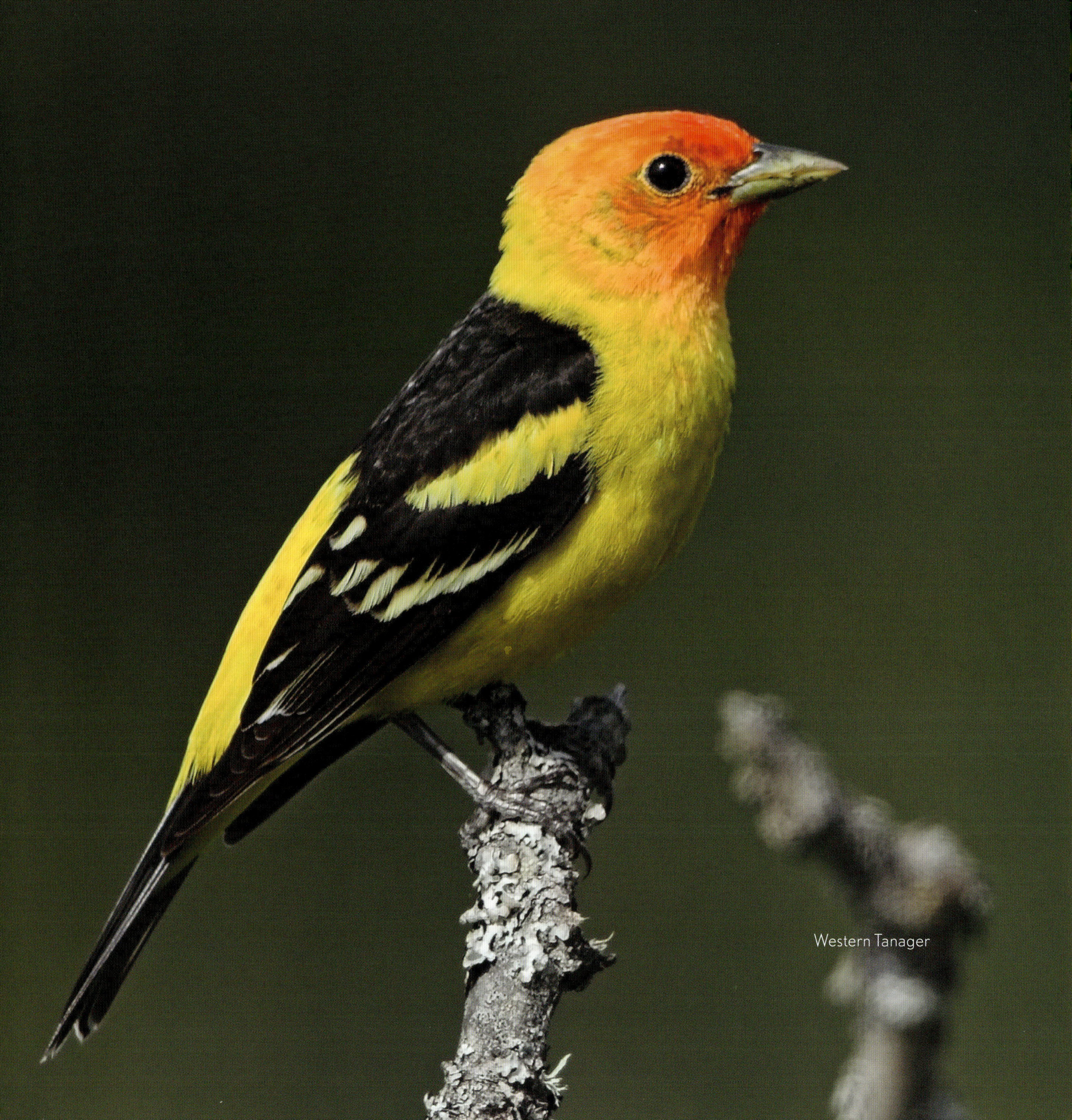

Western Tanager

Introduction

There is no question that British Columbia is a fantastic place to be a birdwatcher. This province is blessed to have the greatest bird diversity in all of Canada. Approximately 300 species of birds regularly breed within the province, and this is attributed in large part to the extremely diverse biogeography. Lush rainforests, miles of rugged coastline, sweeping grasslands, high mountains, alpine meadows and the vast northern forests—British Columbia has a lot to offer to any keen naturalist. When I first moved to this province in 2006, I was overwhelmed by the natural beauty that abounds here; it was so different from what I had left behind in southern Ontario. I could hardly wait to begin exploring.

People are often curious about my photographic interests and cannot help but ask, why birds? I will admit that I find this a difficult question to answer. My default answer is that they are beautiful to watch and that they are challenging and fun to photograph. When I think more carefully about the question, I find a more accurate answer would be that birds simply amaze me. From the tiny Pacific Wren, whose song is far larger than its body size would ever suggest, to the incredibly vibrant yellow and red colours of the Western Tanager, to the aerial capabilities of the swifts, swallows and shearwaters, birds are amazing creatures. Who has not looked up at a Bald Eagle and wished, just for a moment, to trade places with it? Who has not found enjoyment and serenity while listening to the beautiful songs of the birds in a forest? I have no simple or eloquent answer for why I love to photograph birds so much. What I can say, though, is that every time I am out in nature and spending time with birds, I am left in awe of the evolution of these most beautiful of all Mother Nature's creations.

My search for birds has taken me to some spectacular places in this province. I currently live in Victoria on Vancouver Island, and I never get tired of the amazing variety of birds that can be found even in this relatively small region. But each part of the province has a different feel, and each has different bird species that help make these areas unique.

There are so many wonderful places to visit in BC and so many beautiful birds to search for that I find it impossible to pick a favourite. Searching for new species and visiting exciting new places is absolutely one of my preferred things to do. Whether the mountains or the northern forests spark your curiosity, the important thing is to get outside and experience nature. Perhaps it is the sight of a stunning Lazuli Bunting singing from the Okanagan grasslands or the sound of a Townsend's Warbler ringing out from the coastal forests that gets you motivated to get outdoors and go birdwatching. In BC we are so lucky to have endless beauty in our natural landscapes and a wonderful variety of birds to spend our days searching for.

This book is not intended to be a field guide or to display every breeding bird of BC. My knowledge of the avifauna of this province is ever expanding, but I am by no means an ornithologist. There is so much of this province that I have yet to explore and still so much that I have to learn about the birds that live here. I am first and foremost a photographer and naturalist. This book will give you an idea of the birds that can be found in some of the main ecoregions within the province. The book is divided up into five main chapters that highlight one major region each. Each chapter features a selection of photographs of some of the most characteristic or beautiful birds from that region. For some birds, like the American Dipper, it was a challenge to decide under what chapter to classify them. Other generalist birds, like the Raven, could have been included in any of the chapters. The final chapter, "Notes from the Field," attempts to give a behind-the-scenes look at the life of a bird photographer.

One of my favourite aspects of being a bird photographer is that the pursuit of finding and photographing these beautiful and elusive animals takes me to many places that I might otherwise never visit. Trying to find a bird gives me a reason to go for a hike or to hop in my car and go somewhere new. Sometimes I get the shots I have in mind and sometimes I come home empty-handed. In either case, there is usually a smile on my face after I spend a day exploring in nature. I am a true believer in the old saying that life is more about the journey than the destination. I hope that you will enjoy this book and the photographic journey that I took to capture these images of the birds of British Columbia.

All the best,

Glenn Bartley

Glenn Bartley, 2013

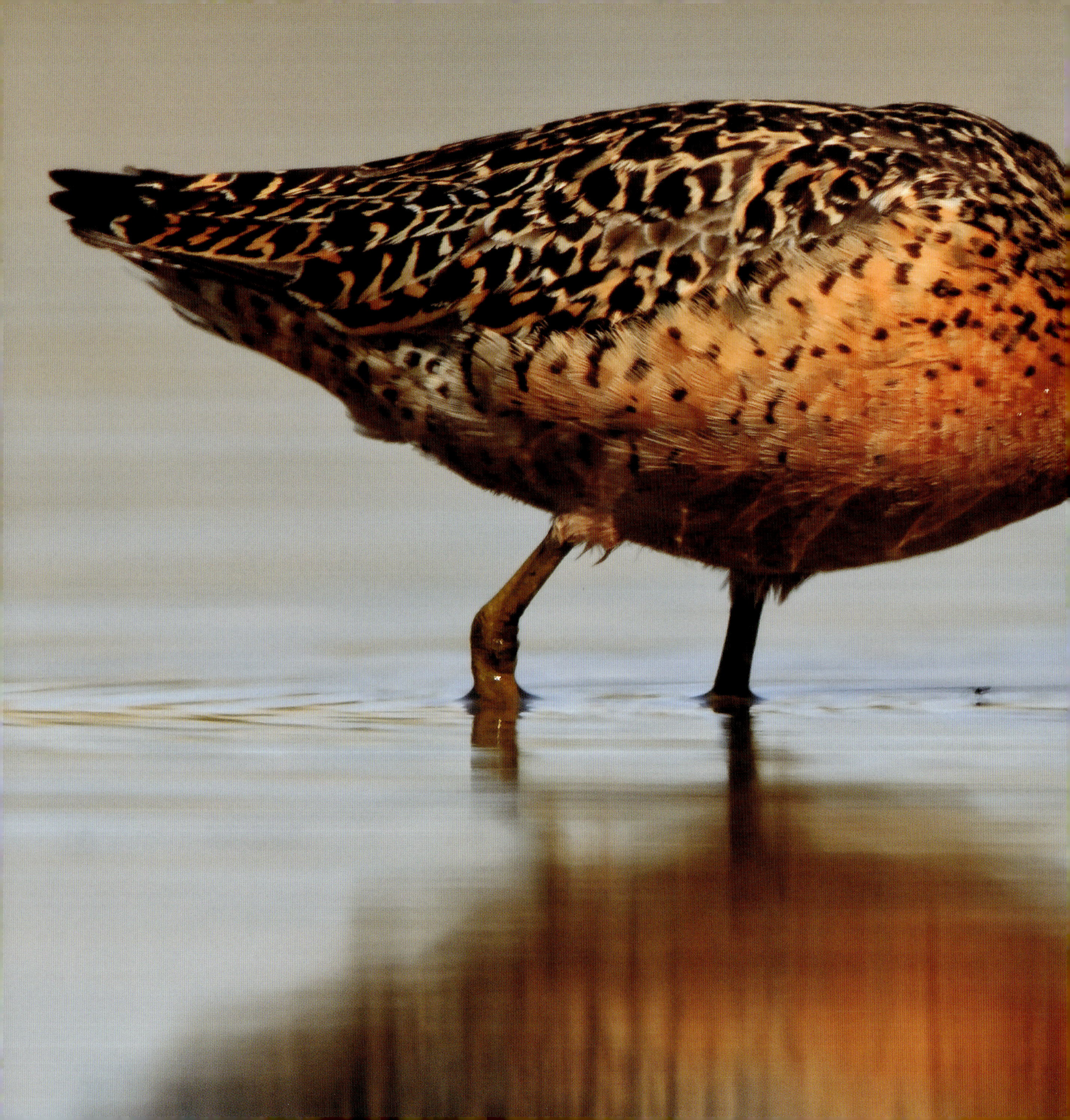

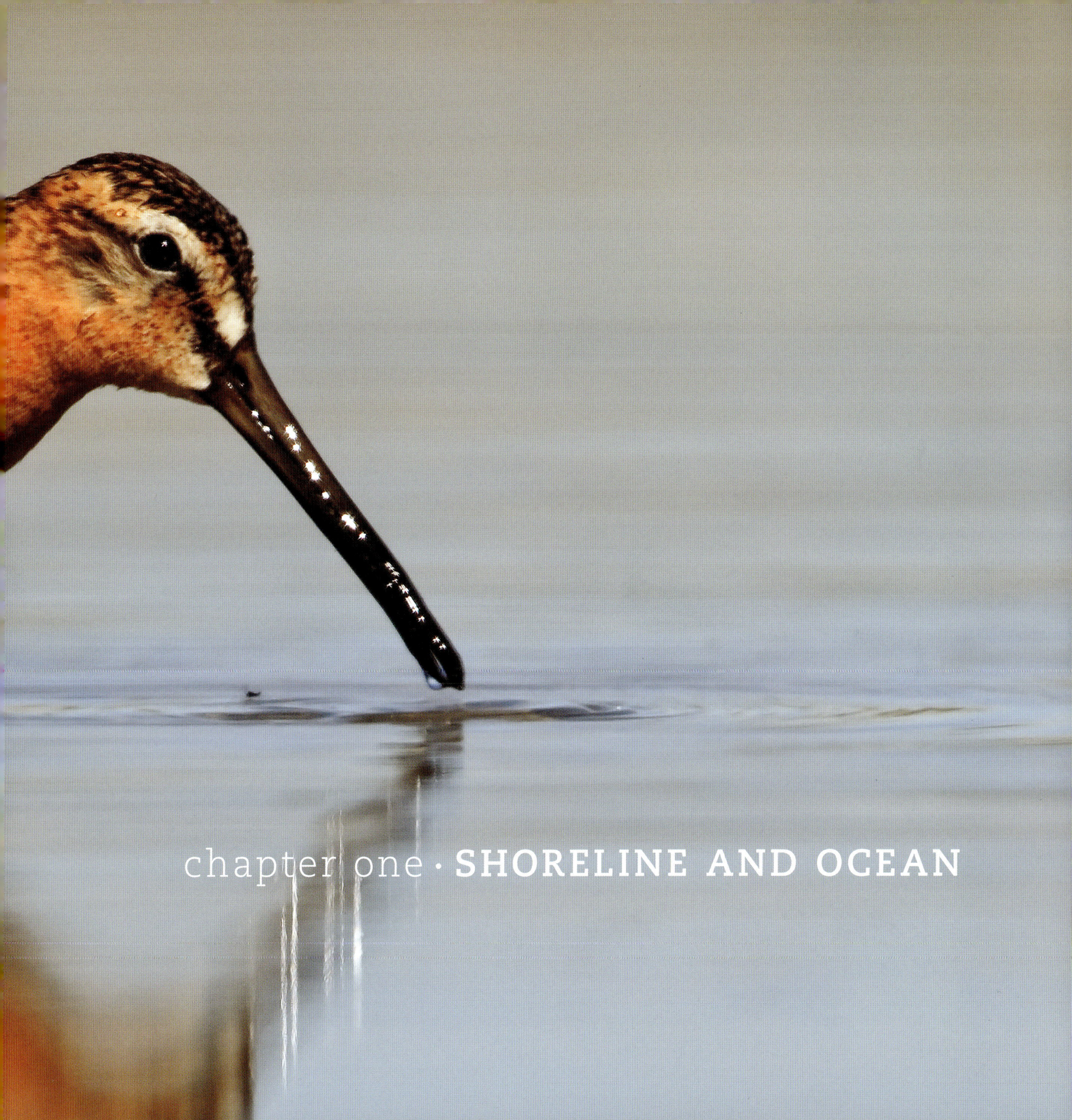

chapter one · SHORELINE AND OCEAN

On the western edge of British Columbia, a collection of very special habitat types exists. Here, along the shoreline, the terrestrial begins to intermingle in an almost playful way with the marine. Each day as the tide advances and retreats, these dynamic ecosystems go through their daily ebbs and flows. This coastal routine takes place in various forms in many different types of environments scattered all along the 25,000 kilometres of BC coastline. Rocky shores and headlands, sandy beaches, mud flats and islands all have diverse ecosystems that support numerous species of organisms, including many birds. Some of these birds find food and refuge in these places year round, while others simply pass through as part of their long migratory journeys. Some stay close to the shoreline and never venture very far from the water's edge, while others are rarely observed from land. The ecological communities along the coast of British Columbia are some of the richest in the world.

THE INTERTIDAL AREA

The intertidal area is the zone between the high-tide line and the low-tide line. It is in constant flux and absolutely teems with life at every trophic level. From the tiniest of microscopic plankton to invertebrates and, of course, birds, these areas are extremely biologically diverse. Those visiting the intertidal area at high tide may not immediately realize that there is such rich abundance of life. But as the water retreats, it leaves behind hidden gifts of all types for birds and other animals to discover. Fully aware of this bounty, shorebirds like Sanderlings, Western Sandpipers and Semipalmated Plovers invade beaches at low tide—frantically running and hopping about, searching for new delicious morsels the sea has left behind. Hordes of gulls, crows and herons emerge from their roost sites to share in the feast too. Meanwhile, the rocky areas of the intertidal zone are wonderful places to find birds like Black Oystercatchers, Black Turnstones and Surfbirds. These birds scurry about the seaweed-covered rocks, searching for invertebrates and molluscs to devour.

Closer to river mouths, the scattered estuaries that exist all along the coastline are fantastic places to find many types of waterfowl. For example, the Fraser River Estuary just outside of Vancouver is located along the Pacific flyway migration corridor. As such, it receives millions of feathered visitors each year. Ducks and geese (including tens of thousands of Snow Geese) flock here each winter in search of food and shelter. Sandhill Cranes are residents that are hard to miss, as they stand about 1.2 metres tall and roam around in large groups. Raptors such as Bald Eagles, Northern Harriers and Short-eared Owls also find these coastal ecosystems ideal places to spend the winter.

MUD FLATS

Mud flats are a type of coastal environment that is often overlooked. It makes sense that they would be—to most people they are mucky, smelly, inaccessible areas that do not stack up favourably when compared to sandy beaches or rainforests. However, there may not be any other coastal habitat that offers such rich feeding grounds for birds as these dynamic bionetworks. During spring and fall migration, these mud flats are absolutely packed with shorebirds that need to feast in order to complete their lengthy migration. Some of the shorebirds that migrate along the coast of BC come from as far away as the southern tip of Chile and travel all the way to Alaska—that's more than 11,000 kilometres.

Keen observers of the feasting shorebirds will note that not all of the species feed in the same area or use the same techniques. The size of the various birds, the length of their legs and their bill morphology give clues as to how each species exploits the habitat. For example, small, short-legged shorebirds like Least Sandpipers and Semipalmated Plovers must stay in the shallow water. From here they can feel around in the mud with their feet and their bills for possible prey. Longer-legged birds like Willets, Dowitchers, Whimbrels and Long-billed Curlews can venture out much farther into the water. With their long bills, they are able to probe deep into the mud for a variety of invertebrates that may have been left behind by the tide. Seemingly aware of the imminent return of the tidal flow, these birds feed systematically, frantically and often without pause. As soon as the mud flats are again under water, the birds are forced to move on or patiently wait for their next opportunity to feast.

JUST OFFSHORE AND THE OFFSHORE ISLANDS

Looking beyond the low-tide mark, it seems obvious that the areas permanently covered by water must be rich with life too. Indeed, this is the case, shown by the many species of waterfowl that feed close to shore. Scoters, Goldeneyes and Harlequins spend winters along the coast in sheltered bays so that they can feast on the clam and mussel beds in these areas. Amazingly enough, birds like the Black, Surf and White-winged Scoters are able to swallow clams and mussels whole and pulverize them in their powerful gizzards.

Farther away from the mainland, there are a number of birds that take advantage of the small islands off the coast of BC. Glaucous-winged Gulls, Pigeon Guillemots and Black Oystercatchers inhabit some of the islands close to shore. These birds find safe places to nest and raise their young on rocky outcroppings, which keep them away from many would-be predators. Still farther offshore are larger and more remote islands whose cliffsides are home to incredible numbers of nesting seabirds. One of the most populated of such islands is Triangle Island, off the northern tip of Vancouver Island, where more than a million seabirds nest on the rocky cliffs or in burrows dug into the soil. Triangle Island is an especially important site for the Cassin's Auklet—up to 70 percent of the world's population nests there in the spring and early summer. Other inhabitants of the island include Tufted Puffins, Common Murres and Rhinoceros Auklets.

THE DEEP BLUE SEA

Beyond the coastline and past the offshore islands lies the vast expanse of the Pacific Ocean. Even here, there are special birds adapted to living and thriving in their pelagic environment. Although rarely seen from land, species like Sooty Shearwaters are very common as they migrate well off the coast. In addition to shearwaters, birds such as albatrosses, auklets, fulmars and jaegers live most of their lives above the open ocean. Except for when they come to land to breed, they rarely come close enough to shore for birdwatchers to get a satisfying look. These birds lead fascinating lives, take part in amazing migrations and, despite their dull colours, are beautiful in their own ways.

It is amazing to be miles out at sea and spot an enormous Black-footed Albatross gliding in toward you. They are able to soar effortlessly on their long, narrow wings. Without flapping at all, they can zoom past the moving boats. By capitalizing on their 1.8-metre wingspan and by taking advantage of the gradient of wind speeds above the ocean, these birds efficiently circle above the ocean in search of food and use very little energy in the process. Albatrosses, and indeed all of the seabirds known as "tubenoses," have an incredible sense of smell. These highly developed olfactory capabilities help albatrosses, fulmars and shearwaters find food on the surface of the ocean from miles around.

Photographing ocean-dwelling birds can be daunting. Finding these pelagic species in the vast ocean is a real challenge; to capture a compelling image, you have to get quite close to the birds. To view some species, there is no choice but to join a pelagic birdwatching expedition that will venture many kilometres from shore. These excursions target areas known to have rich feeding grounds for the birds. Once in the right habitat, the tour operators will often throw scented bait overboard, attempting to appeal to the keen sense of smell of the tube-nosed seabirds.

A second strategy for photographing birds of the deep blue sea is to hop in a kayak and paddle out offshore. While not for the faint of heart, the low perspective in the water offers an intimate glimpse into the lives of these ocean-dwelling birds.

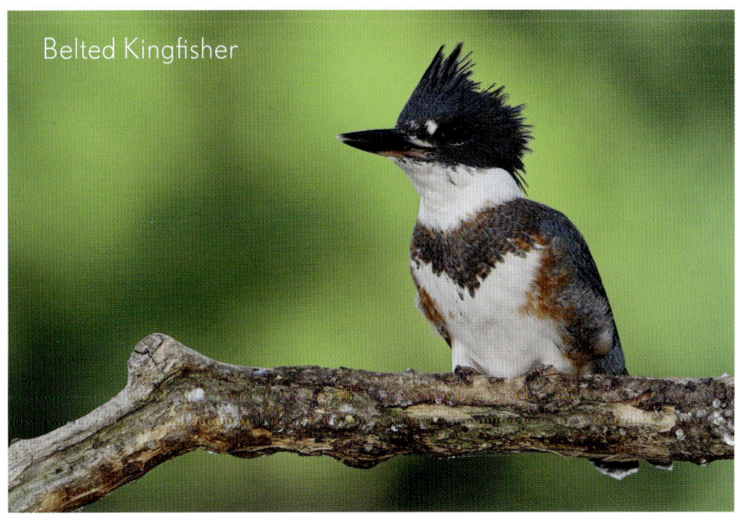
Belted Kingfisher

Black Turnstones are found along the BC coast throughout the fall and winter. In spring they migrate farther north to Alaska, their primary breeding grounds.

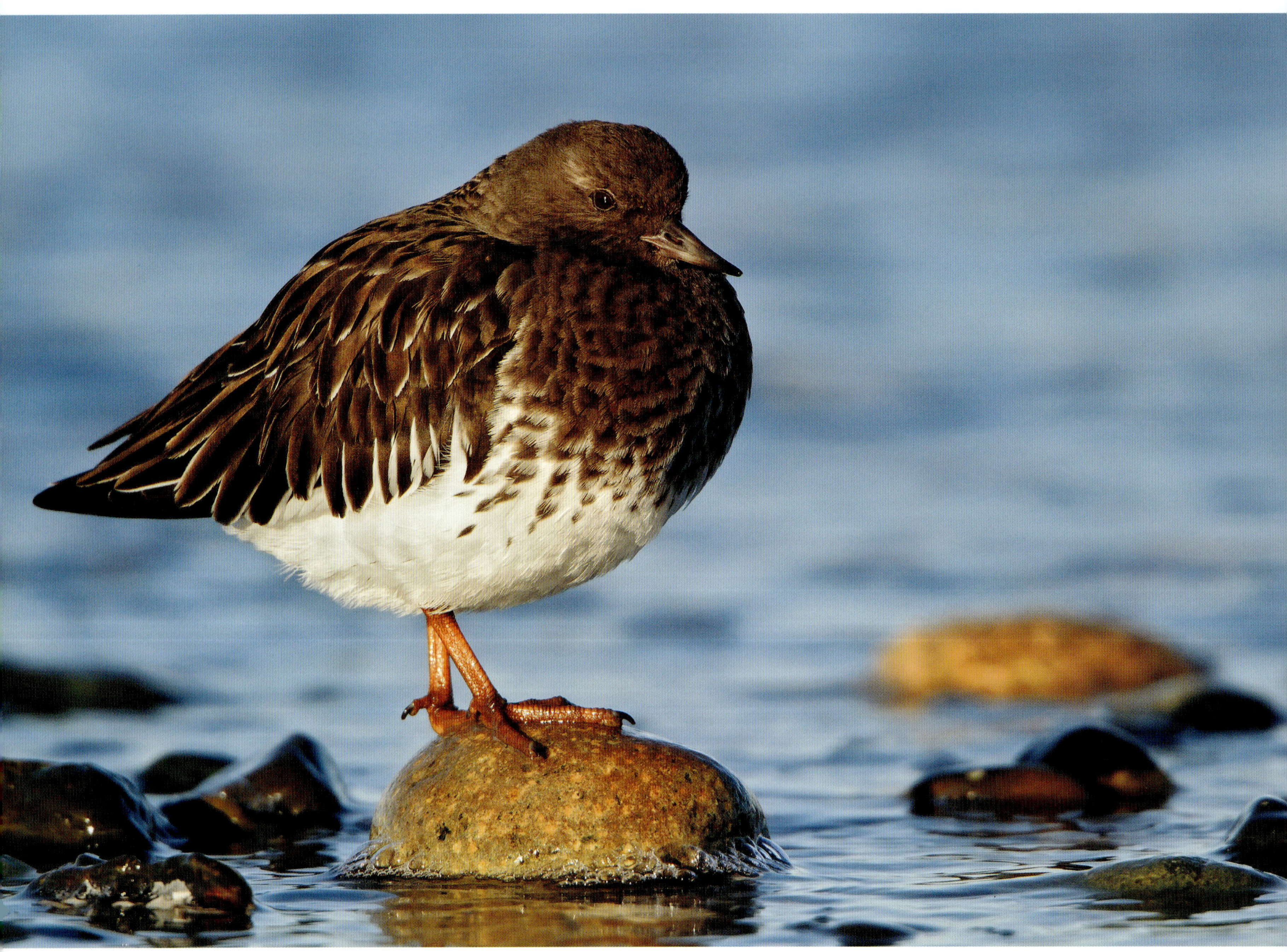

A Black Oystercatcher admires its reflection while feeding.

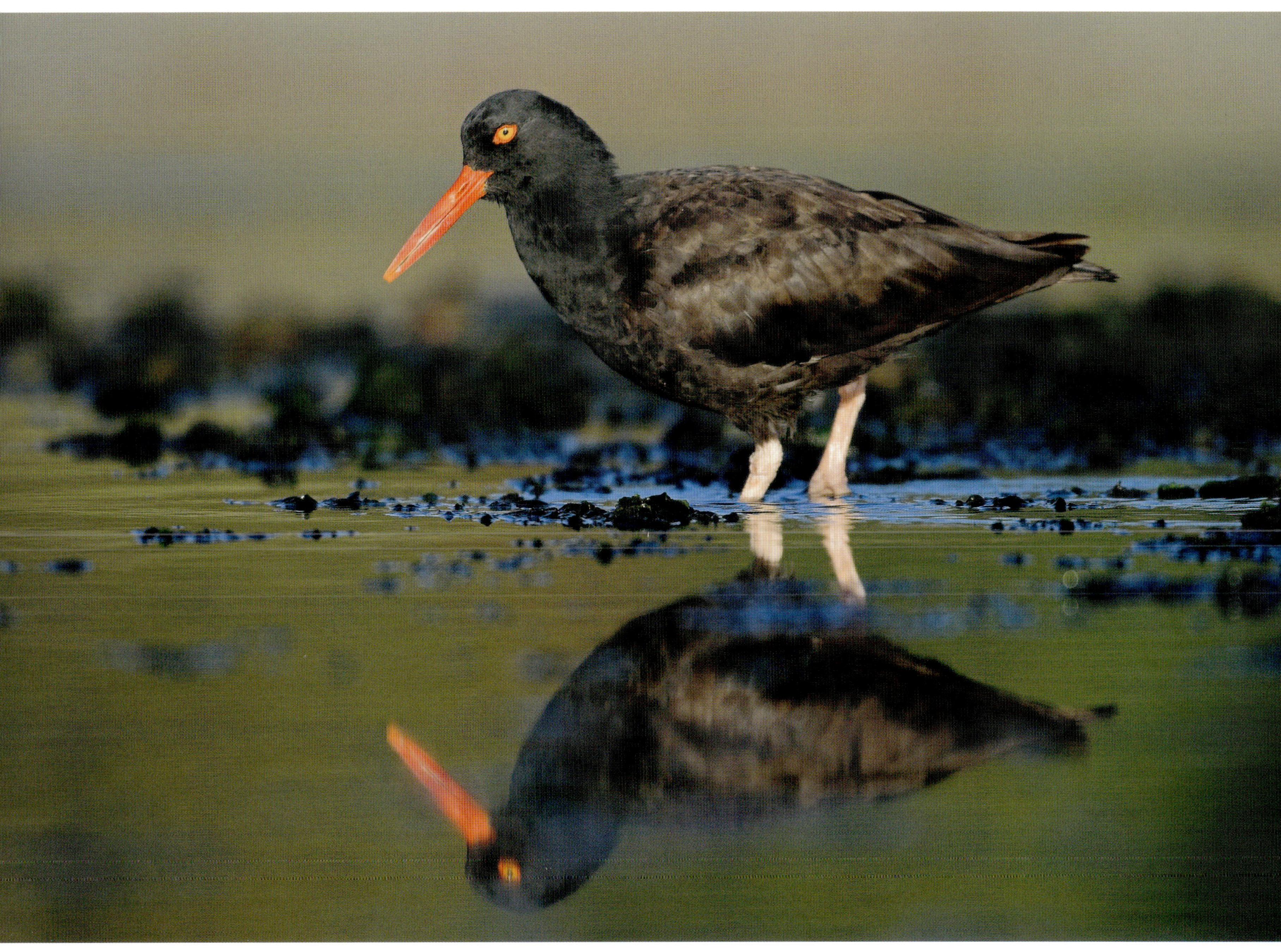

Far from shore, a Black-footed Albatross cruises gracefully through the air. These birds have an amazing sense of smell and can detect food from miles away.

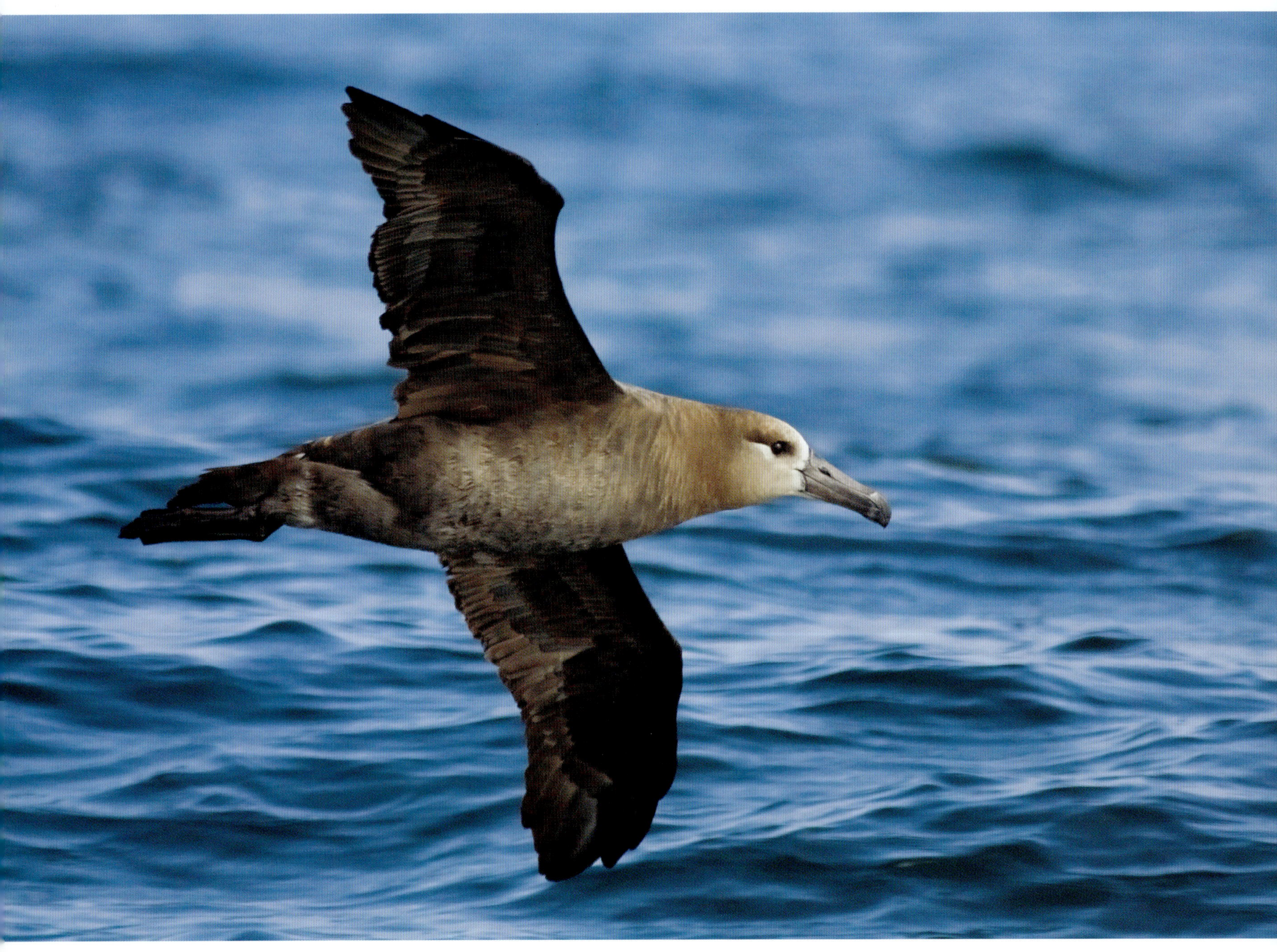

A Whimbrel feeds along a sandy beach during its southward-bound fall migration.

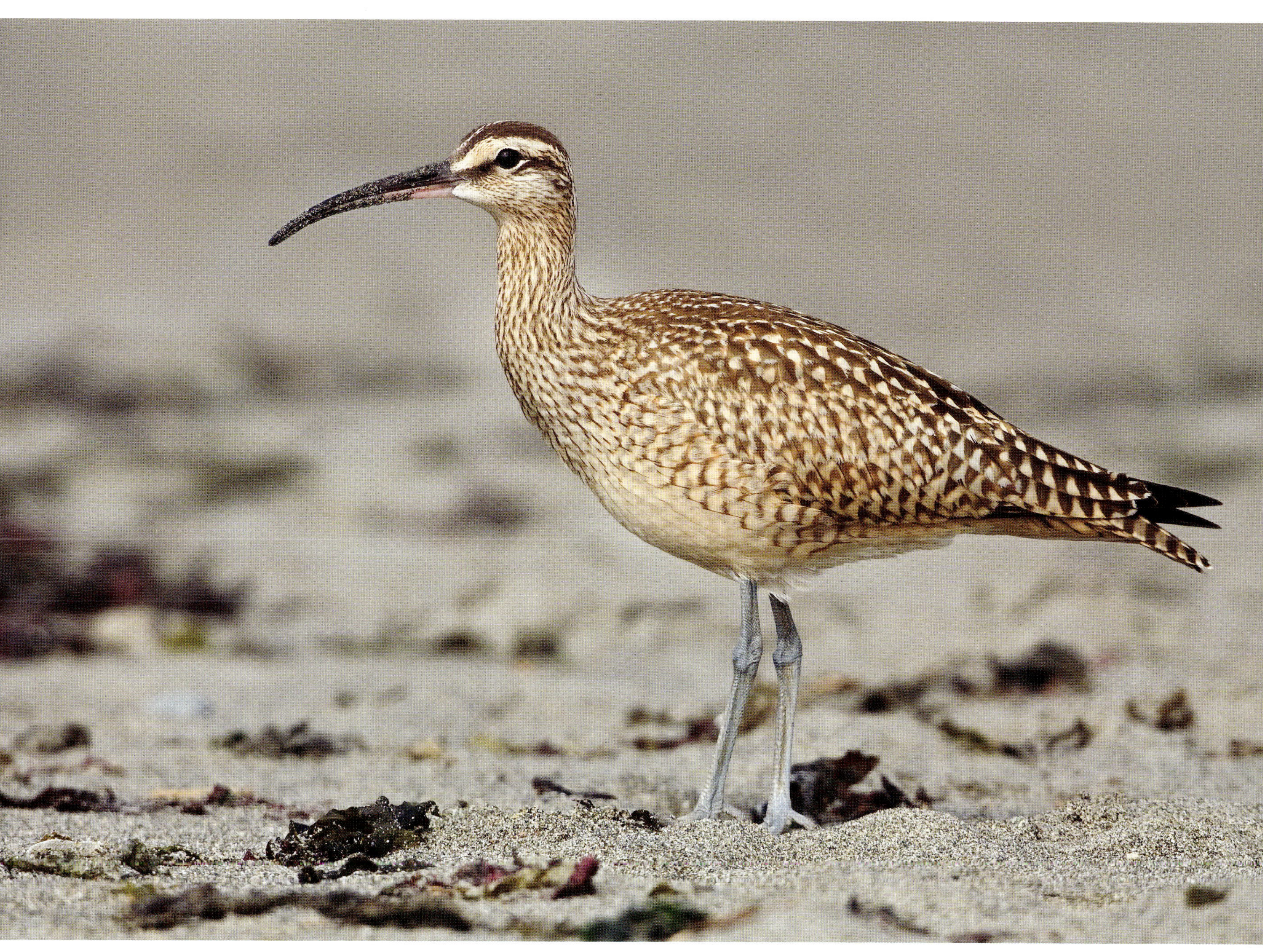

Common Murres are colonial nesting seabirds that form huge colonies on rocky cliffsides. They are capable of diving to incredible depths in search of food.

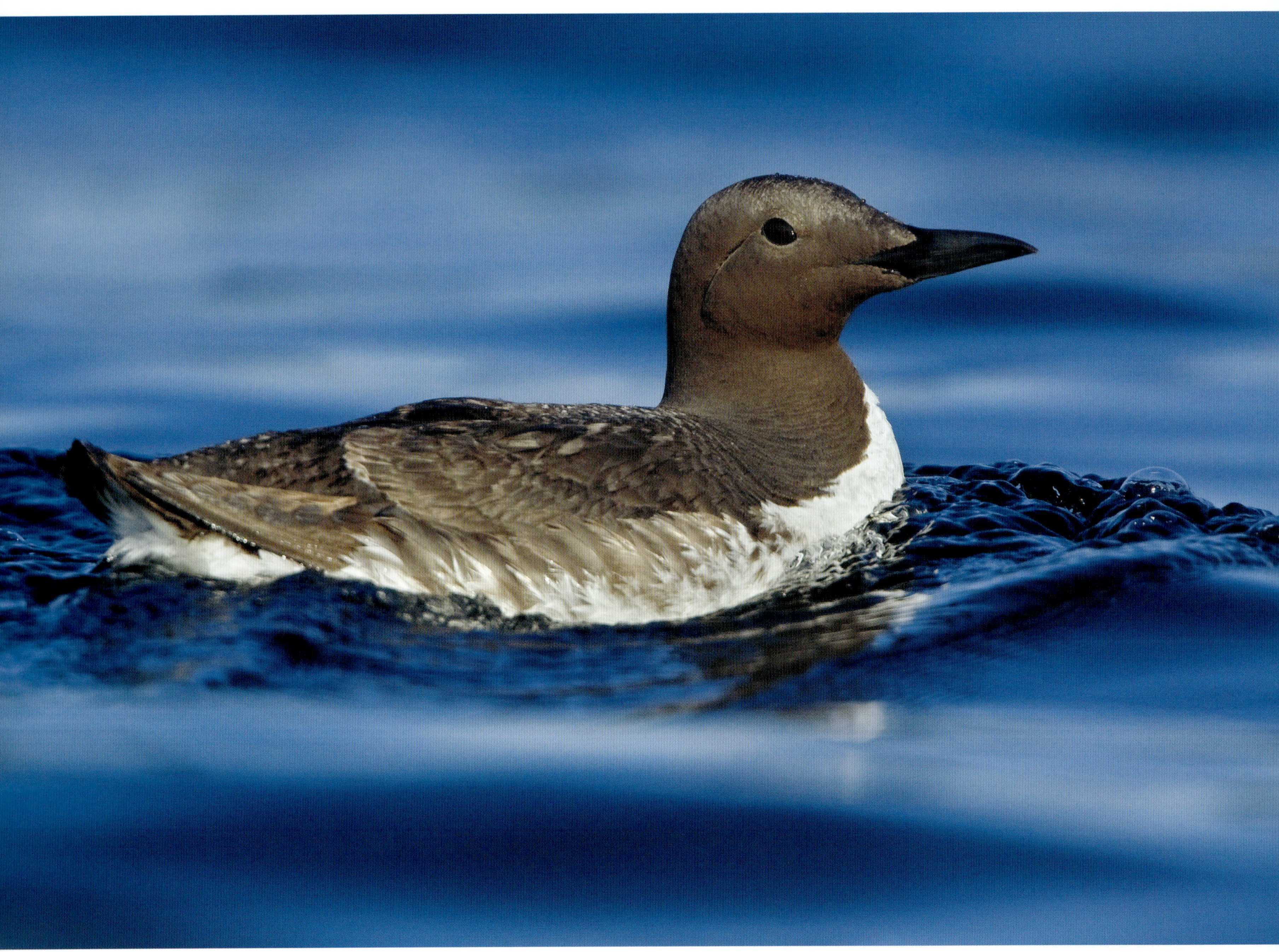

Snow Geese breed in the high Arctic but fly south for the winter, finding refuge in coastal ecosystems such as the Reifel Bird Sanctuary in Delta.

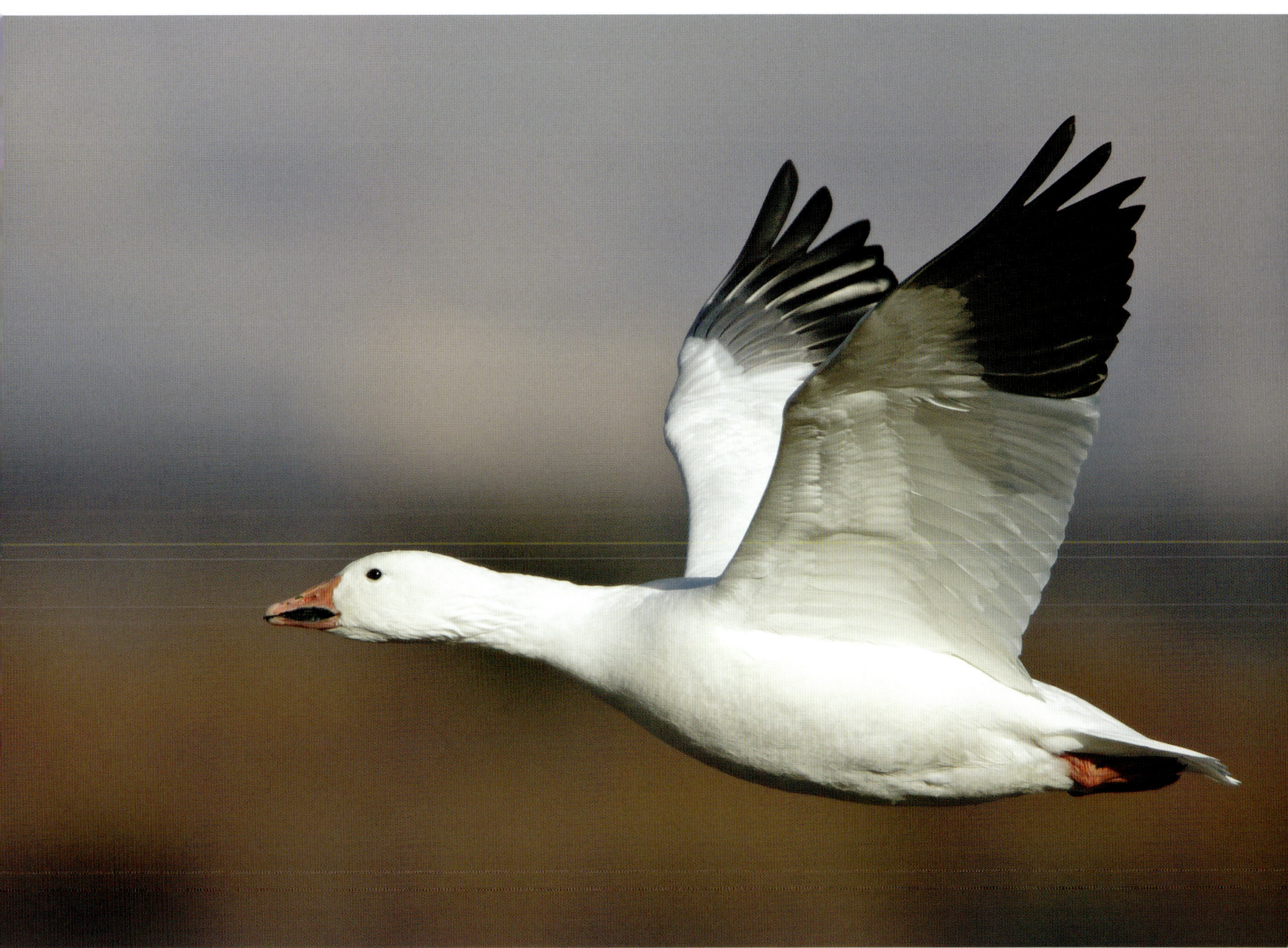

Like most members of the Alcidae family of birds, Tufted Puffins nest on rocky cliffs and islands. Triangle Island, off the northern tip of Vancouver Island, is home to approximately 30,000 pairs of these beautiful seabirds. ALAN MURPHY

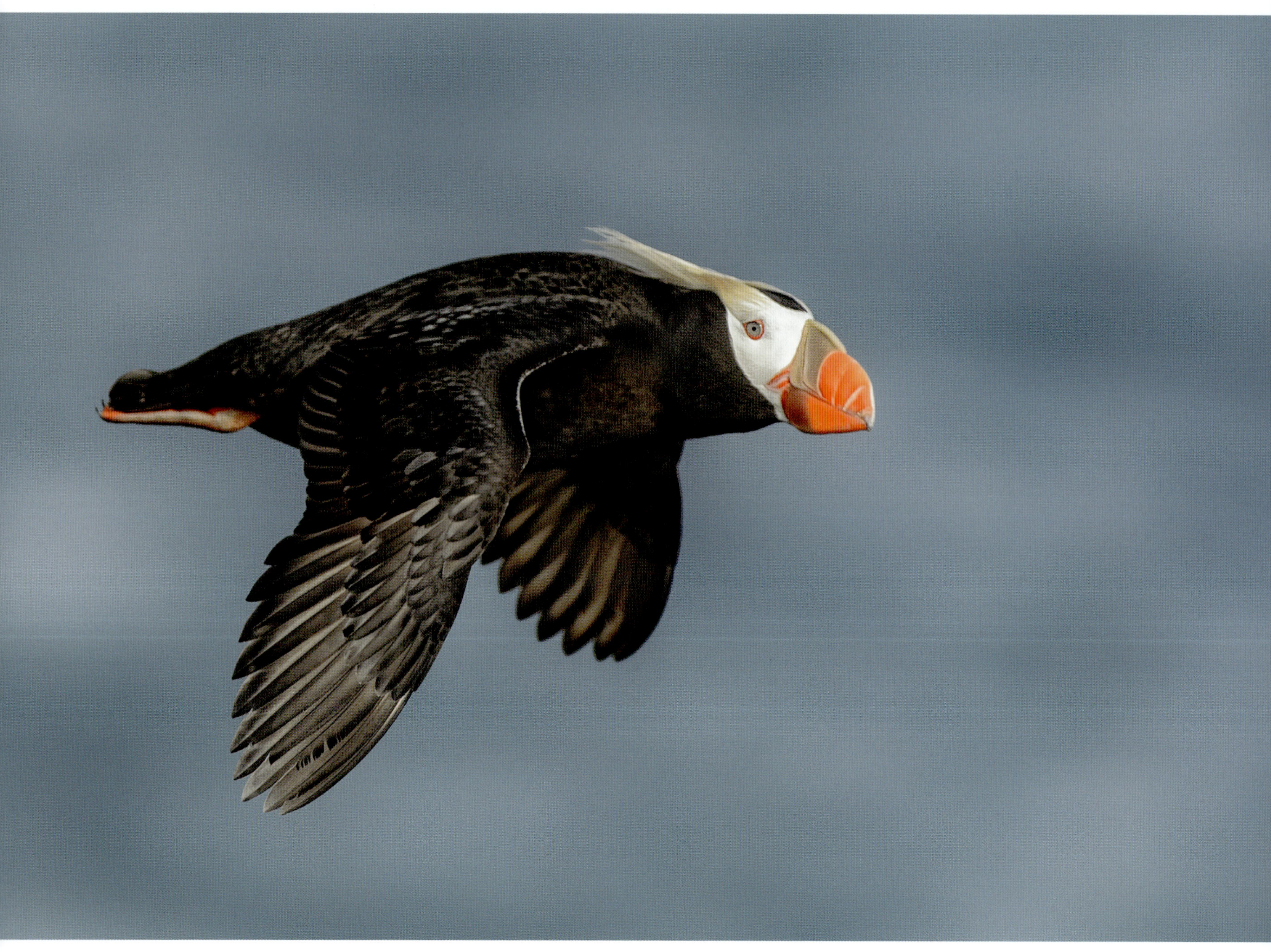

Sooty Shearwaters take part in extraordinary annual migrations from their breeding grounds in the south Pacific to the Arctic. Recent research has shown that some birds fly more than 70,000 kilometres each year.

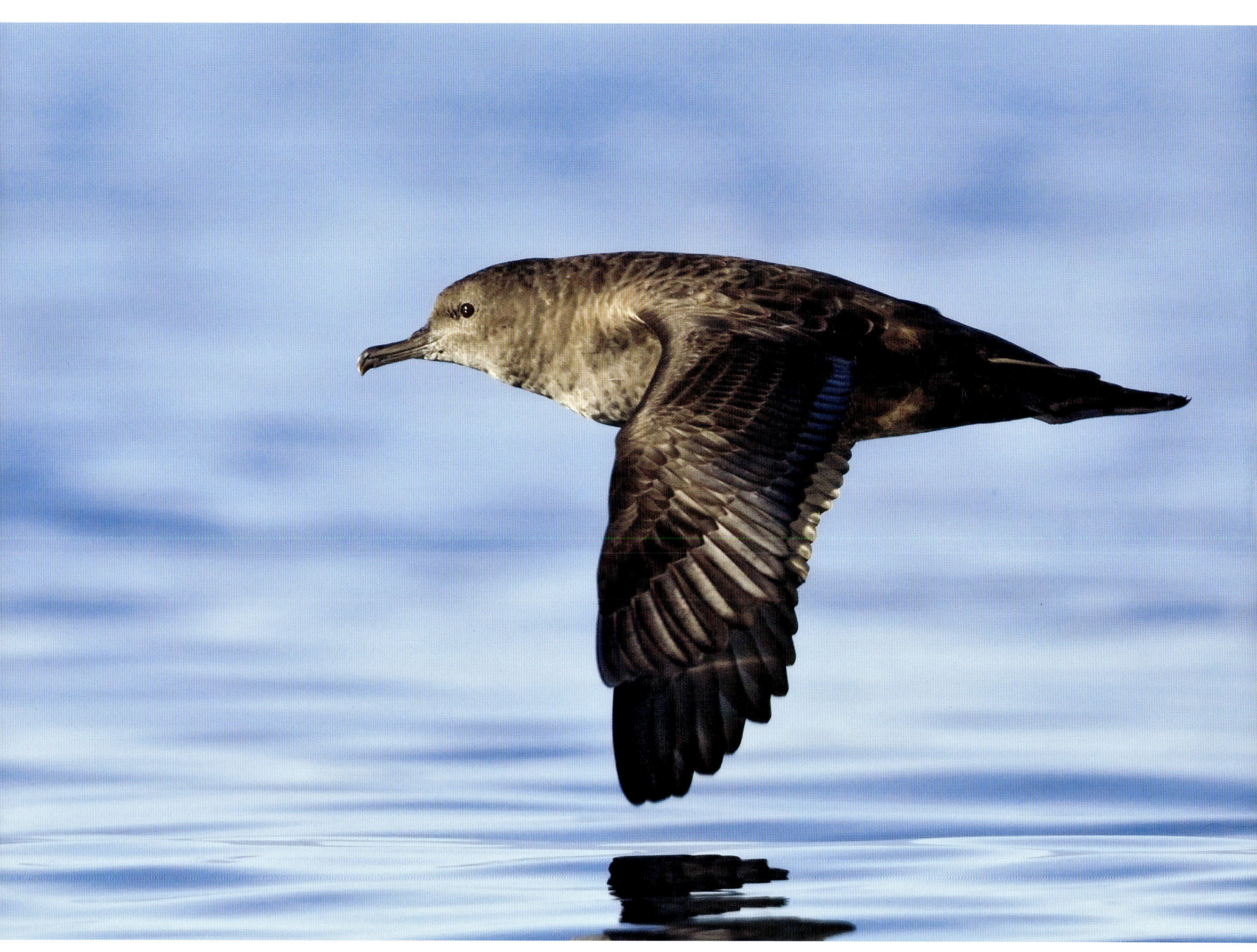

A male Harlequin Duck poses proudly along the shoreline of Vancouver Island.

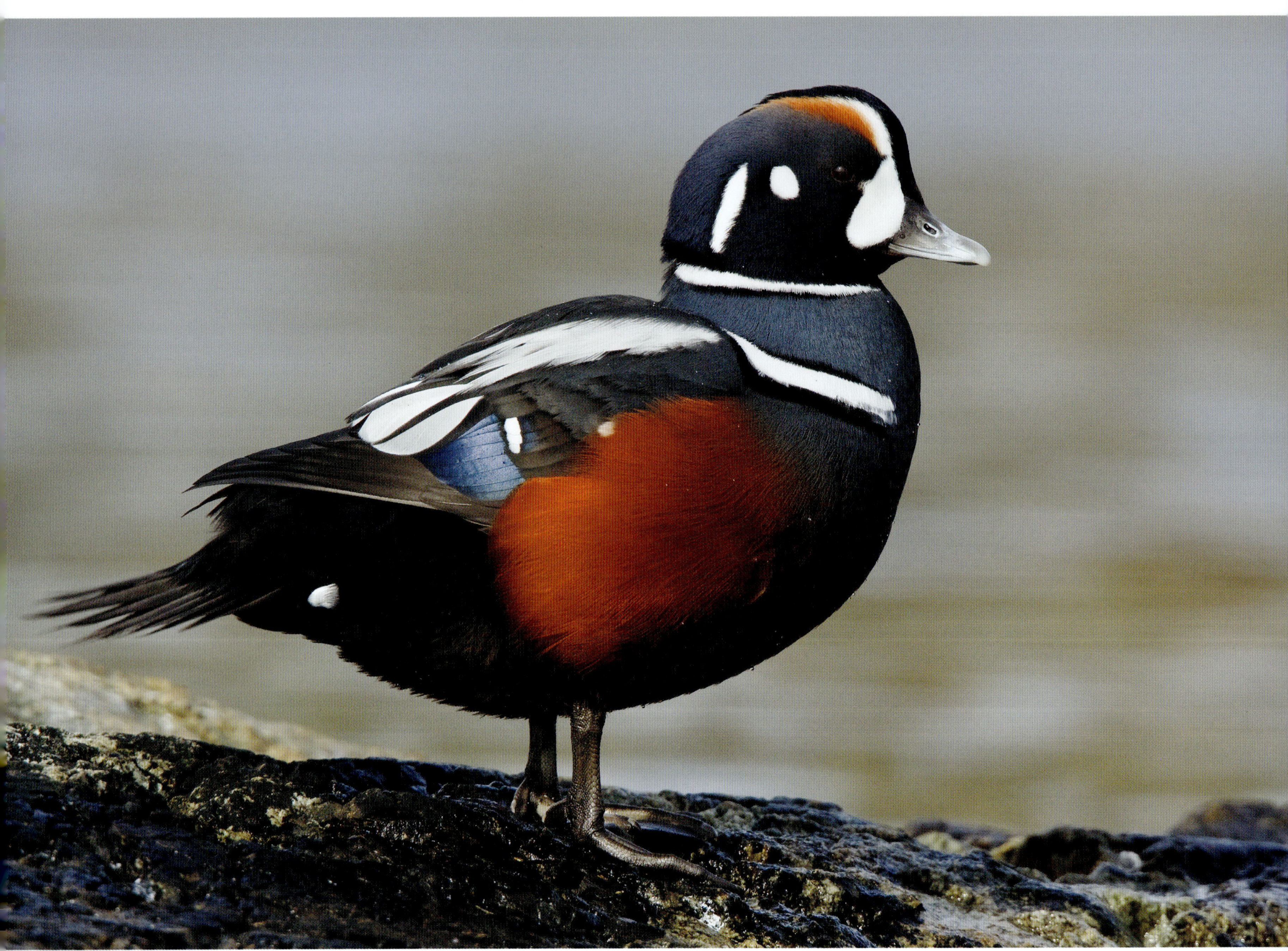

The bizarre-looking Rhinoceros Auklet certainly lives up to its name with the prominent "horn" that extends from its beak during the breeding season.

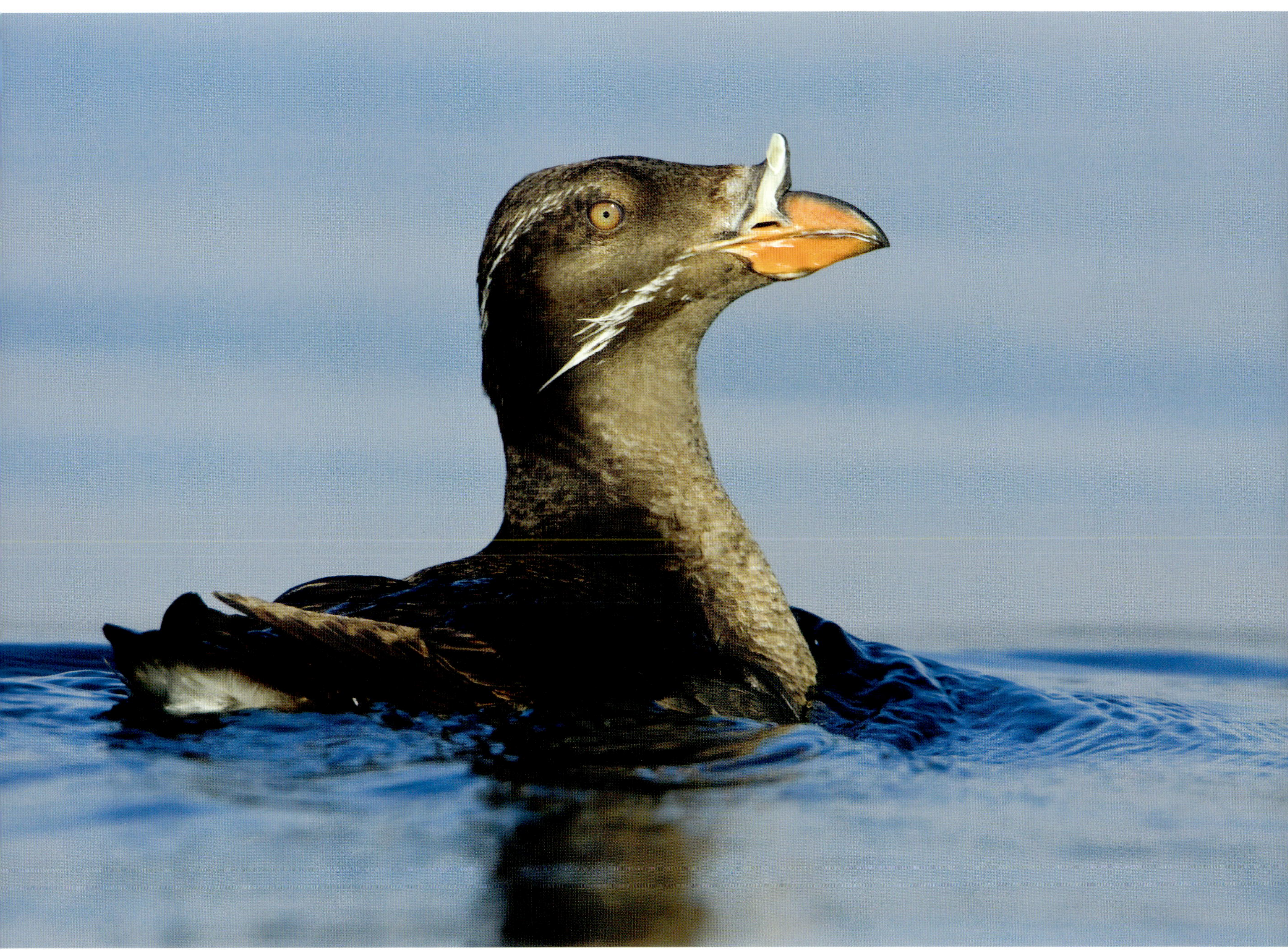

A Sanderling searches for food in a mud flat during its lengthy migratory journey.

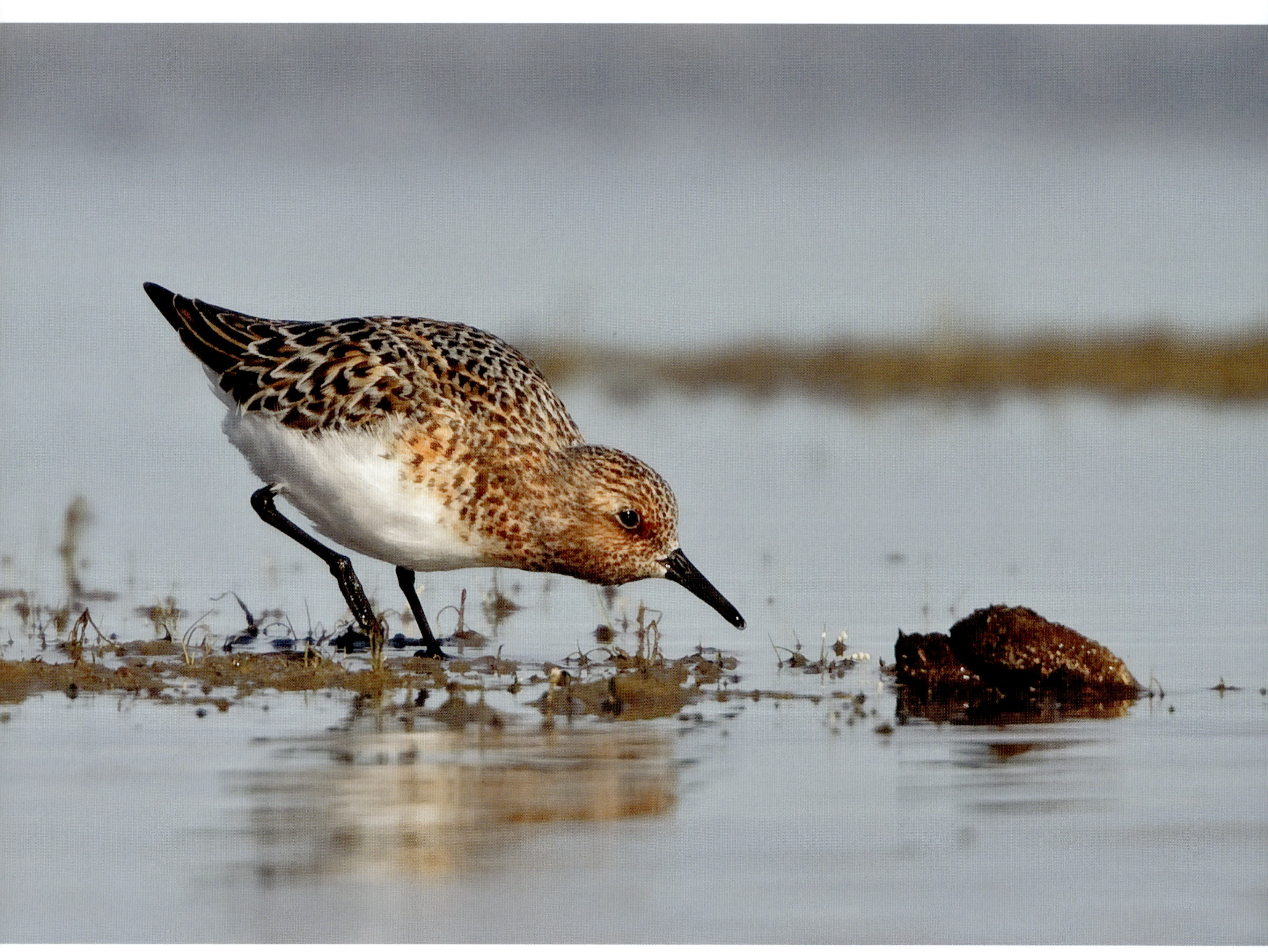

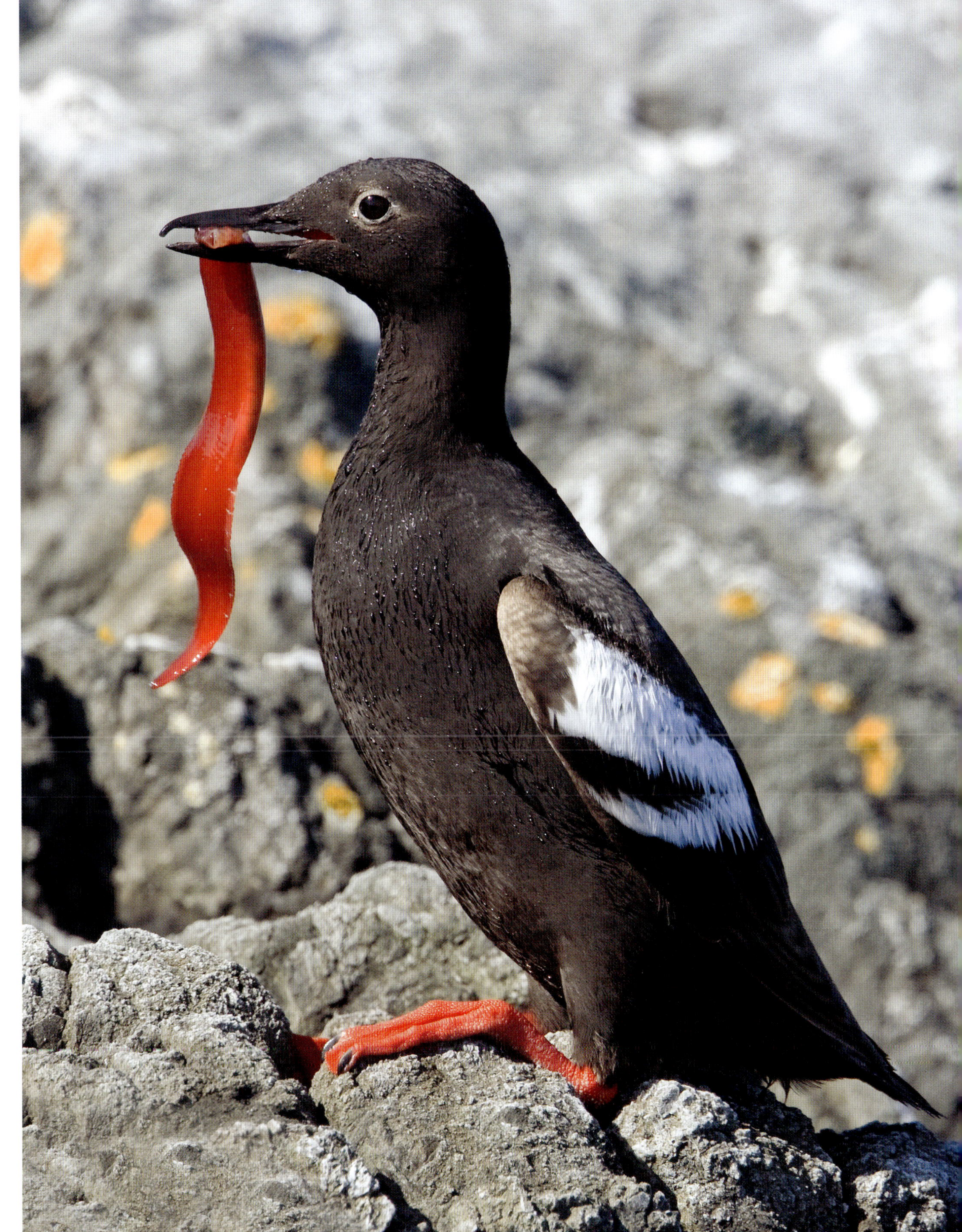

A Pigeon Guillemot shows off the day's catch on an offshore rocky islet. Looking at the colour of the bird's feet and its prey, it's hard not to wonder if these birds derive their skin colour from what they eat.

The intertidal area is a favourite place for birds like this Western Sandpiper to search for food.

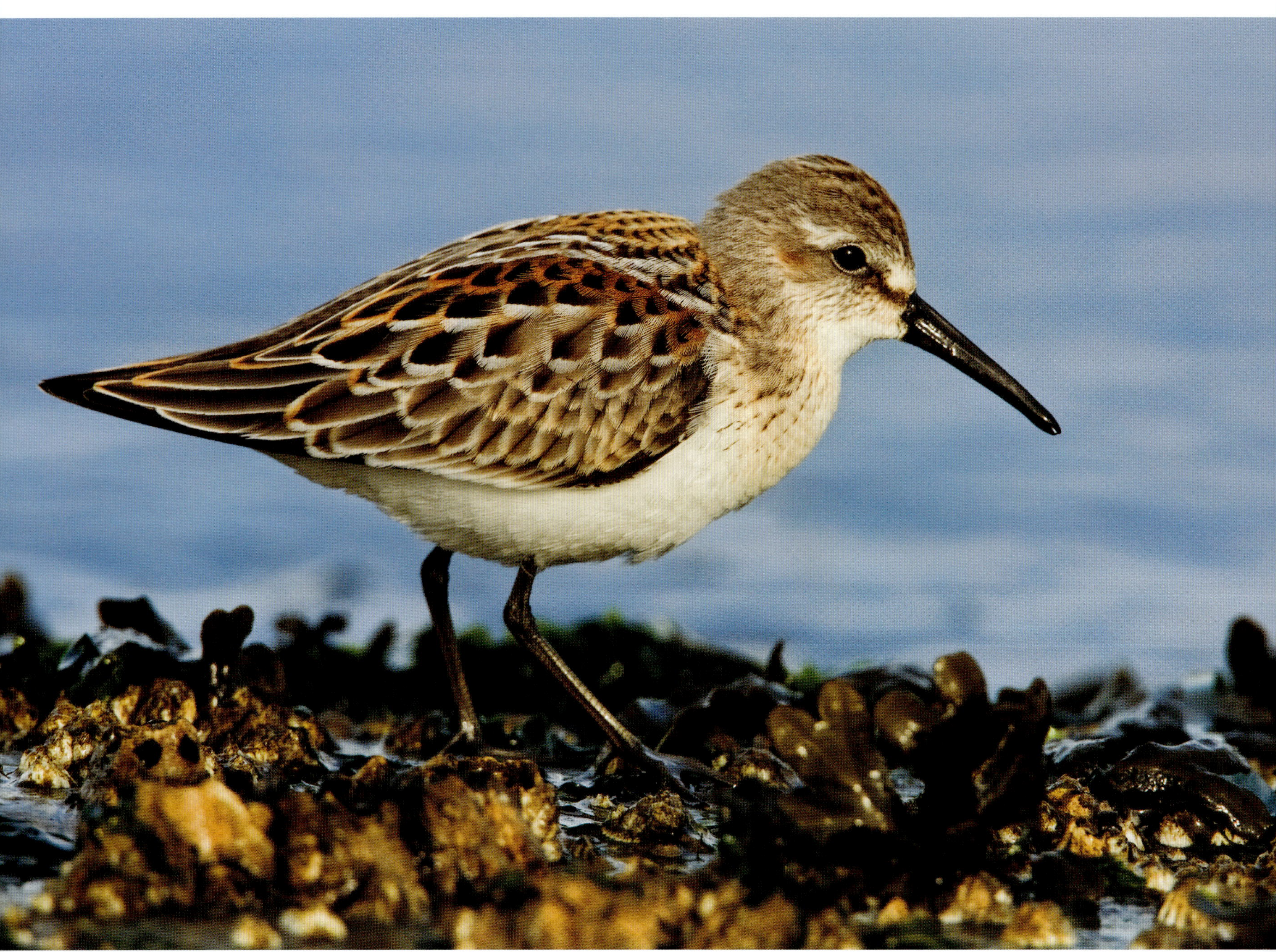

Watching seabirds navigate the aquatic environment is incredible. The ease with which birds such as this Ancient Murrelet dive and swim through the water in search of food is fascinating and exemplifies their versatility.

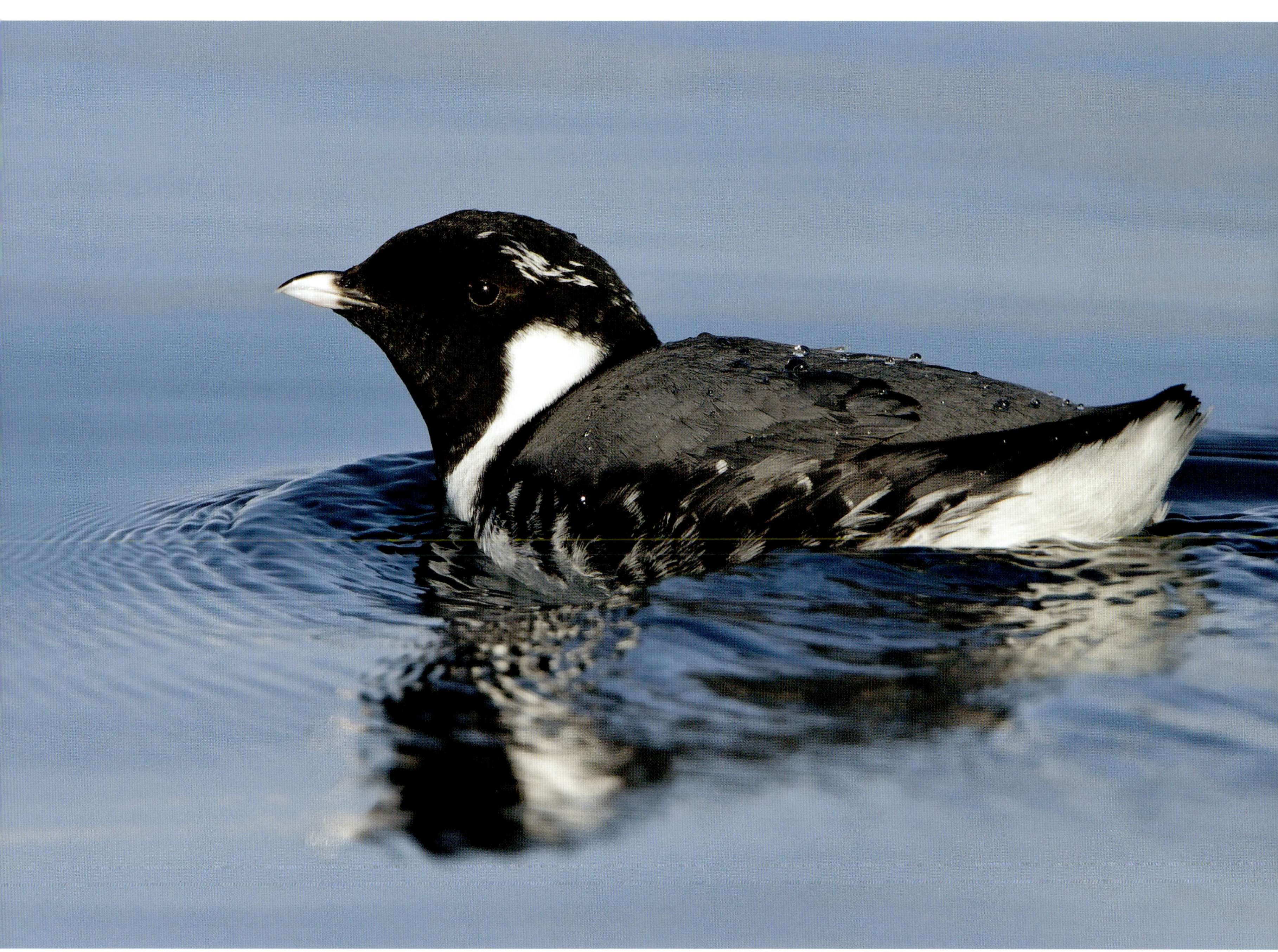

Sandhill Cranes are impressive birds; standing about 1.2 metres tall and often very vocal, they are hard to miss.

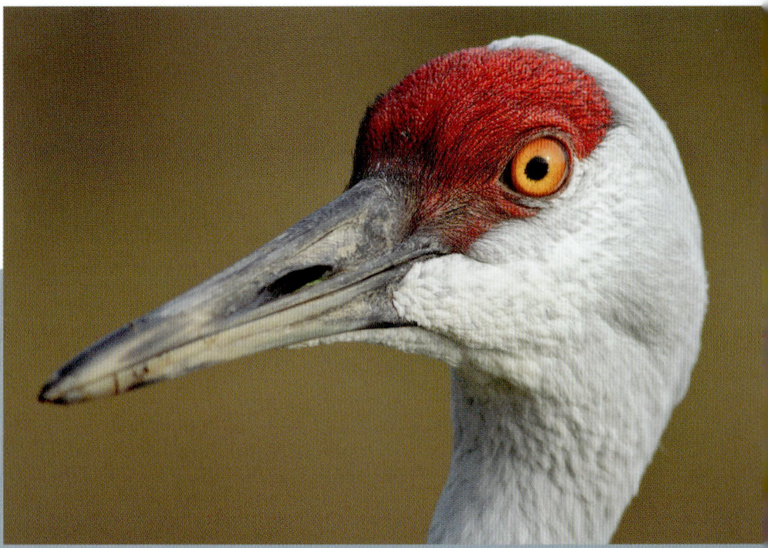

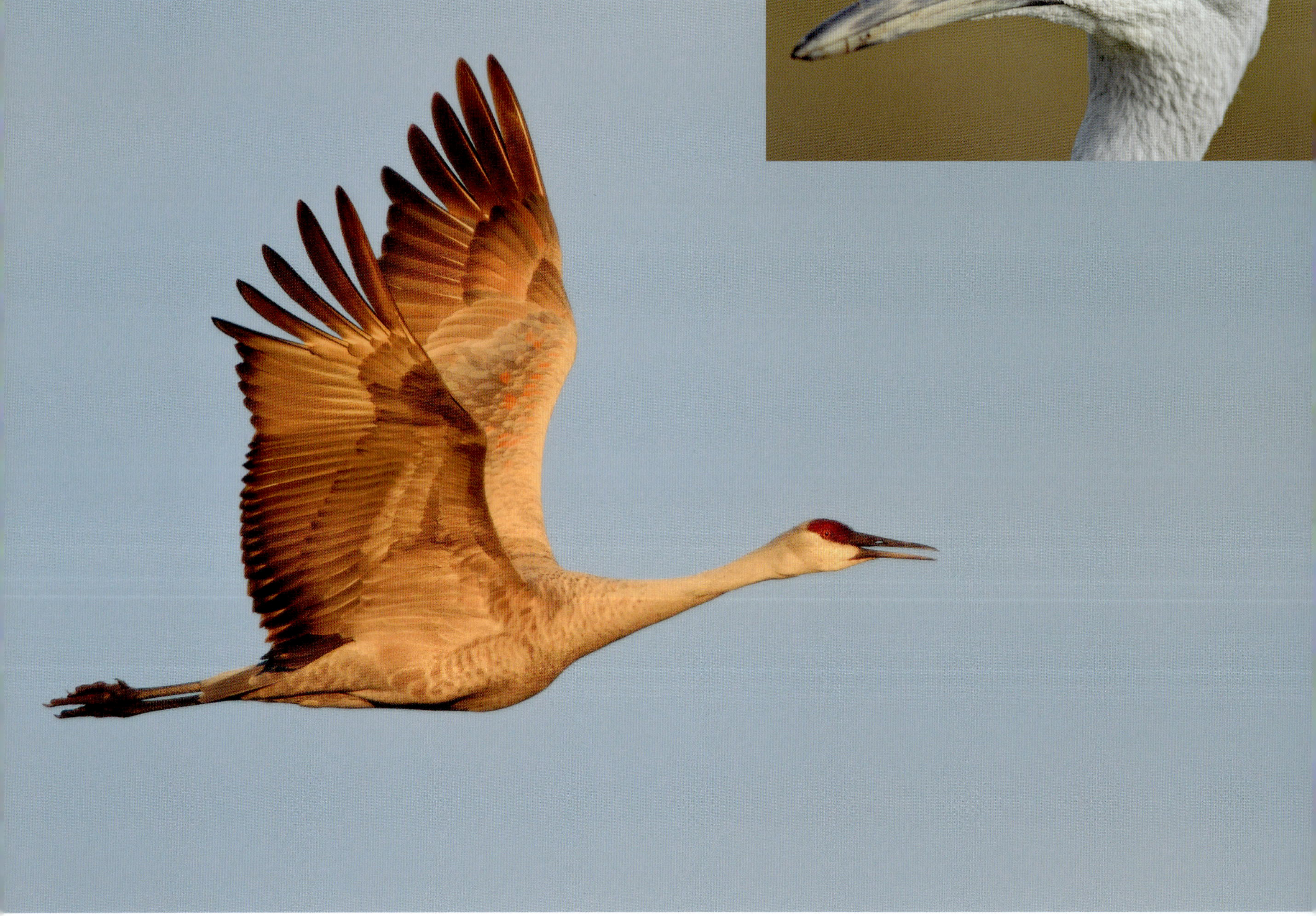

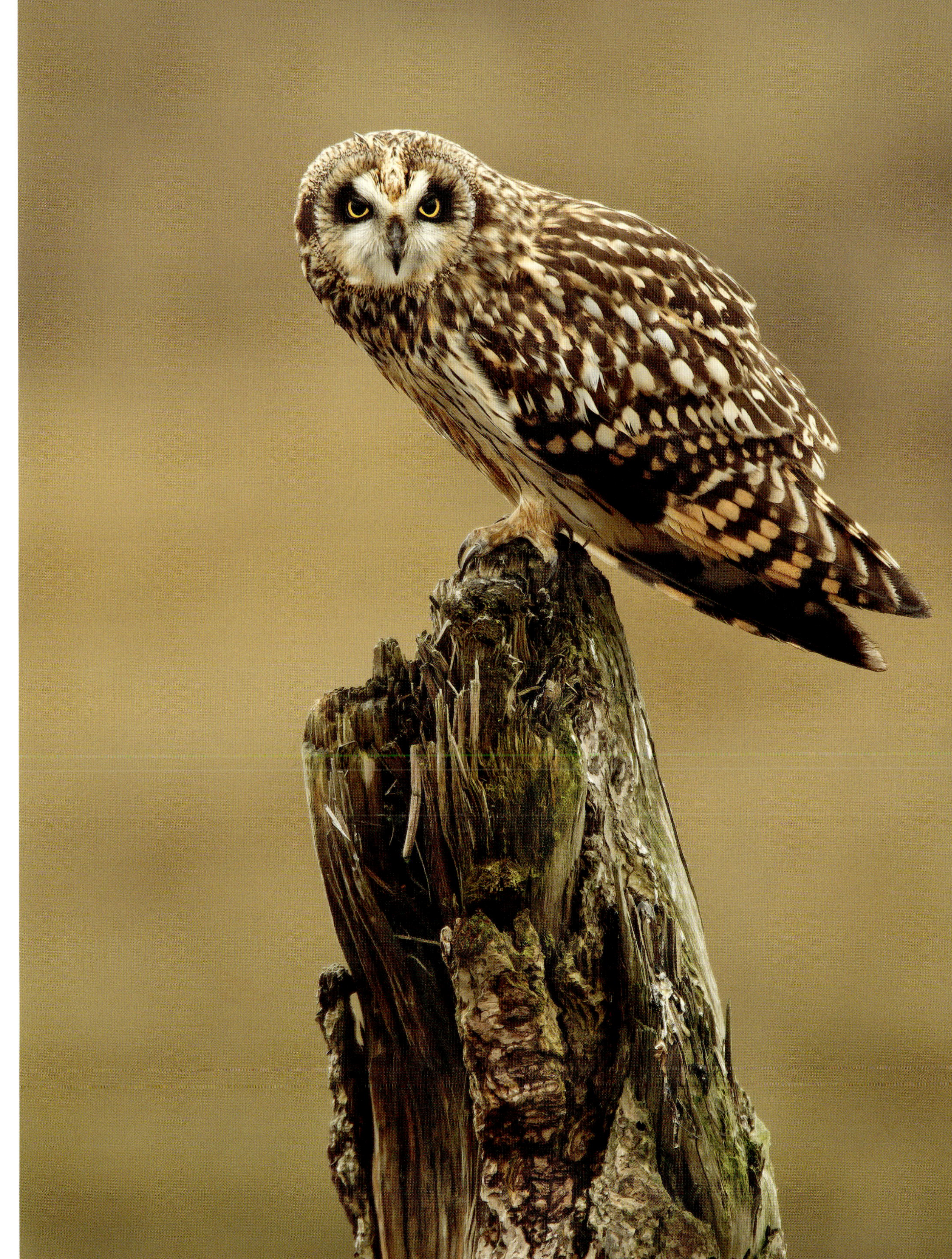

The estuary ecosystems that form at river mouths are ideal places for Short-eared Owls to search for rodents.

JARED HOBBS

A Surf Scoter flies just above the surface of the ocean. The large bill and white patch on the back of its neck make it easy to identify, even from a distance.

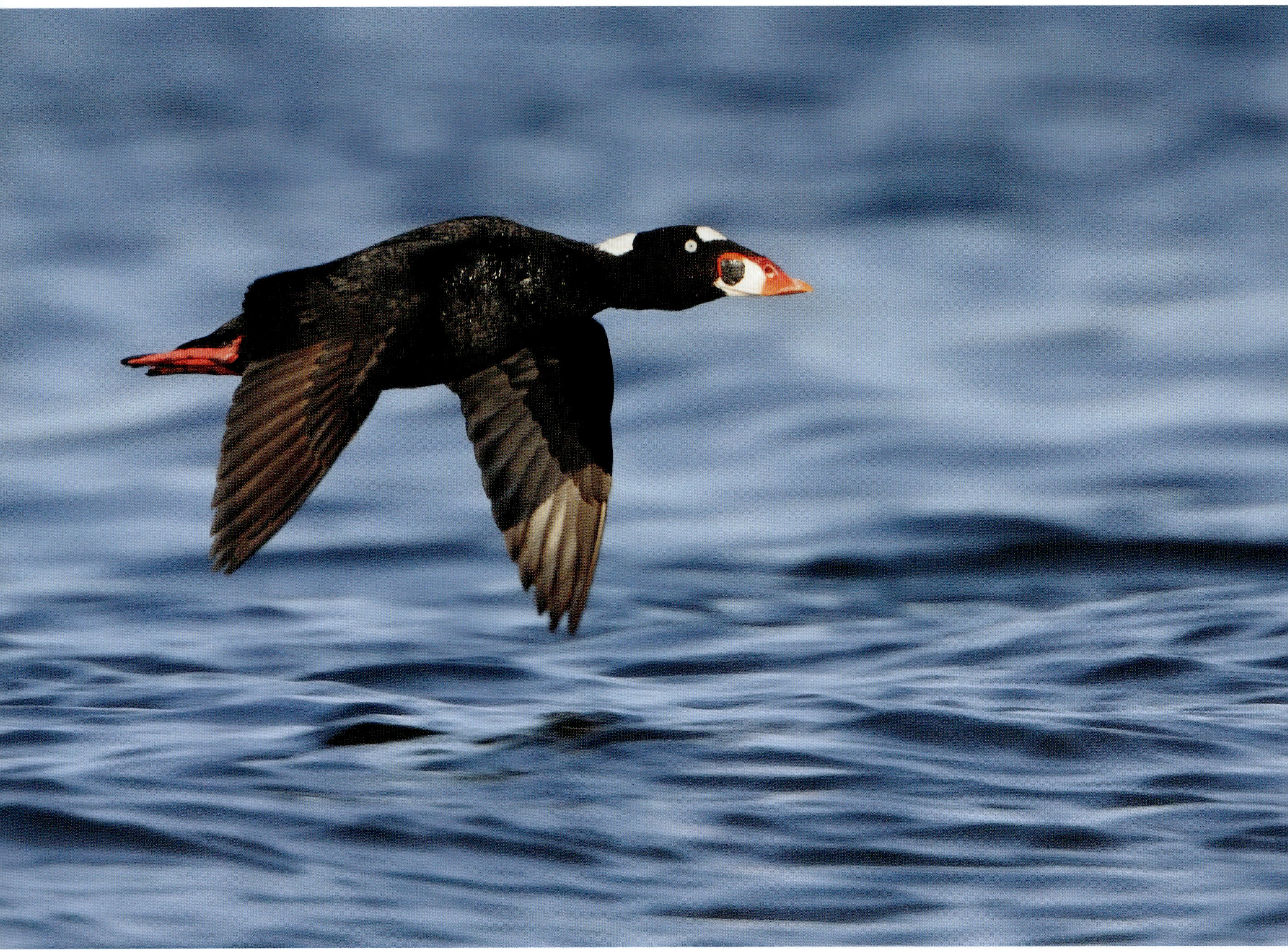

A second species of Scoter that inhabits the waters off the coast of BC is the White-winged Scoter, named for the white patches on its wings.

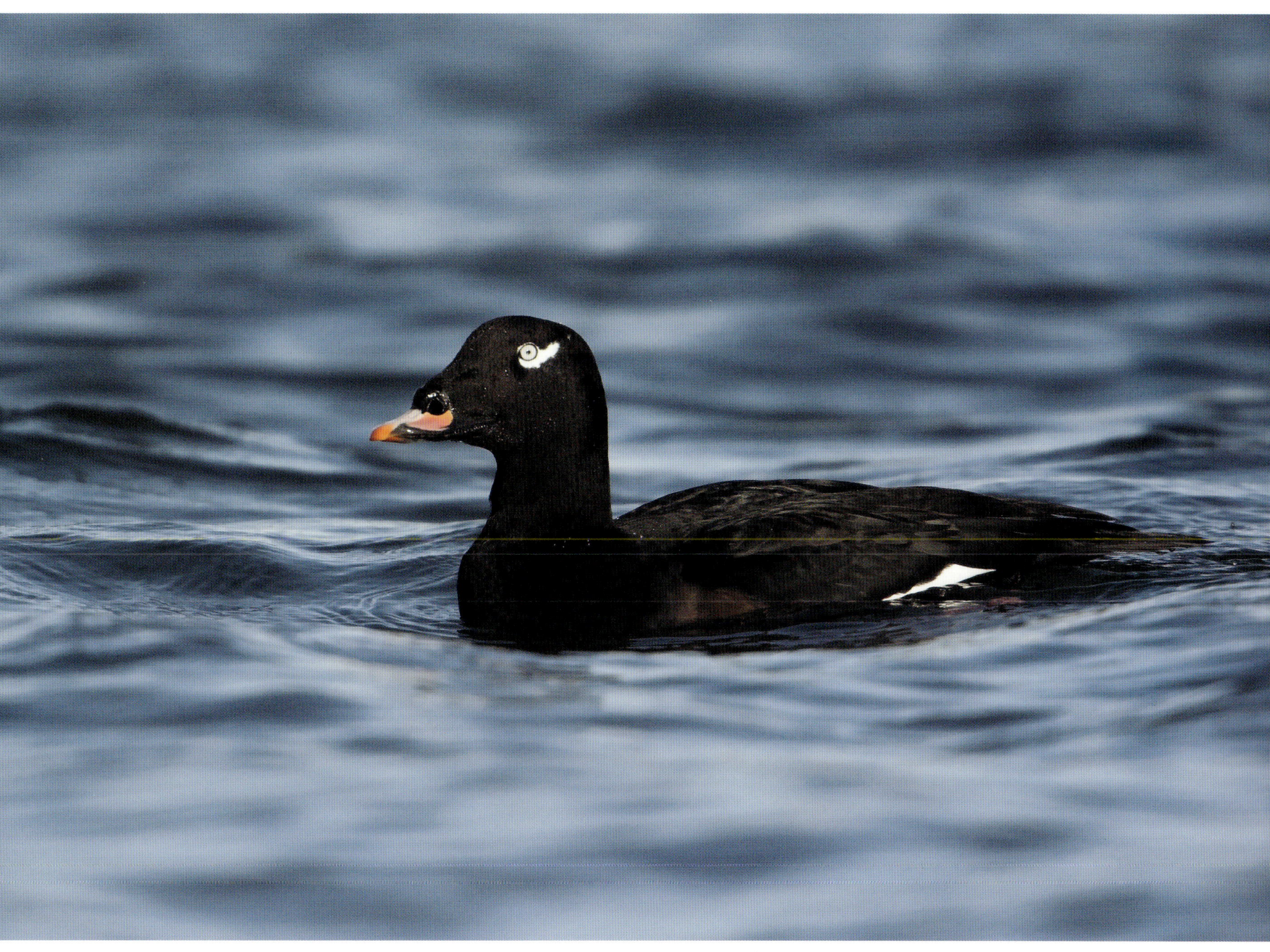

The third member of the *Melanitta* genus is the Black Scoter. Like all Scoters, it feeds primarily on molluscs, which it gathers from the ocean floor and crushes in its muscular crop.

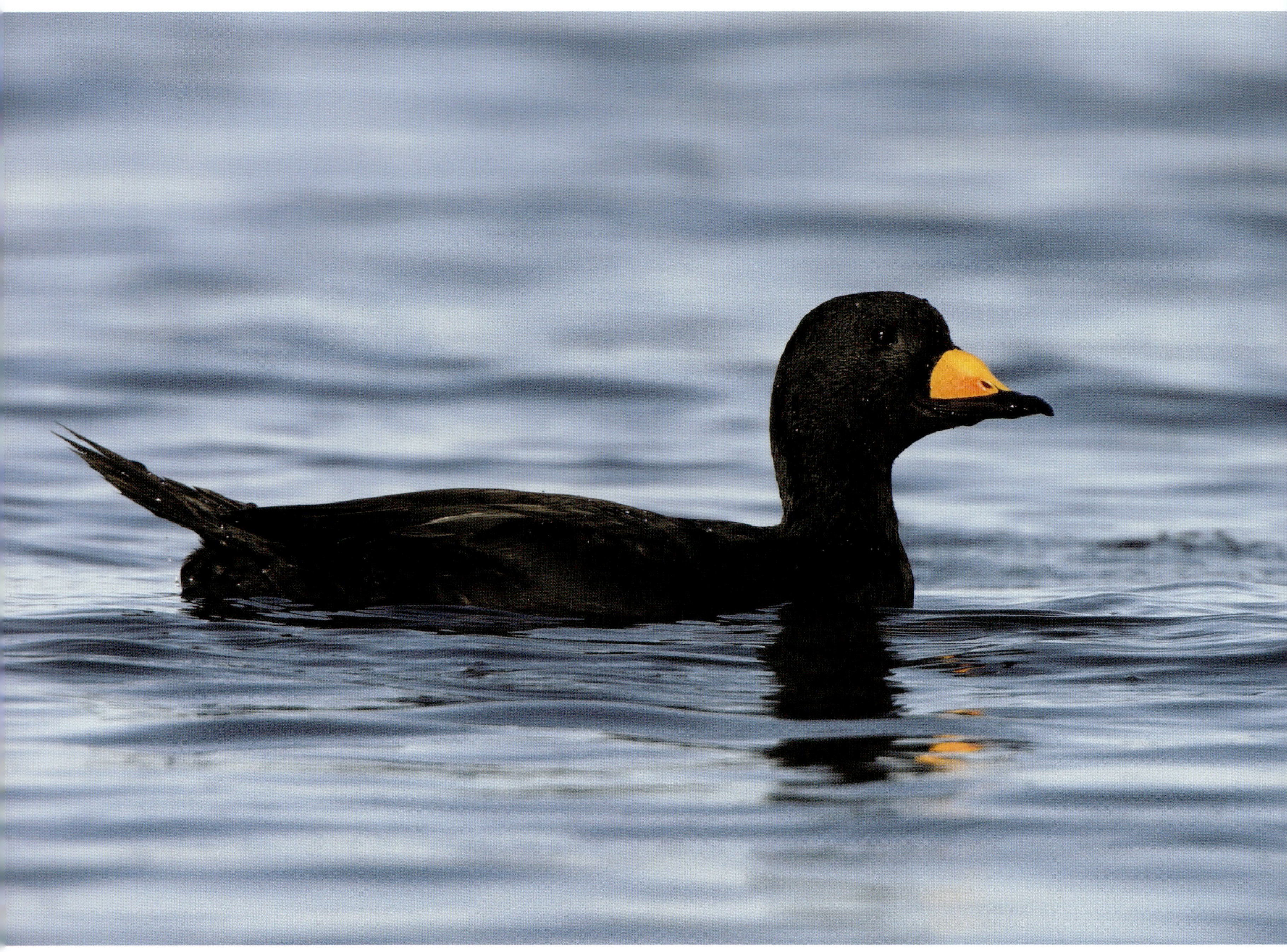

The Glaucous-winged Gull is a large species of gull that is common off the coast of BC. Although they generally breed on offshore islands, they also use urban rooftops (much to the dismay of local residents). Inset: Baby Glaucous-winged Gulls look more like dandelions than seabirds.

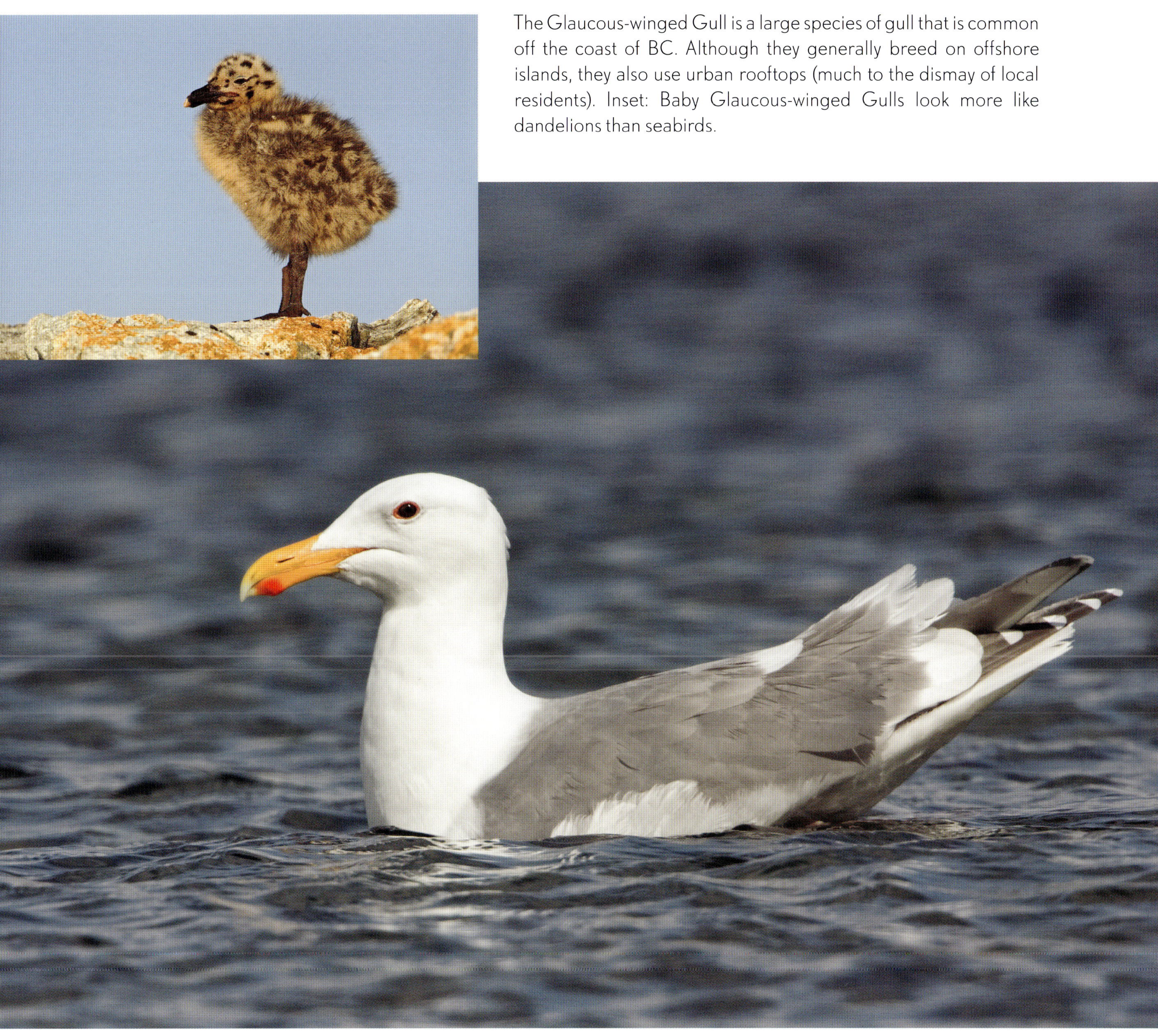

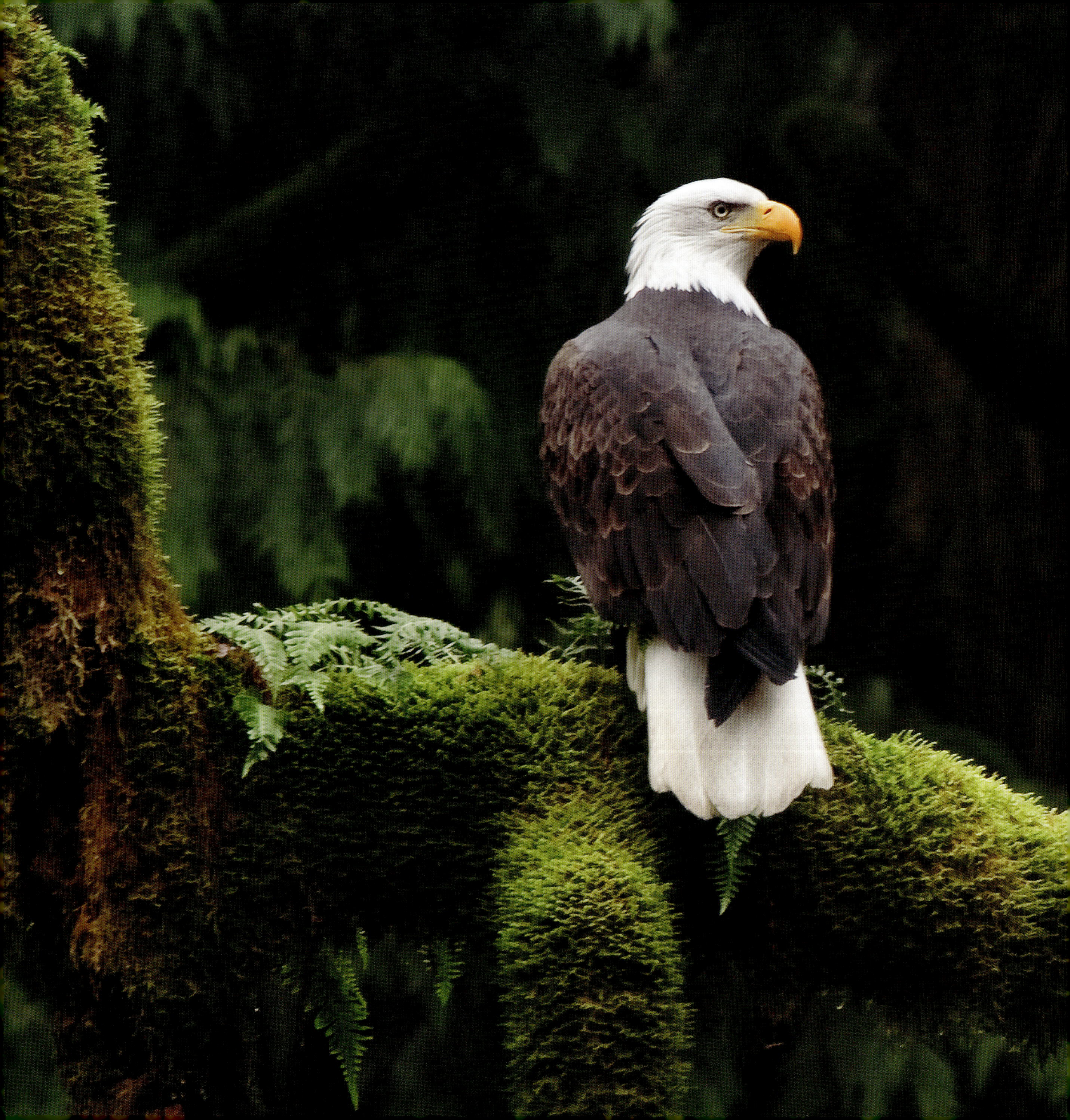

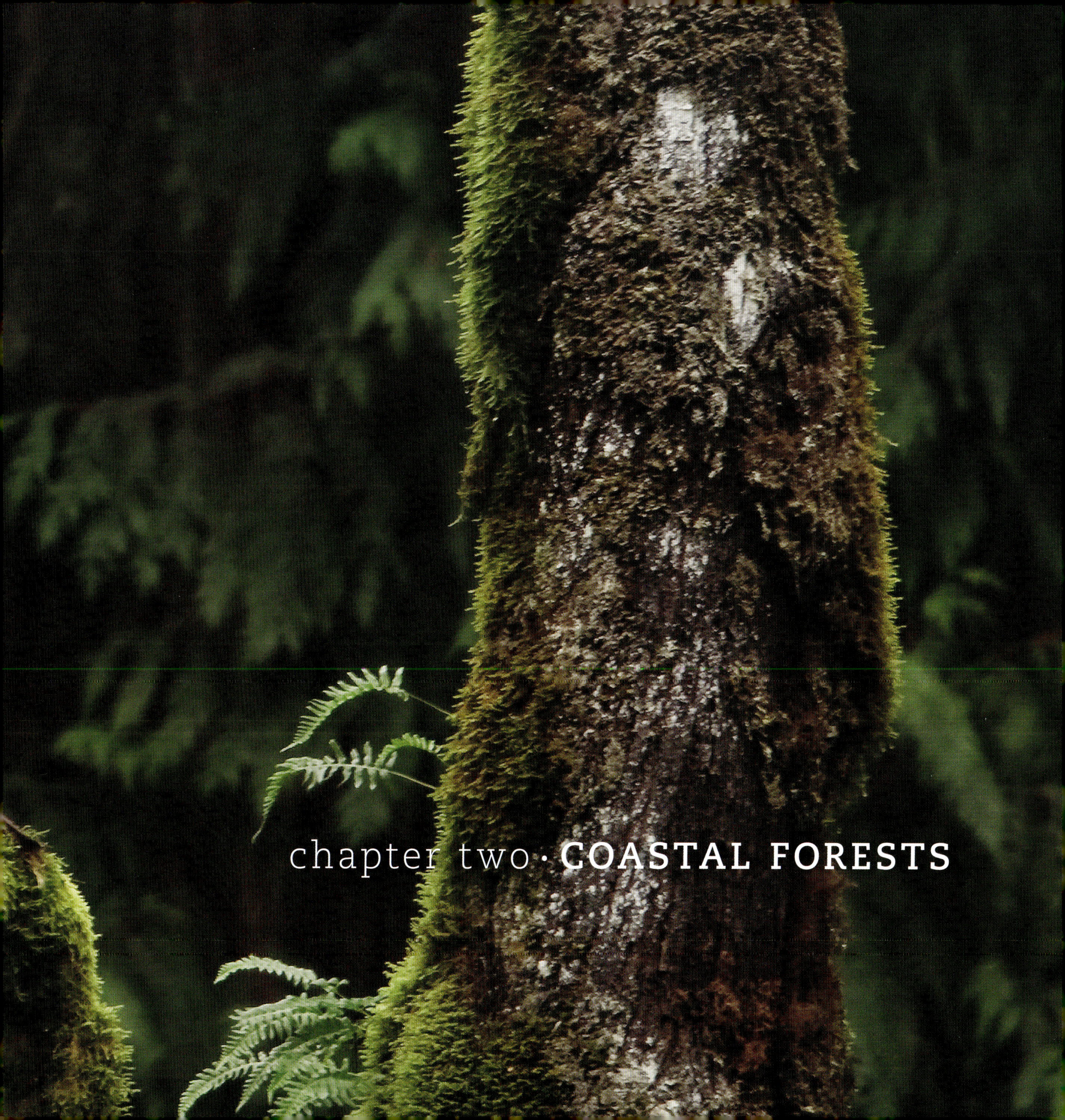

chapter two · COASTAL FORESTS

Perhaps more than any other symbol of the province, it is the iconic old-growth rainforest trees covered in moss and shrouded in mist that first come to mind when someone thinks about British Columbia. Located west of the Coast and Cascade Mountain ranges and descending down to the coastline, these rainforests are home to the biggest trees in all of Canada. Walking through a coastal rainforest and standing among the giant, centuries-old trees, it is hard not to feel small and insignificant. And sometimes, feeling small is a good thing. Being humbled by these miraculous forests forces us to respect them. It makes us immediately aware of the brevity of our lives on this Earth and the fact that we are but a small part of Mother Nature's master plan.

A temperate rainforest in BC has a certain feel to it. Cool dampness hangs thick in the air, permeated by the scents of cedar and humus, and the acoustic characteristics resulting from nearly every surface being covered in moss add to its unique feeling. When it comes down to it, though, it is the immense size of the trees that characterizes the coastal forests of BC. These cedar, fir, spruce and hemlock trees grow to such towering heights primarily because of two factors—precipitation and temperature. The high amounts of precipitation and the moderate temperatures of the west coast allow the trees to grow rapidly and combine to create a third factor—the absence of forest fires, which allows the trees to survive to incredible ages. The oldest Yellow Cedar trees on the north coast of BC are thought to be more than 2,000 years old. These ancient coastal forests are wonderful places to explore and to search for the many species of birds that live in them. To the knowledgeable birdwatcher, the sights and sounds of these birds contribute greatly to the overall feeling of the rainforest itself.

YEAR-ROUND RESIDENTS

Some birds can be found in the coastal forests throughout the entire year. These year-round residents are always there to greet visitors to their home, and each has its own personality and way of saying hello. While the curious Chestnut-backed Chickadee is likely to come in for a close-up inspection, the shy Varied Thrush is more apt to stay out of sight and be heard rather than seen. Troops of Steller's Jays would be hard to miss with their bold behaviour and raucous calls. On the other hand, it would be easy to walk by a roosting Barred Owl and never even know it was there. The squeaky call of a Red-breasted Nuthatch often gives its presence away as it travels down a tree trunk searching for insects. Pileated Woodpeckers call loudly as they fly overhead. Other year-round residents of the coastal forests include Ravens, Bald Eagles, Northern Pygmy Owls, Spotted Towhees, Bewick's Wrens and Red-breasted Sapsuckers, to name a few.

SPRING SPLENDOUR

Although birds can be found in this region throughout the year, there is perhaps no better time to explore the coastal rainforests of BC than in the springtime, when the air comes alive with birdsong. Many of these songsters are migratory birds that have come to BC from as far away as Central and South America to breed and raise their young. One of the loudest and most persistent singers is the tiny Pacific Wren, whose relentless song can be heard throughout the lower realms of the forest. Another denizen of the temperate rainforest is the Townsend's Warbler, whose song rings out from the tops of the towering trees. Birds like the Brown Creeper bridge the gap between forest floor and canopy. These busy birds seem to be almost always hard at work searching for spiders, insects and other tasty morsels hidden underneath the bark of trees. Other migratory birds that come to the coastal forests of BC each year include Western Tanagers; Wilson's, Black-throated Gray, Yellow, MacGillivray's and Orange-crowned Warblers; Olive-sided and Hammond's Flycatchers; Chipping Sparrows; Band-tailed Pigeons; Black-headed Grosbeaks; and Cassin's and Hutton's Vireos. With all of the resident and migratory species in their best plumage and singing their hearts out, it is difficult to imagine a better time than the spring to be out birdwatching.

FALL FRENZY

If any time compares to the spring for diversity and excitement of exploring the coastal forest, it would have to be autumn when the salmon return to their coastal rivers to spawn and end their life cycle. During this time many areas along the coast experience a burst of life when tremendous amounts of food become available. The promise of an easy meal brings in birds of all kinds from far and wide. Perhaps the most spectacular bird to join the feast is the Bald Eagle. During salmon spawns, it is not uncommon to see dozens of these majestic raptors feeding on the carcasses of dead fish or loafing around in the treetops—no doubt wishing they had not eaten so much. Another incredible bird that takes advantage of the feeding frenzy is the American Dipper. These fascinating little birds are incredibly adept in water and will scurry around beneath the surface searching for all kinds of aquatic invertebrates, fish and even salmon eggs. The salmon spawn is such a special event that birds that would ordinarily not be found deep inside a rainforest, such as gulls and Common Mergansers, cannot refuse the bountiful supply of food.

What amounts to a fantastic spectacle for nature lovers, birdwatchers and photographers also plays a vital role in the nutrient cycle of the forest. Birds serve a purpose in returning valuable nutrients from the aquatic environment back to the terrestrial zone. After they devour huge amounts of dead salmon, they excrete the nutrients back into the forest. These age-old interactions exemplify the connectivity inherent throughout the natural world that we so often take for granted.

INTERCONNECTIVITY

Interconnectivity is a theme that can easily be seen throughout the coastal forests of BC. One excellent example is the timing of the return of the migratory Rufous Hummingbird. These birds, the smallest in North America, make amazing journeys each spring to travel all the way from their winter homes in Mexico to BC, where they breed and raise their young. Their migration is perfectly timed to coincide with the spring eruption of the flowering salmonberry shrubs upon which they feed. Another example of interconnectivity can be seen in the Marbled Murrelet—a fascinating and exquisite seabird that lives along the Pacific coast. Unlike other members of the Alcidae family (which includes murres, murrelets, puffins, auks and guillemots) Marbled Murrelets do not nest in large groups on rocky islands or outcroppings. Instead they fly far inland each night and nest in solitude in the towering old-growth forests of the Pacific Northwest. These birds depend equally upon the sea and their ancient forest homes to survive. In this way, they seem to perfectly characterize the connections in nature and between the earth and the ocean.

CAPTURING THE SHOT

The rainforests of BC are truly magical places with tremendous biological diversity and are home to a wonderful variety of birds. Yet, as fantastic a place as the rainforest is, it does present a number of challenges when it comes to photographing birds. Perhaps the most obvious one is that rainforests tend to be shady and dark. With little natural light to work with, there is often no choice but to rely upon flash. Finding a way to balance the natural ambient light and the artificial "fill" light is a skill that must be mastered before entering the rainforest environment. A second major challenge to photographing birds in rainforests is that the trees are extremely tall. Many species of birds spend most of their time in the canopy and rarely come low enough to offer a satisfying look, let alone photograph. Rainforest bird photography can be difficult, but it brings great rewards if one is willing to patiently wait, study and observe the patterns of nature and the lives of its avian inhabitants. For me, the time and patience required to successfully photograph rainforest birds only adds to the experience, as it means that I am forced to spend even more time in these spectacular places.

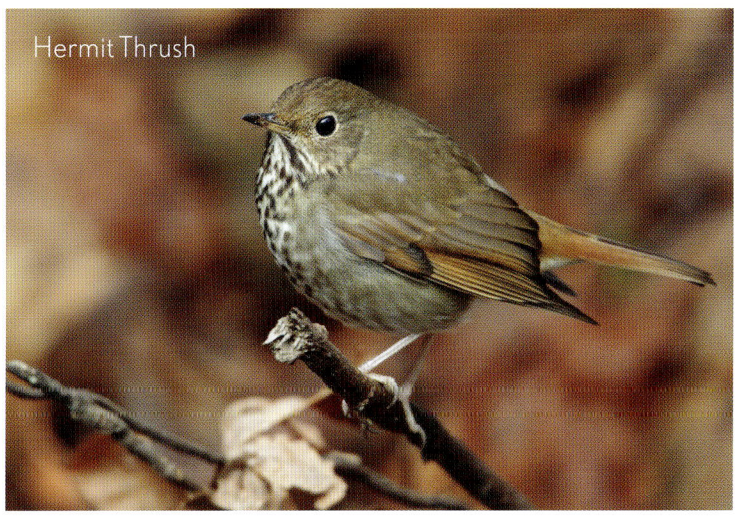
Hermit Thrush

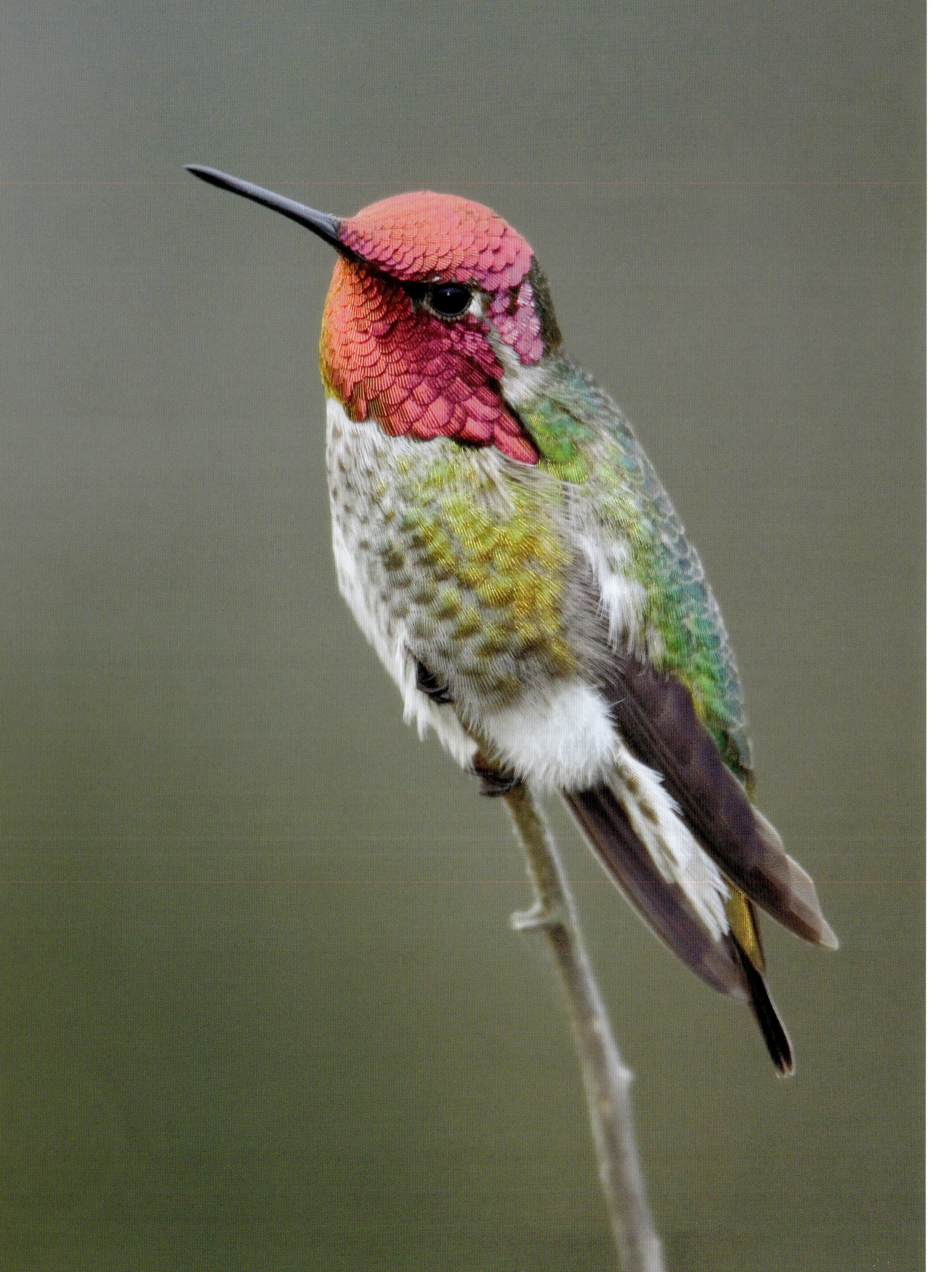

This Anna's Hummingbird shows excellent iridescent plumage. As the full spectrum of light hits the bird's facial feathers, most of the wavelengths are absorbed. Only the pink spectrum is reflected back, resulting in this fantastic display of structural colouration.

In the southwestern corner of the province, Black-throated Gray Warblers are a welcome addition to the spring avifauna.

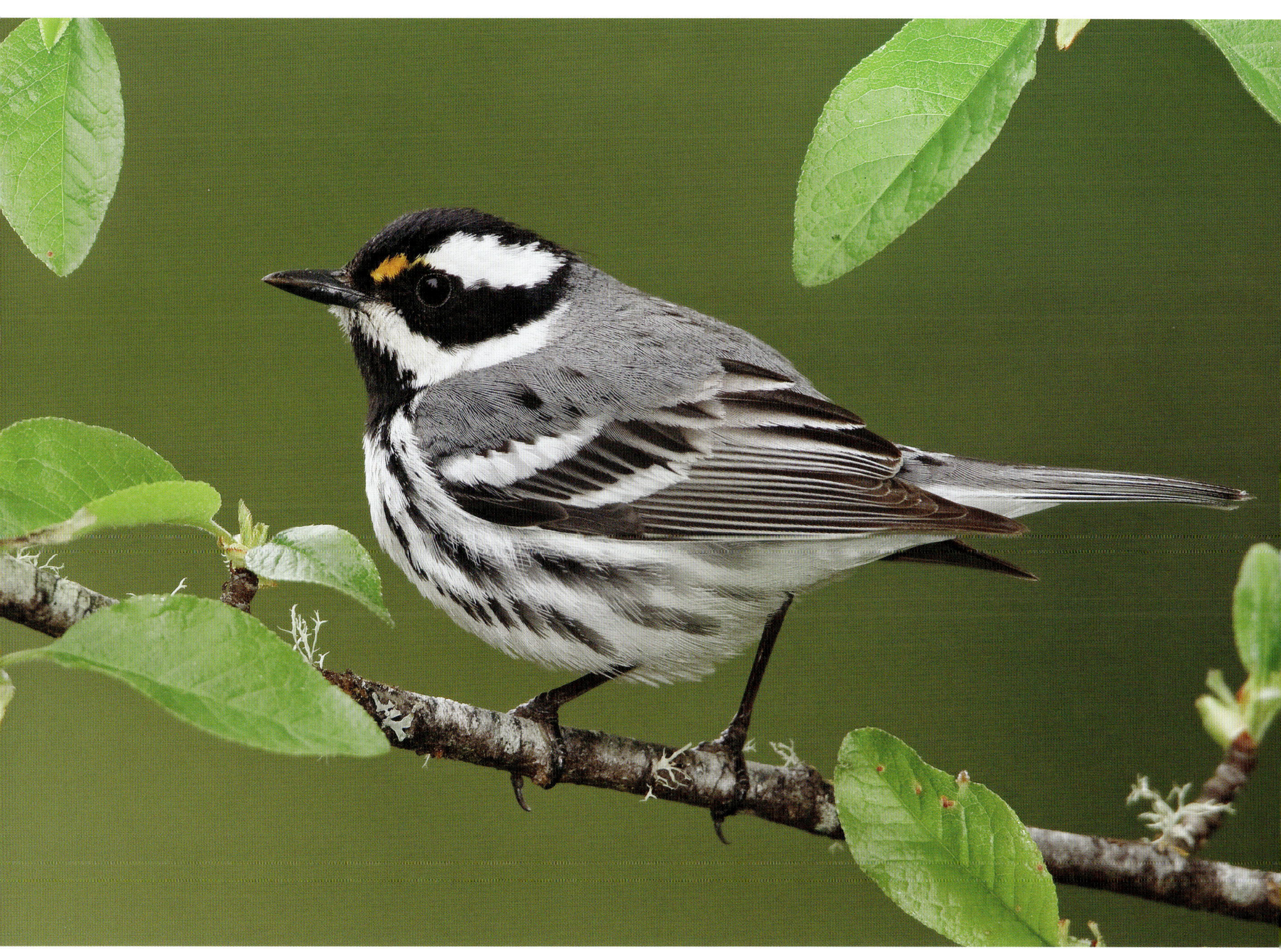

The plumage of Fox Sparrows is highly variable depending on where you find them in North America.

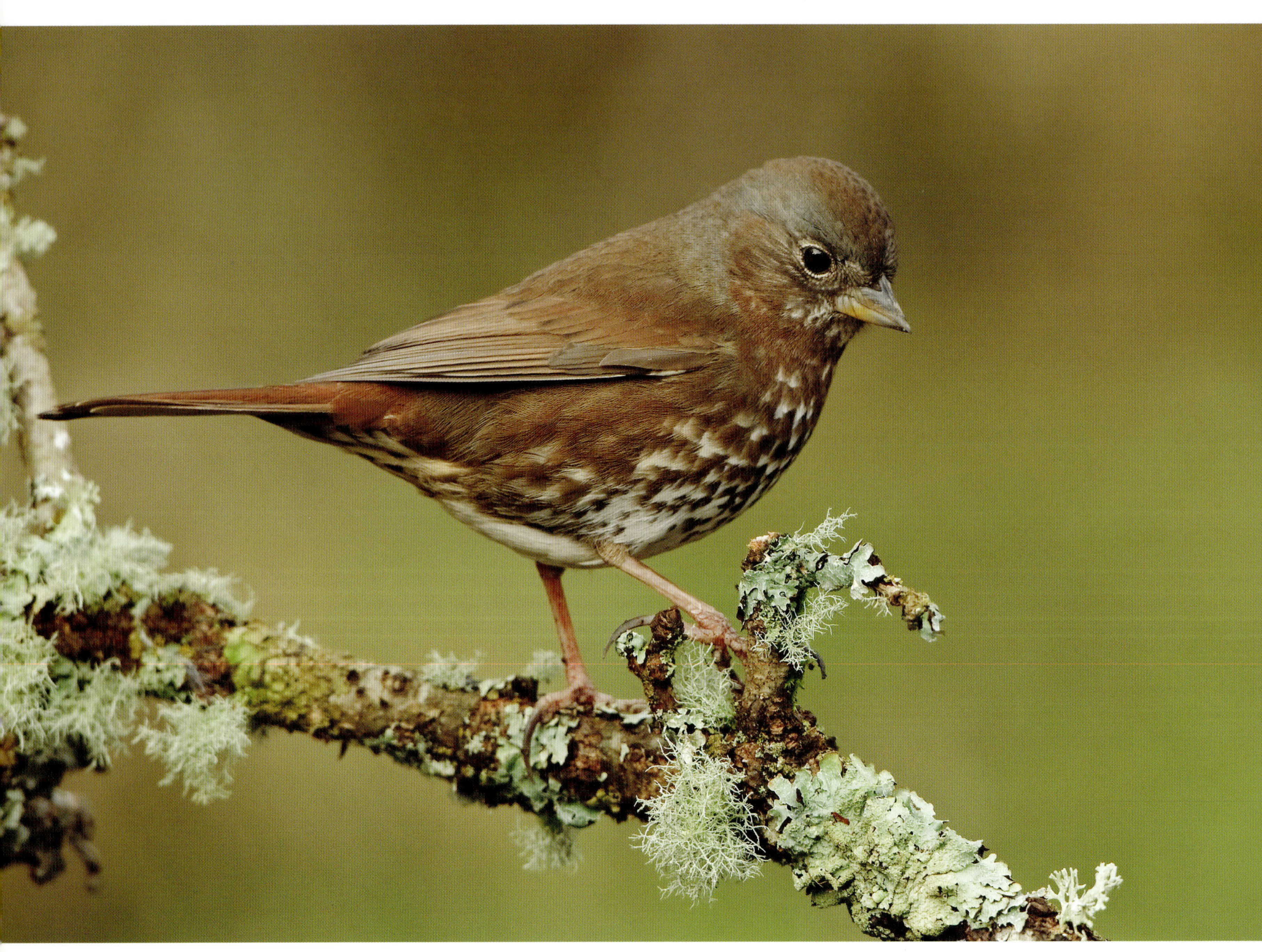

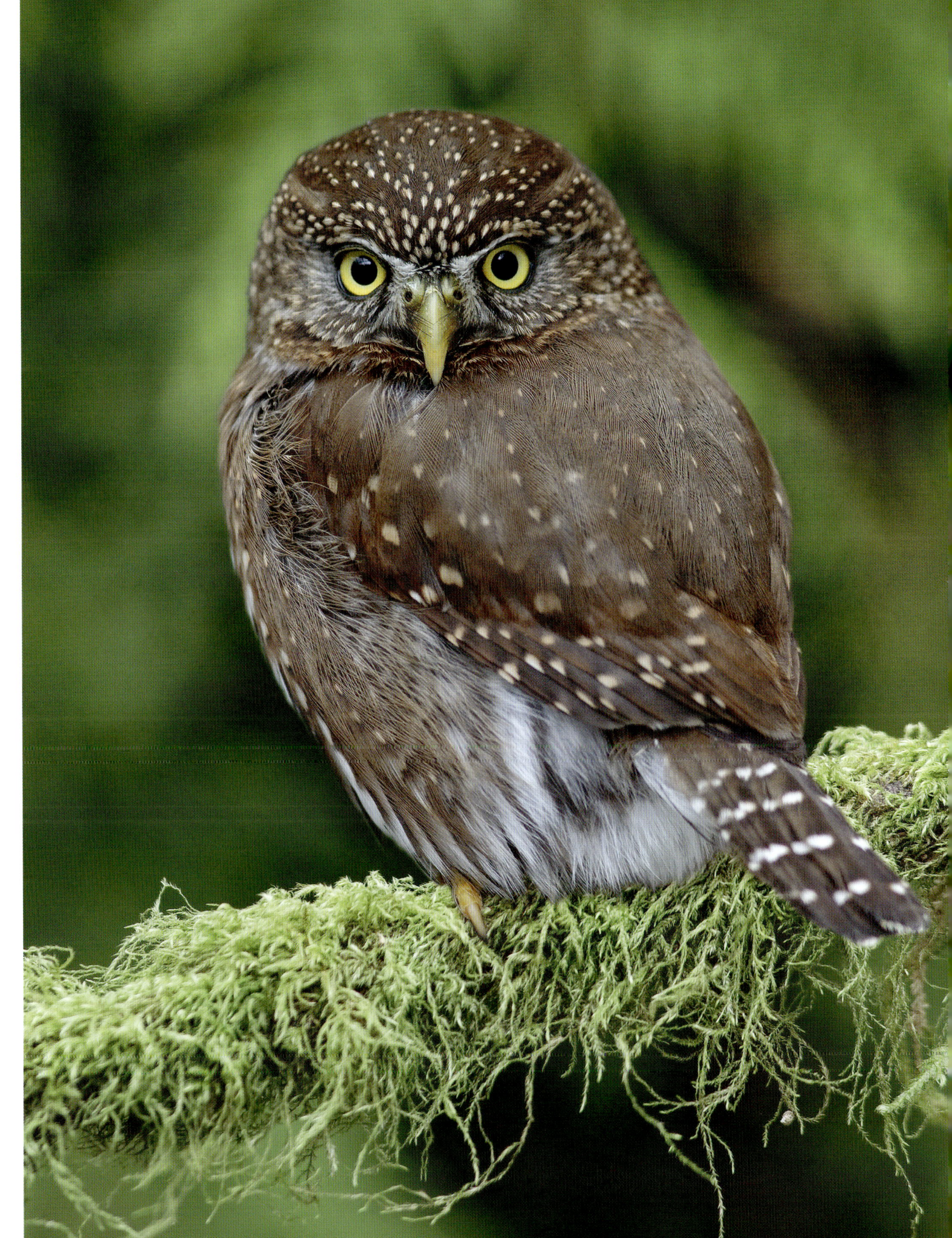

A tiny Northern Pygmy Owl perches on a mossy branch in the coastal rainforest.

The brilliant red eye and rufous flank make this Spotted Towhee easy to identify.

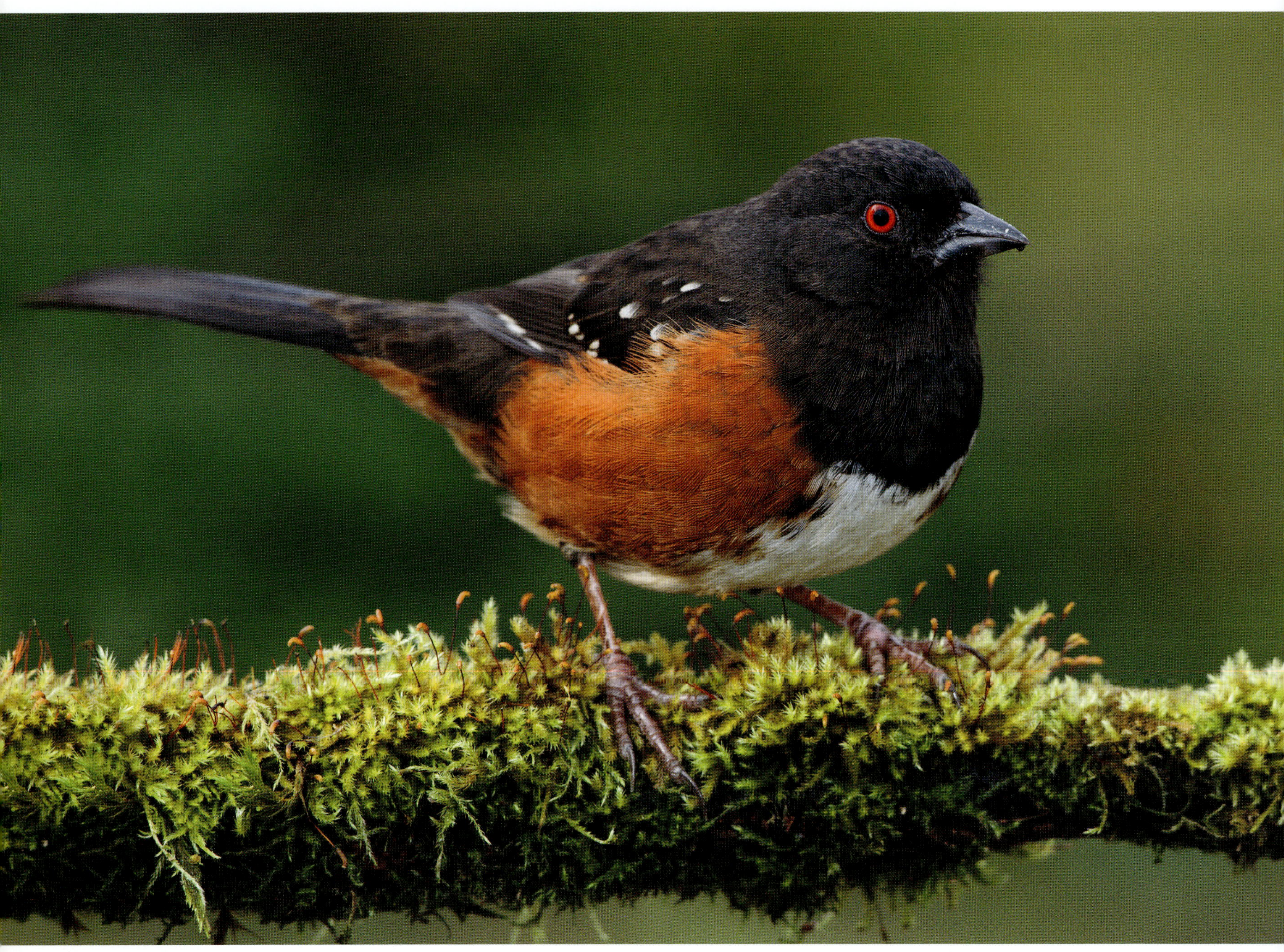

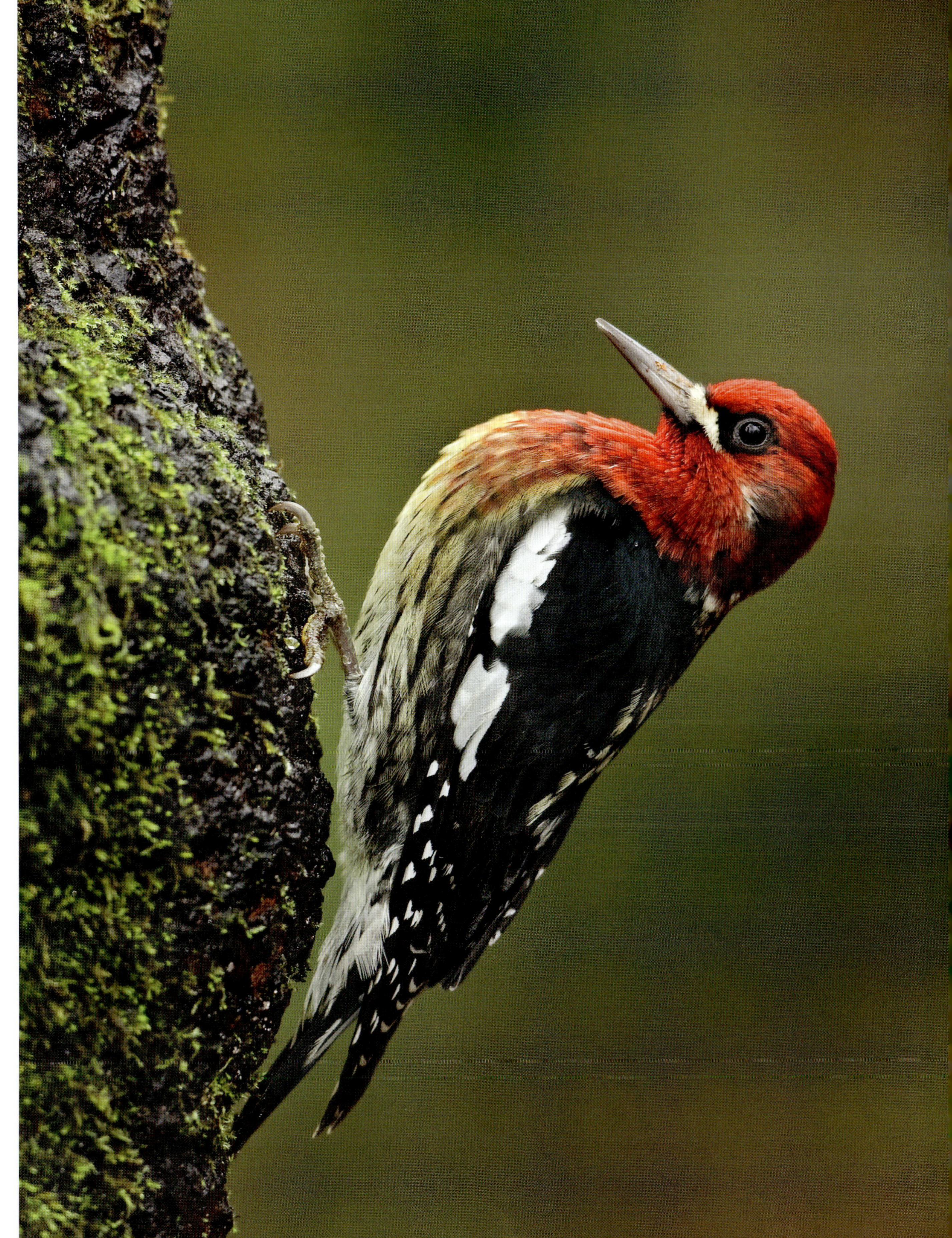

As warmer spring temperatures allow the sap to flow in a Bigleaf Maple, this Red-breasted Sapsucker drills into the tree, which it will visit regularly to drink the nutritious sap.

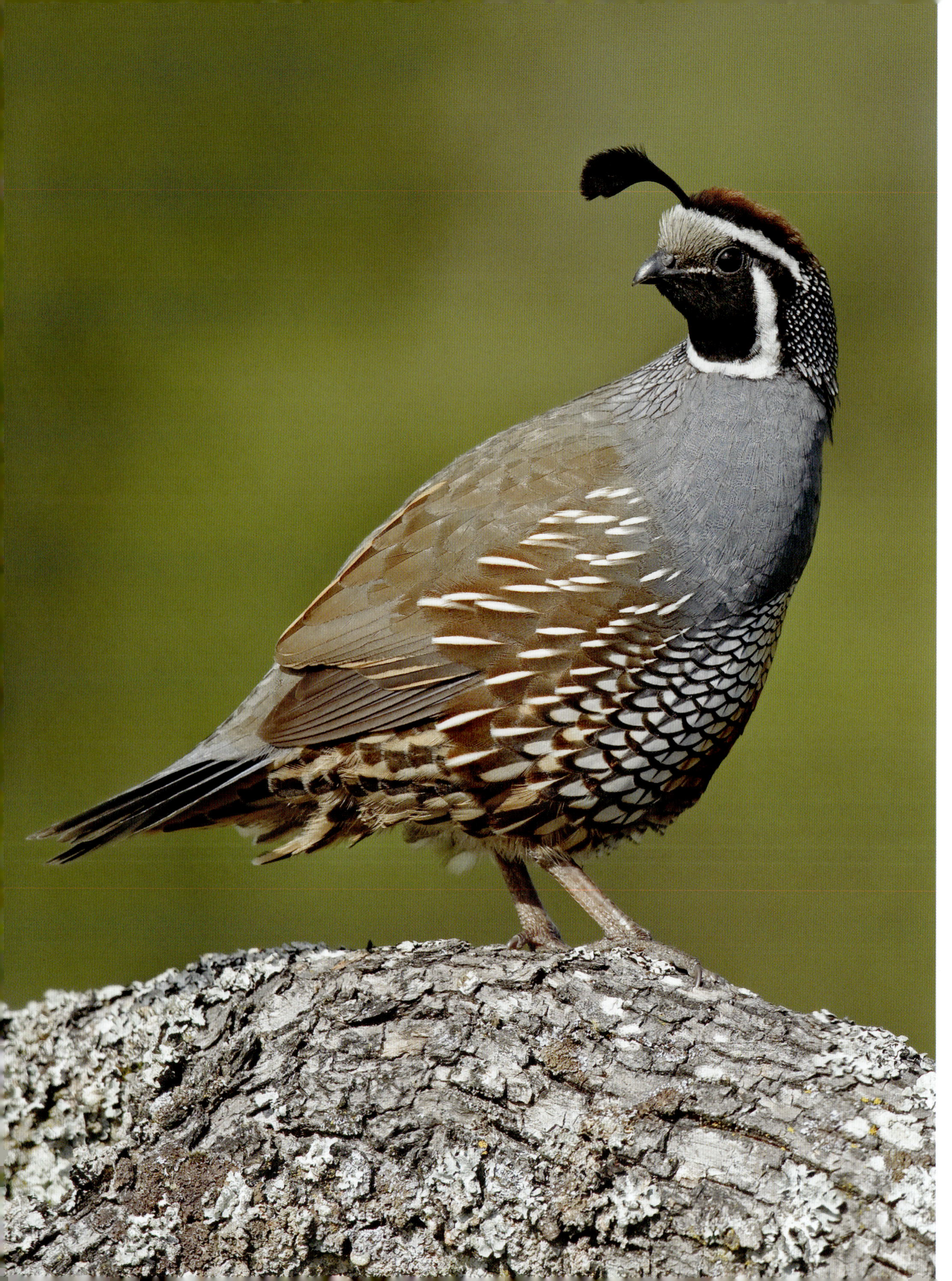

A male California Quail poses briefly to allow observers to appreciate his beautiful plumage.

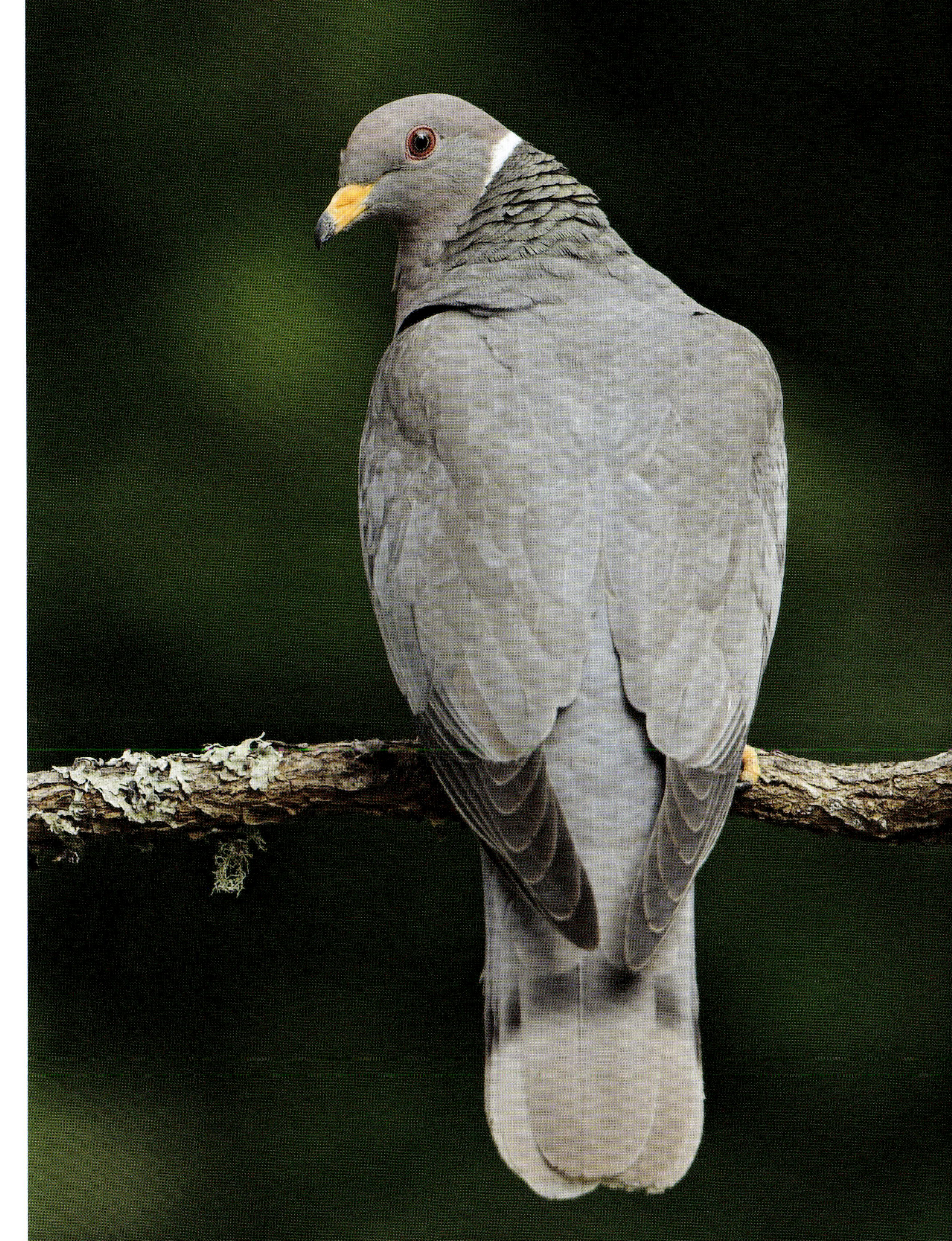

Band-tailed Pigeons spend their winters in the Andes before returning to southwestern BC to breed each summer.

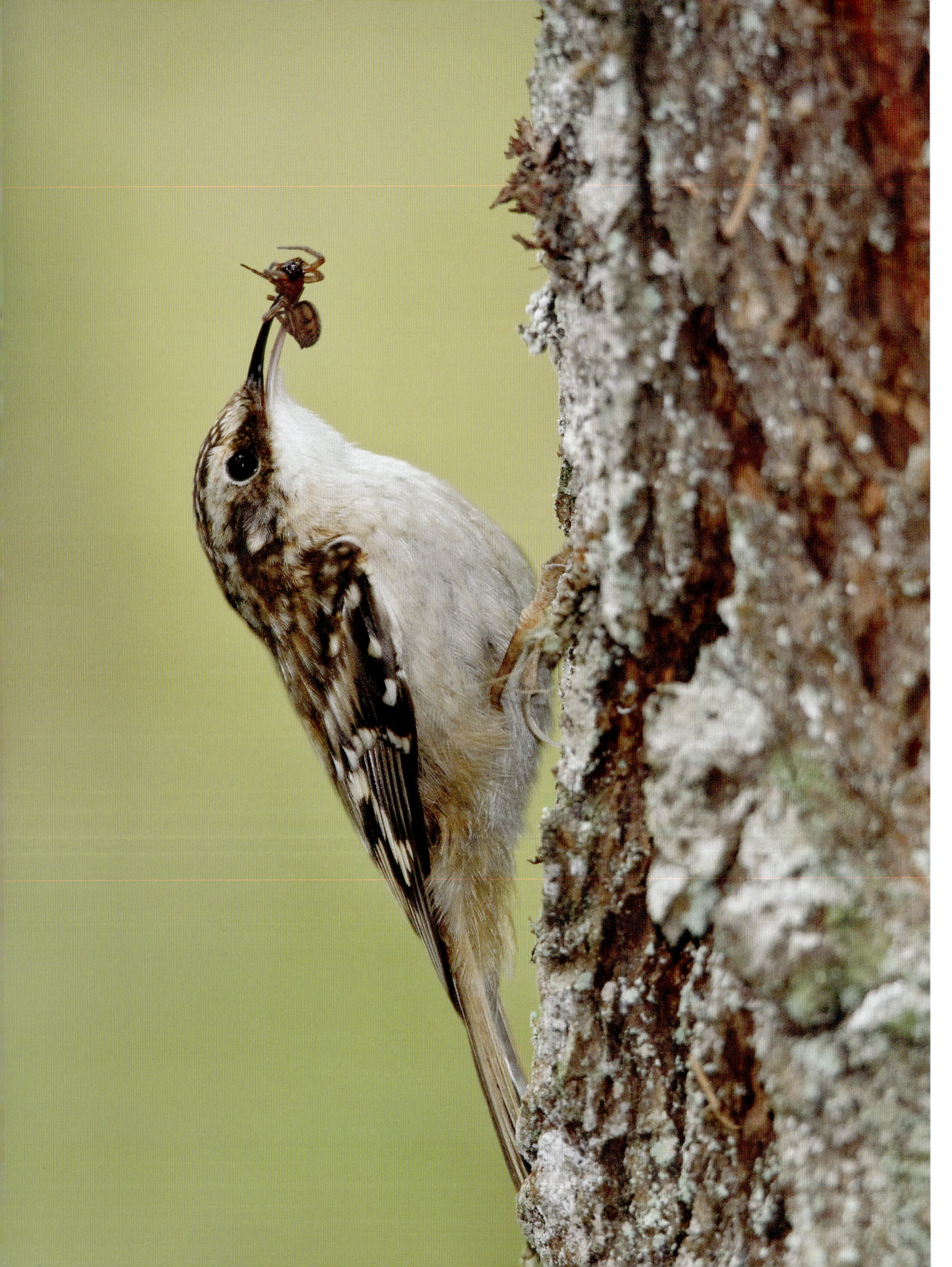

A Brown Creeper extracts a spider from the bark of a coastal Douglas Fir before continuing on its way up the tree.

A curious Chestnut-backed Chickadee descends from the treetops to investigate a backyard bird feeder on Vancouver Island.

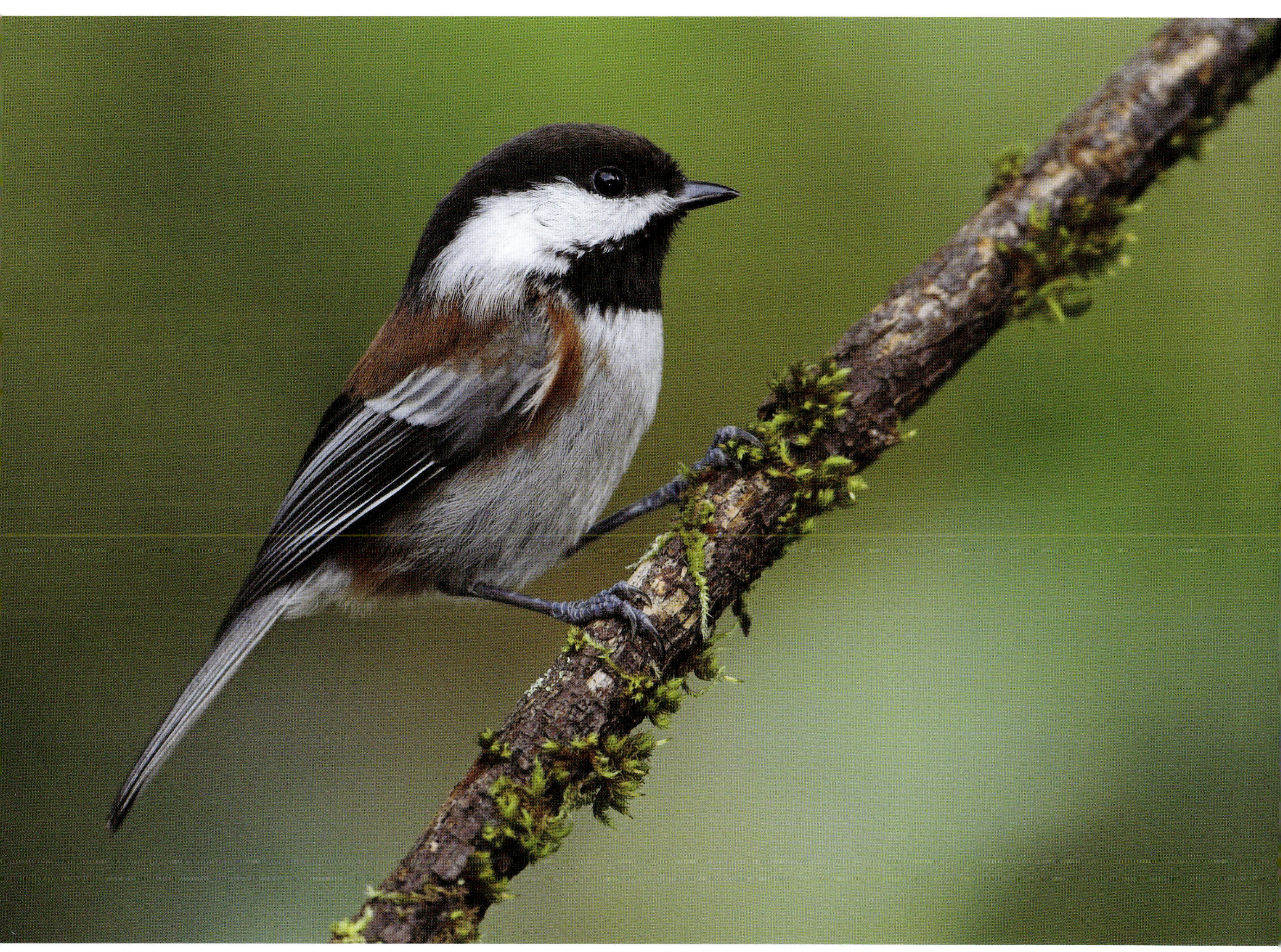

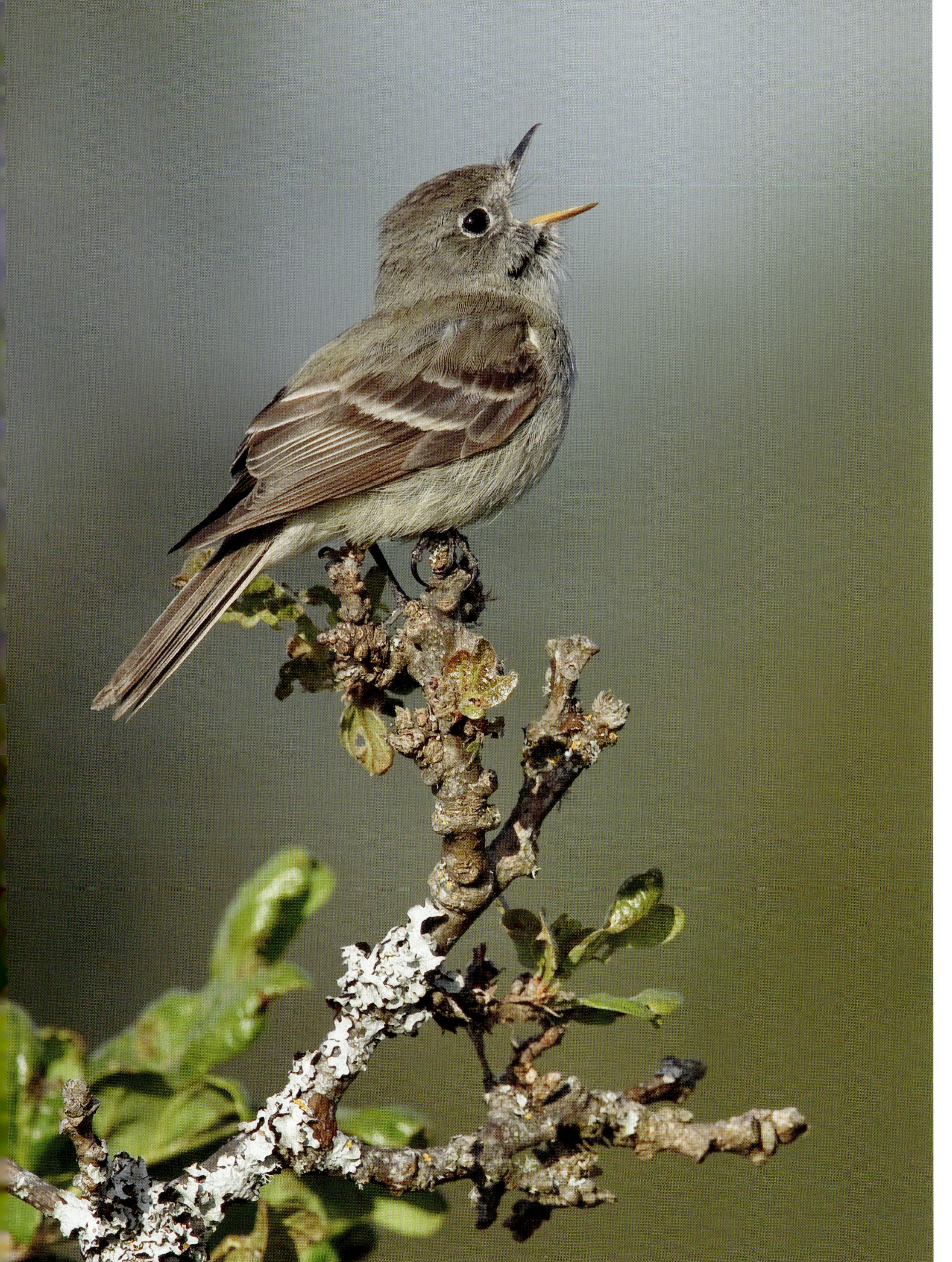

When spring returns to BC, birds such as this Hammond's Flycatcher hurry back from their wintering grounds to establish breeding territories. Male birds generally return first and immediately begin singing as a way to stake their claim to a favourable site.

The high-pitched metallic trill of a Varied Thrush is a wonderful sound that resonates through the rainforests of coastal BC.

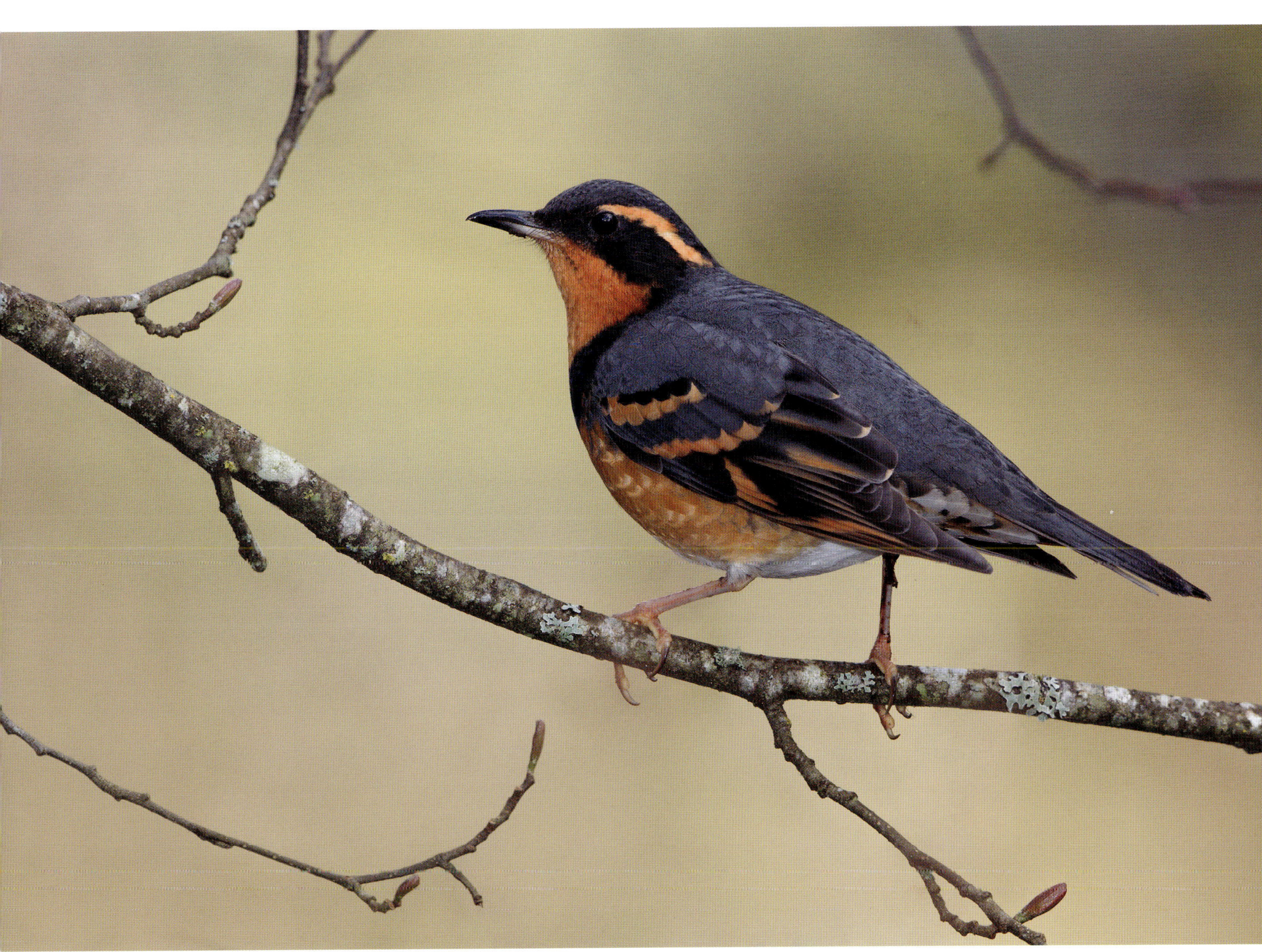

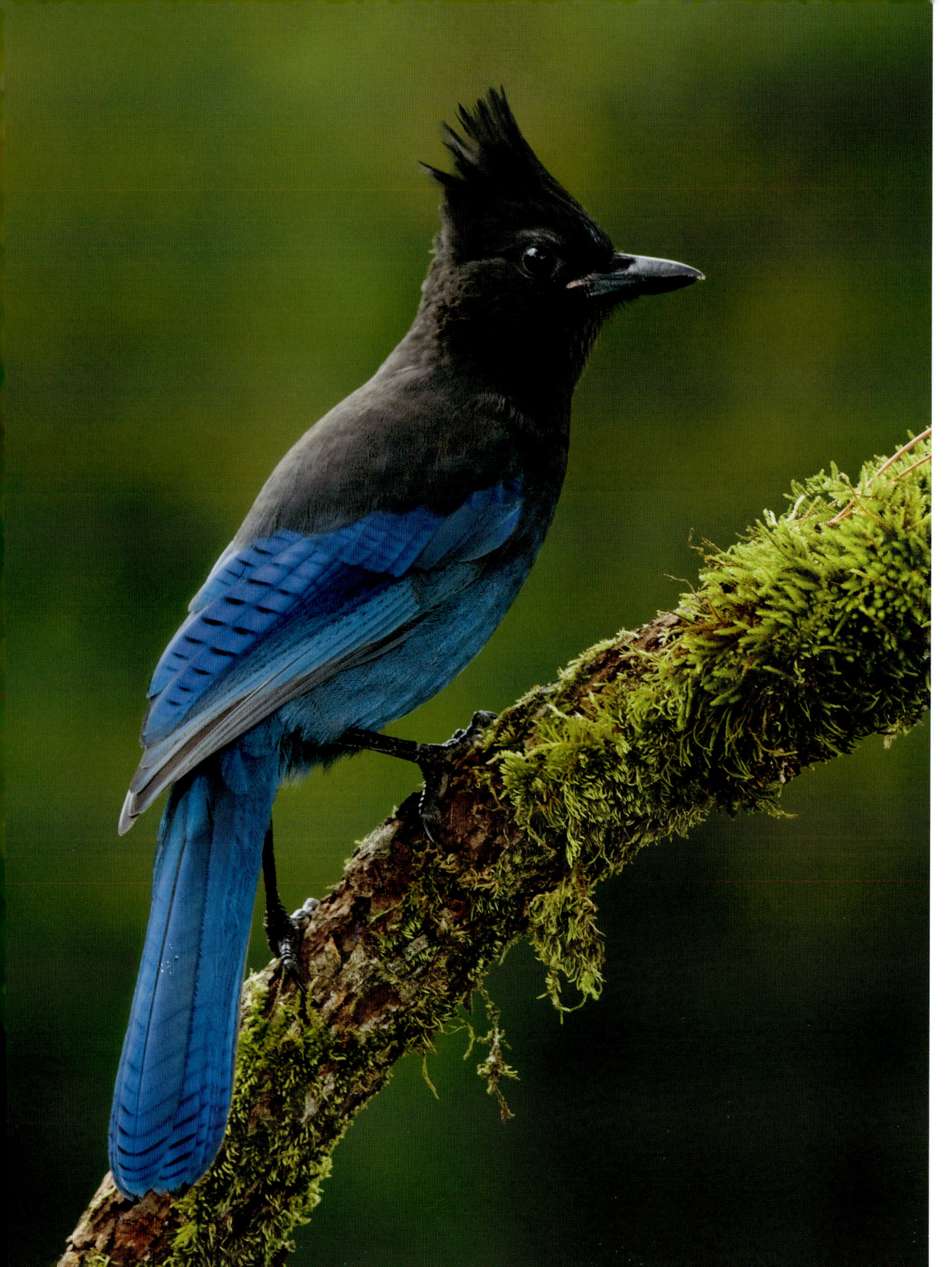

The Steller's Jay is BC's provincial bird. Their raucous calls and big personalities make them extremely conspicuous throughout the coastal forests.

Marbled Murrelets are seabirds that breed in old-growth coastal rainforests. Without sizable trees, they are unable to find adequate nest sites. As a result of their habitat needs and the deforestation that has occurred along BC's coast, these birds are now endangered.

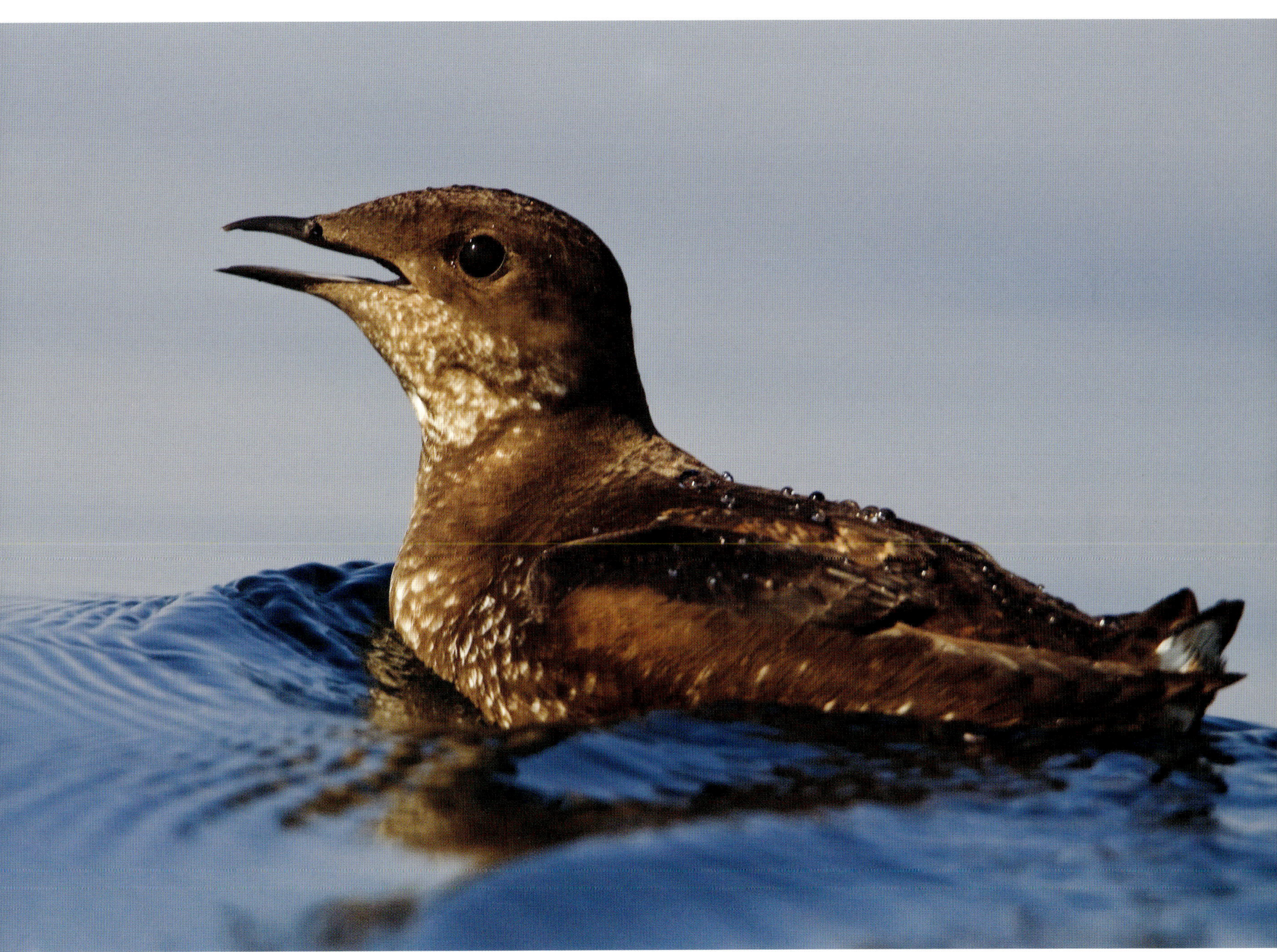

All wrens have lots of personality, and this Bewick's Wren is no exception.

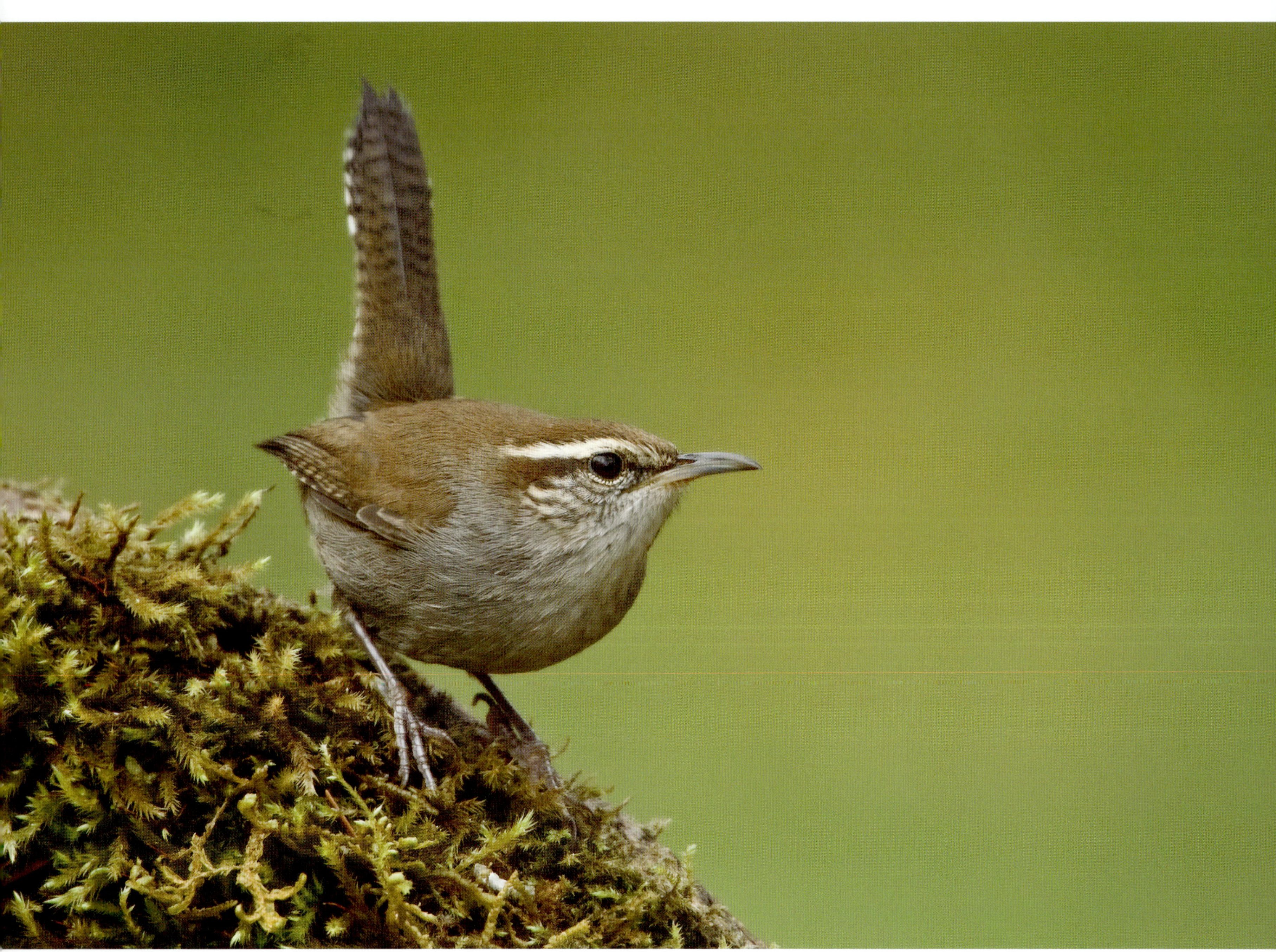

Cassin's Vieros can be found throughout the southern part of the province; this one was found calling from its territory on Vancouver Island.

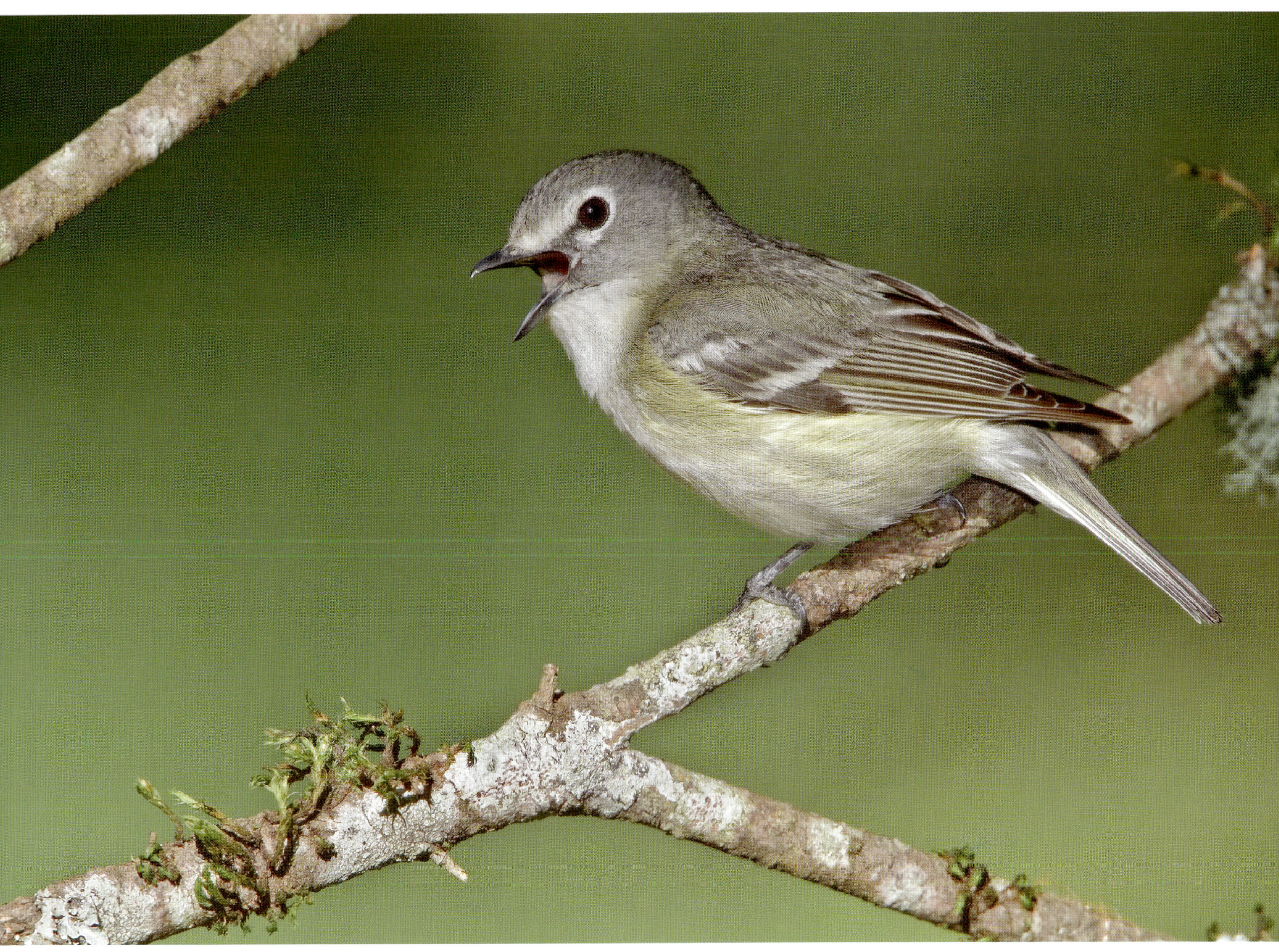

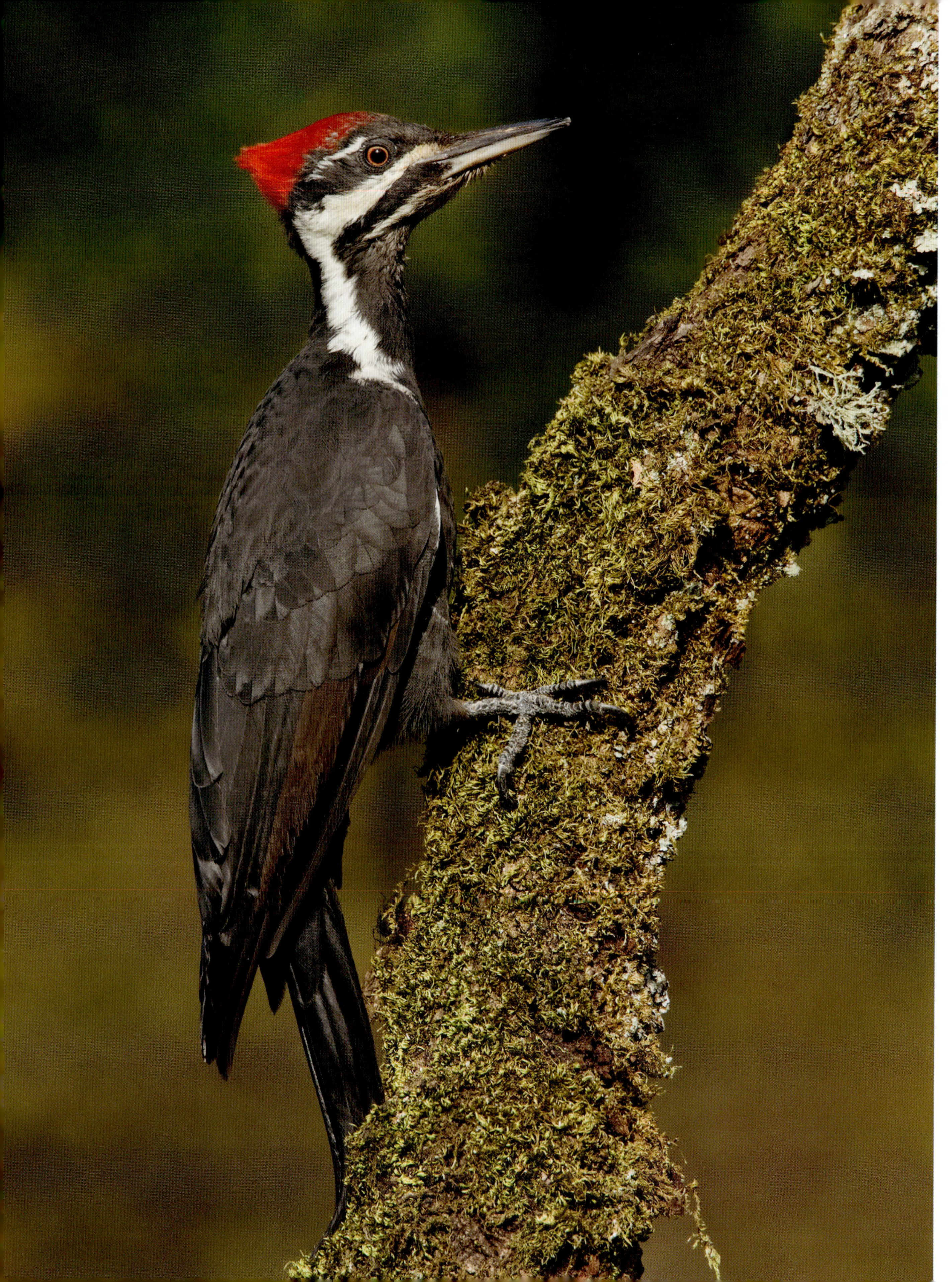

Largest of all of the North American woodpeckers, Pileated Woodpeckers are remarkable birds. They often excavate large square holes in trees as they search for insects.

MacGillivray's Warblers are very secretive birds. They tend to stay hidden in the thickets for much of the year. Male birds, however, emerge to sing and defend their territory in the early part of spring.

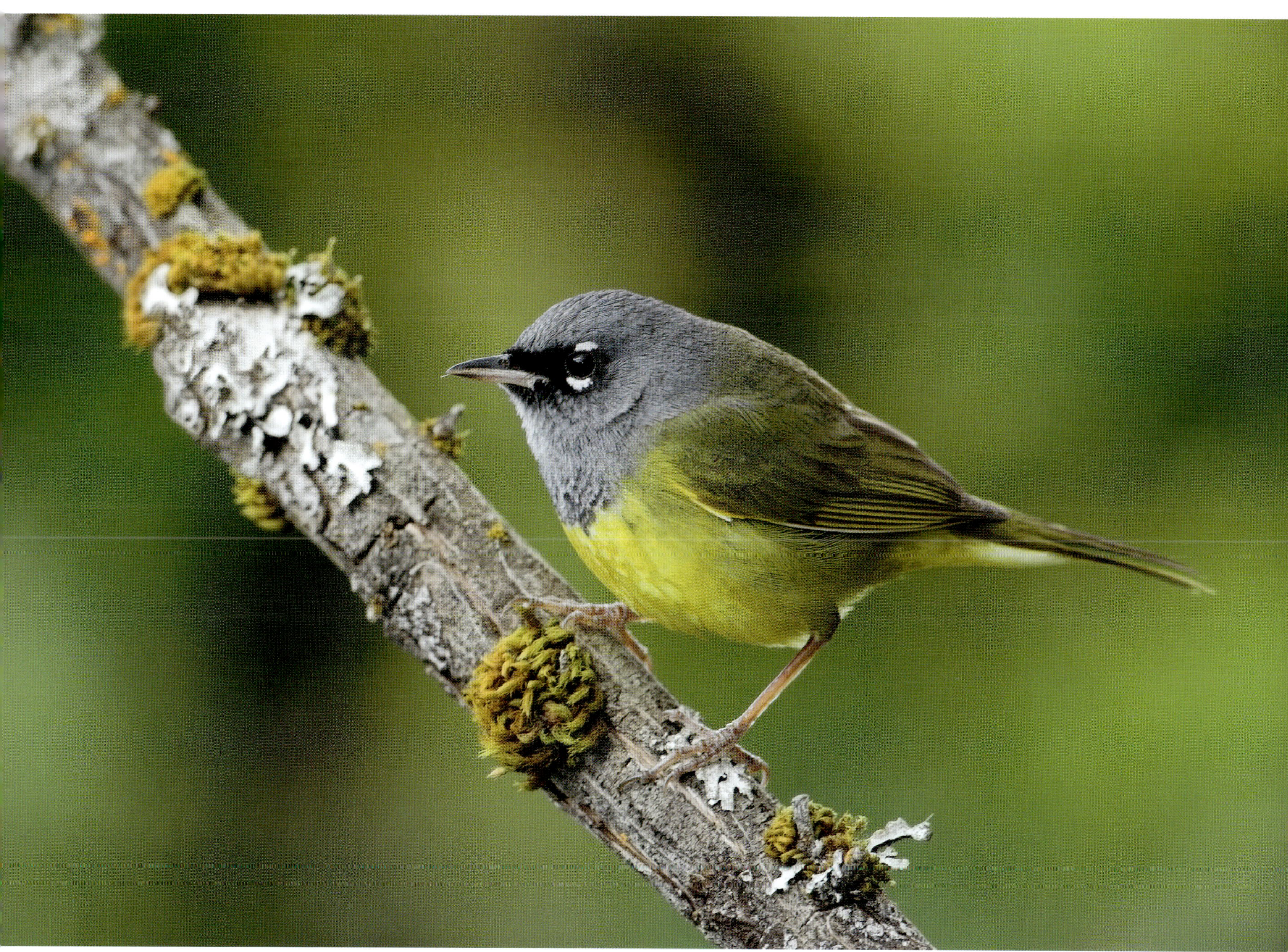

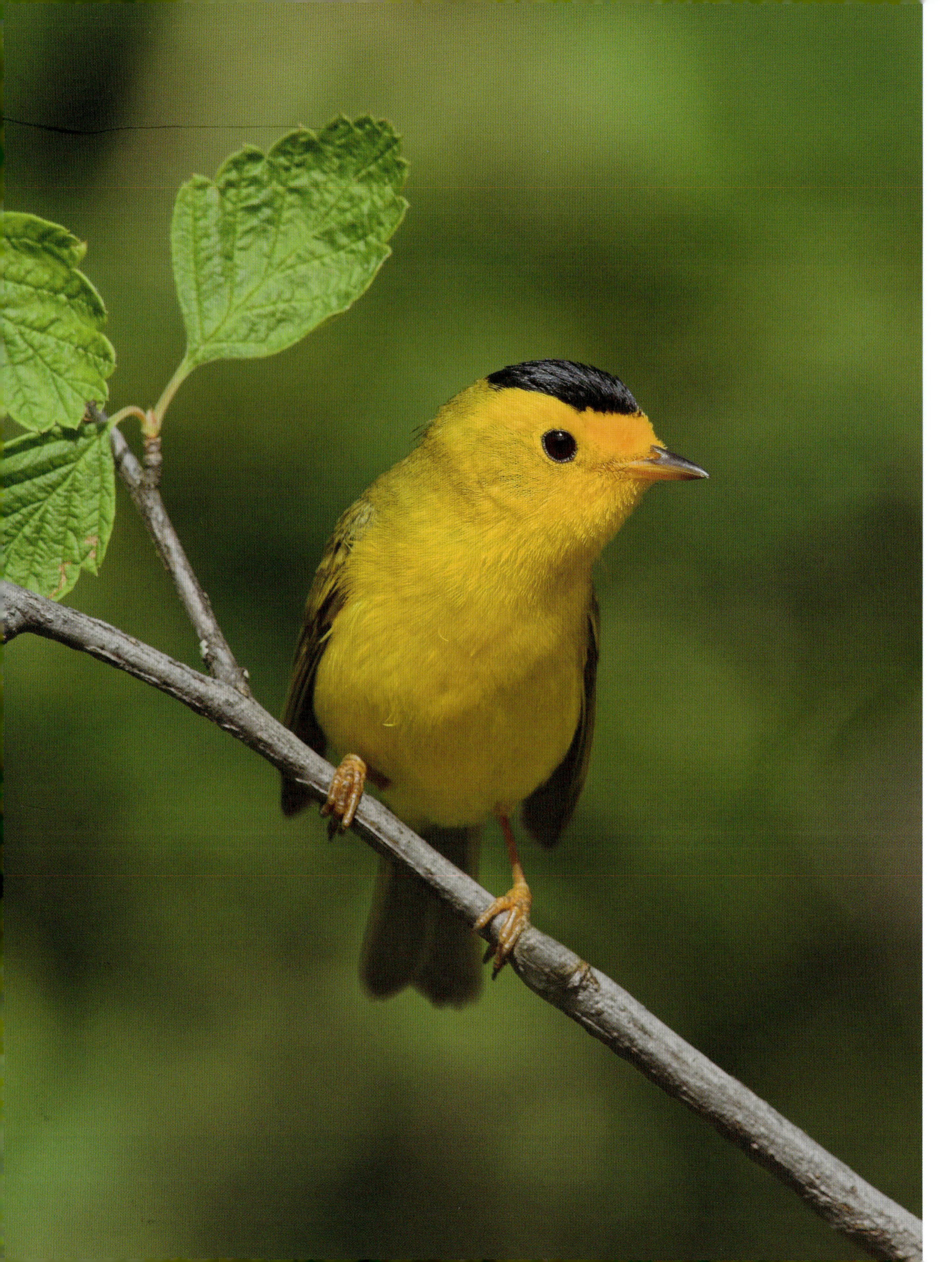

The black cap and yellow plumage of the Wilson's Warbler make it easy to identify. This species can be found throughout the province.

Red-breasted Nuthatches generally work their way down the trunk and branches of a tree as they search for morsels of food that other birds may have missed.

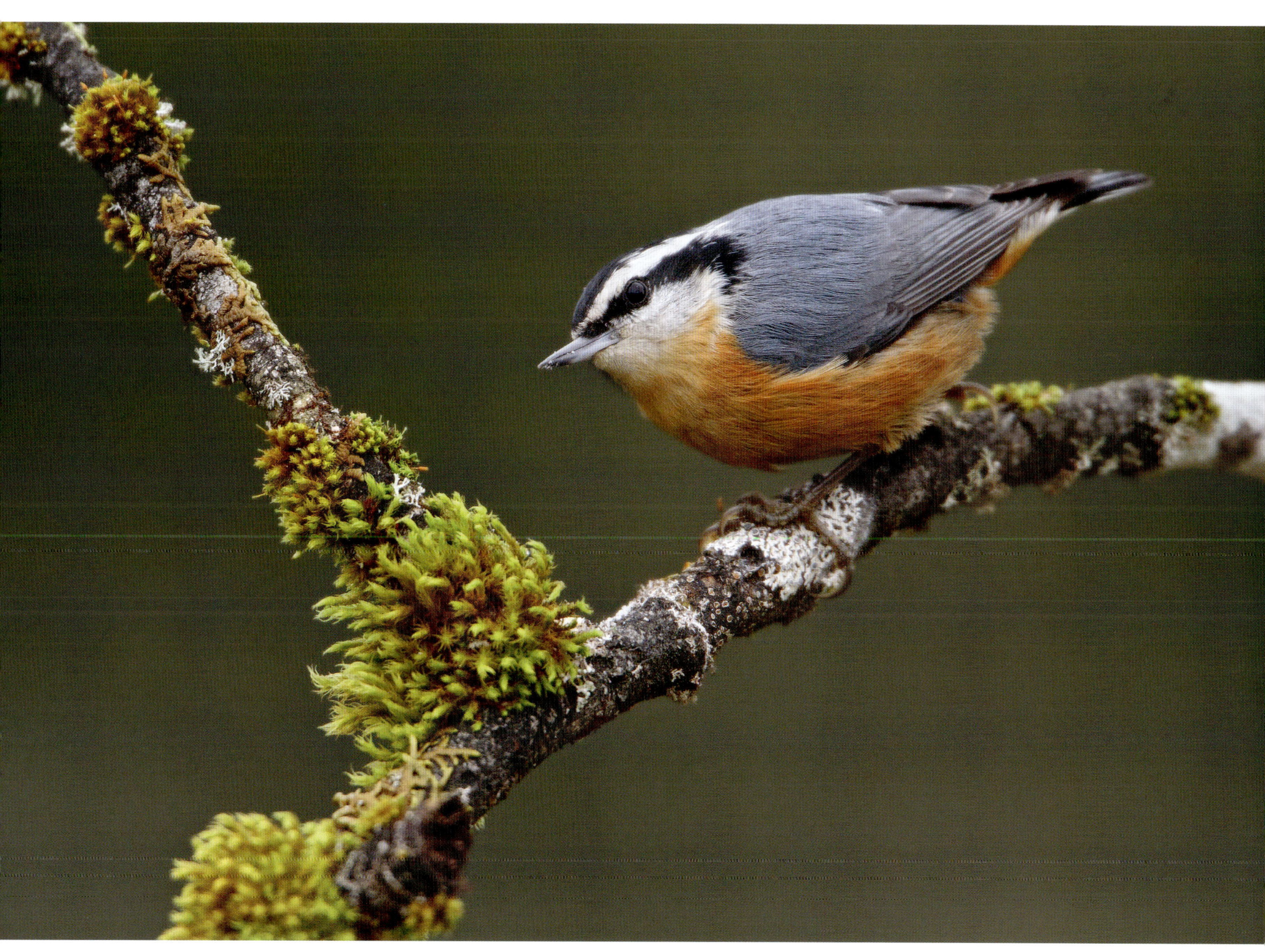

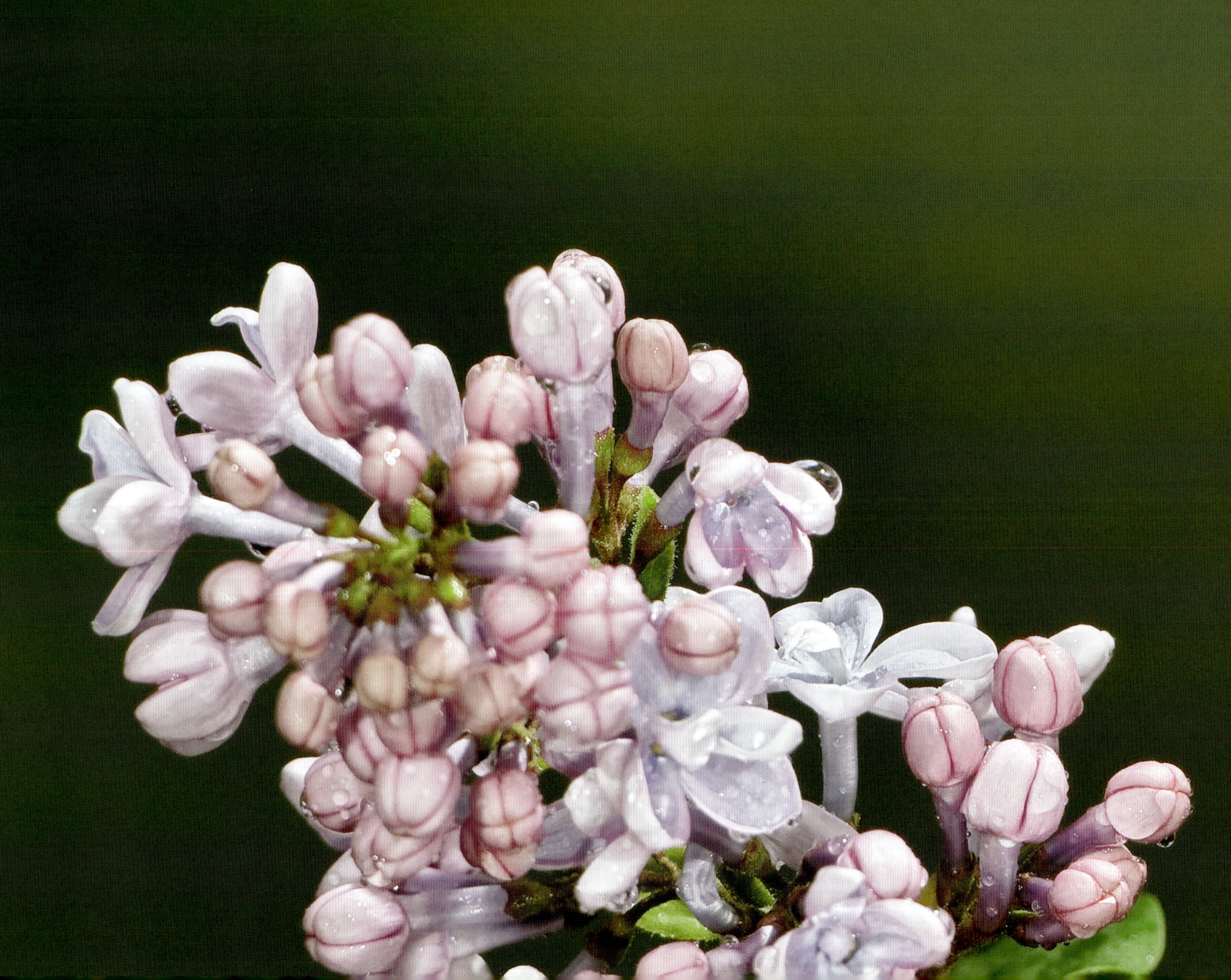

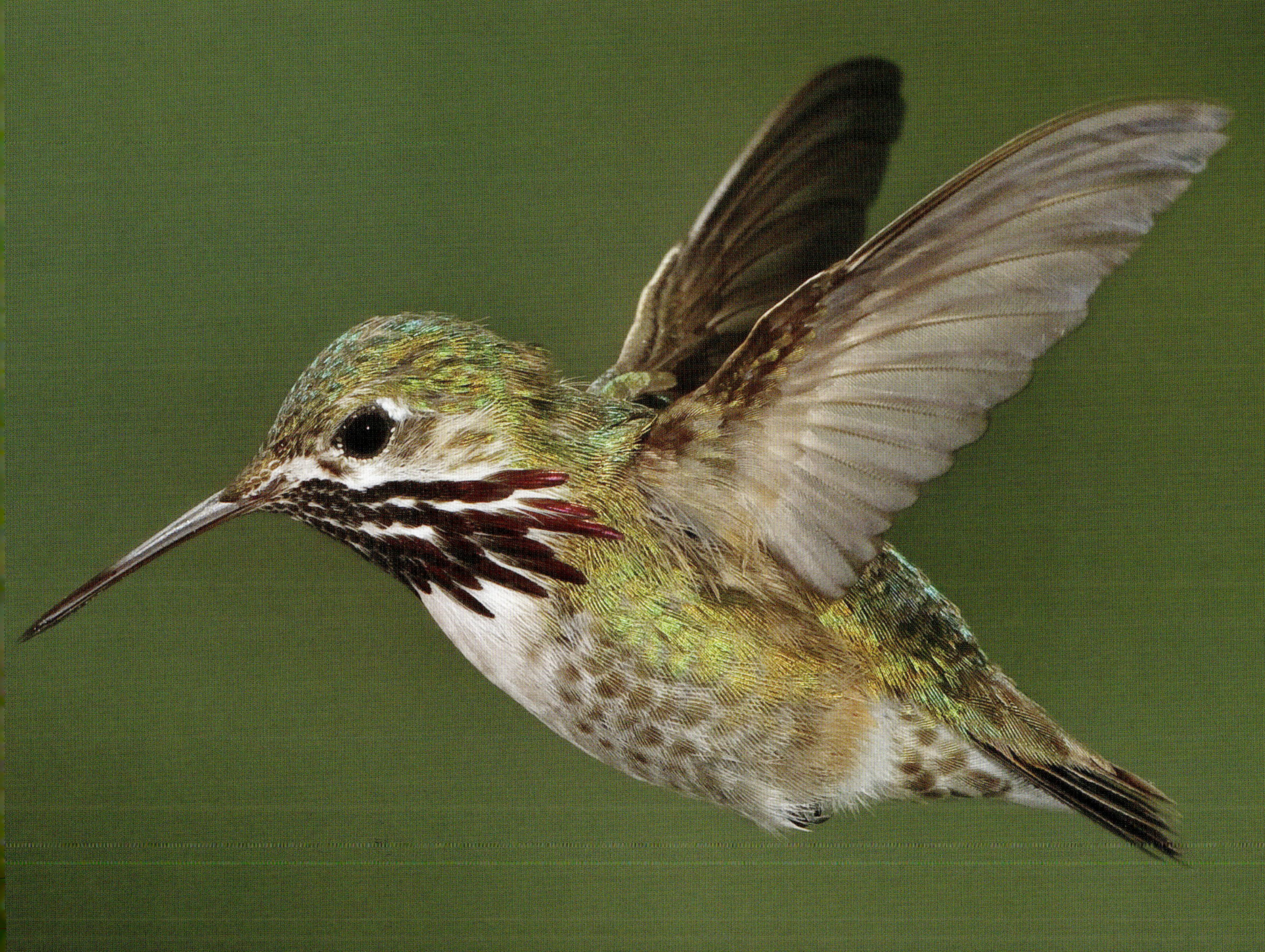

chapter three · **THE INTERIOR**

The climate of a given region and the type of ecosystem that has come to exist there are often the result of the topography of the Earth. This fact is obvious in eastern BC, where the colossal Rocky Mountains are responsible for shaping the weather patterns and dictating what species of plants and animals can thrive throughout much of the province. The same mountains that cause the warm Pacific air masses to cool, condense and fall as rain on the west coast of the province are also responsible for the extremely dry areas that form on the lee side of the mountains. These intermountain valleys, which form in the rain shadows of the mountains (sometimes known as "steppes"), are areas that are generally too dry for trees to flourish. In these areas, drought-tolerant grasses and shrubs are the dominant form of vegetation.

Snaking their way along the river valley bottoms, these grassland areas are found primarily in the southern Interior, the Peace River parklands in the north and on parts of southern Vancouver Island. These grassland and meadow areas are extremely special ecosystems within BC that support a unique variety of flora and fauna. In fact, the Garry Oak meadows of Vancouver Island are among the most threatened and rare ecosystems in all of Canada. Parts of the southern Interior of the province are even home to "pocket desert" ecosystems that most people would never dream could be in Canada. While these areas are not deserts in a traditional sense, their name gives an indication of just how arid parts of BC can be. These grasslands and dry, open environments typify much of the southern Interior of BC and are home to a wide variety of birdlife.

GRASSLAND SPECIALISTS

For many species of birds in Canada, the dry interior is the only, or at least the best, place to find them. Grassland birds like Brewer's Sparrows and Sage Thrashers find a home here and nowhere else in Canada. Cliffs and rocky outcroppings in the Okanagan Valley are home to Rock Wrens and are the only place in Canada where Canyon Wrens can regularly be spied. Where the dry grasslands are interrupted by fresh water, riparian zones can be found and these areas are home to birds such as Bullock's Orioles, Black-headed Grosbeaks, Gray Catbirds and Yellow-breasted Chats. Meanwhile, birds such as Say's Phoebes, Western Meadowlarks, Vesper Sparrows and Lazuli Buntings are more easily encountered in the dry Interior than elsewhere in the province.

INTERIOR FORESTS

Moving up the slopes from the valley bottoms and steppes, there exists a transition zone between grasslands and woodlands where sparse open forests are dominated by Ponderosa and Lodgepole Pines. These two species of trees have developed strategies for living in these dry areas where water is scarce and frequent fires are the norm. The Ponderosa Pine grows a long taproot to extract water from deep within the ground. It also has a thick outer bark that is resistant to all but the most intense forest fires. The Lodgepole Pine uses a different strategy that looks forward to future generations. It deposits huge numbers of fire-resistant seeds into the soil, setting the stage for their seedlings to successfully colonize the area after a forest fire.

These open forests provide an ideal place to find the carpenters of the bird world—woodpeckers. Perhaps in part due to the colossal impact of the mountain pine beetle, which has ravaged large parts of the province in recent years, these birds find ample space to nest, feed and raise their young in these transition zones. The dry open forests of the southern Interior are the only place in Canada where White-headed Woodpeckers and Williamson's Sapsuckers can be found. Another unique species of woodpecker that resides in the dry Interior is the Lewis's Woodpecker. This beautiful bird is unmistakable, with its glossy green back and pink underbelly. Aside from its striking plumage, this species is unlike any other woodpecker in its unusual feeding strategy. Instead of searching for insects to devour from within the tree as most woodpeckers do, the Lewis's Woodpecker actually hunts for them from an elevated perch, much like a flycatcher would.

The open forests of the dry Interior are also excellent places to find birds such as Pygmy and White-breasted Nuthatches, Cassin's Vireos, Common Poorwills, Northern Saw-whet Owls and Western Tanagers.

CLIFFSIDES

Two of the most fascinating birds to watch in the Interior of BC are also two of the fastest animals on the planet—the White-throated Swift and Peregrine Falcon. For the most part, these two birds could not be more different. Swifts are small insect-eating birds that are more closely related to hummingbirds than to any other family. Falcons, on the other hand, are powerful raptors and among the fiercest predators in the natural world. And yet, these two very different birds have a couple of things in common: they both inhabit cliffsides and they are both masters of the sky. These two species are true aerial acrobats, capable of mind-blowing speed and manoeuvres that are mesmerizing to watch.

It is an amazing experience to stand atop a cliff in the south Okanagan Valley and watch White-throated Swifts flying about. They glide through the air with such agility and apparent ease that it is hard to imagine that they are not having fun. As they zip in toward the cliff face to feed on insects, they seem oblivious to human presence and at times will fly by only a few feet away from binocular-toting observers. Listening to the sound of their tiny wings cutting through the air and admiring their streamlined appearance evoke comparisons to aerodynamic fighter jets. Perhaps most impressive, though, is the Swift's ability to seemingly vanish into thin air. A closer look will reveal that the birds have actually flown into a small crevice in the rock face, where they roost and build their nests. Nevertheless, watching these birds fly into their tiny cracks at nearly full speed boggles the mind. Their agility is almost beyond comprehension.

In comparison to the playful swifts, a dark silhouette looms ominously as another master of the sky patrols the area in search of its next meal. Its long pointed wings, striped underside and slate-gray mask give away its identity as one of the most powerful raptors in the world—the Peregrine Falcon. These birds often hunt from an elevated position before diving down onto their unsuspecting prey. During these dives, the Peregrine Falcon can reach unbelievable speeds of up to 320 kilometres per hour, making them the fastest animal in the natural world. Watching them fly while they hunt is an astonishing sight, as they are both powerful and agile. While Peregrine Falcons can be found throughout most areas of Canada, the cliffsides of BC's Interior make ideal nest sites, as they provide a safe refuge to raise young and also allow for open areas over which to hunt.

Photographing the fastest animal on the planet is, of course, not easy. Nevertheless, late one spring I made my way into a cliff in the Interior where I knew Peregrine Falcons were nesting. I planned my visit to coincide with the stage when they would have their most voracious appetite, just before the chicks reached their fledgling stage. I figured the parents would be busy hunting and bringing in prey, which would lead to more opportunities for me to photograph them.

Not wanting to disturb the birds, I hid myself underneath a thin layer of camouflage material on top of the cliff and waited for the birds to appear. Knowing where the birds were heading gave me an advantage when it came to planning the shot, but the birds seemed to appear out of nowhere and deliver their precious cargo before I could even raise my camera, let alone lock focus and shoot. In a heartbeat they would drop off a meal and then dart off again to capture their next meal. The frustration was almost unbearable. All told, I spent some 30 hours on that cliff, waiting to capture the perfect image. Despite the heat, nervous moments on the edge and the exhaustion of concentrating for such long periods of time, it was a thrill to spend so much time with these birds and eventually walk away with an image I was proud of.

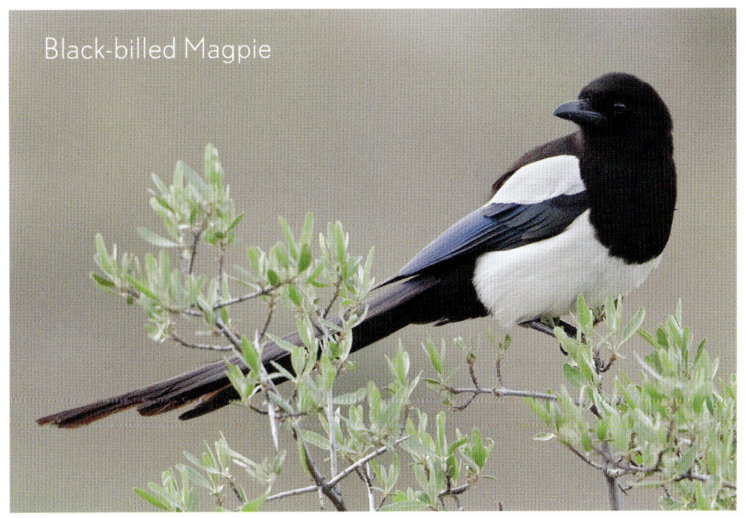
Black-billed Magpie

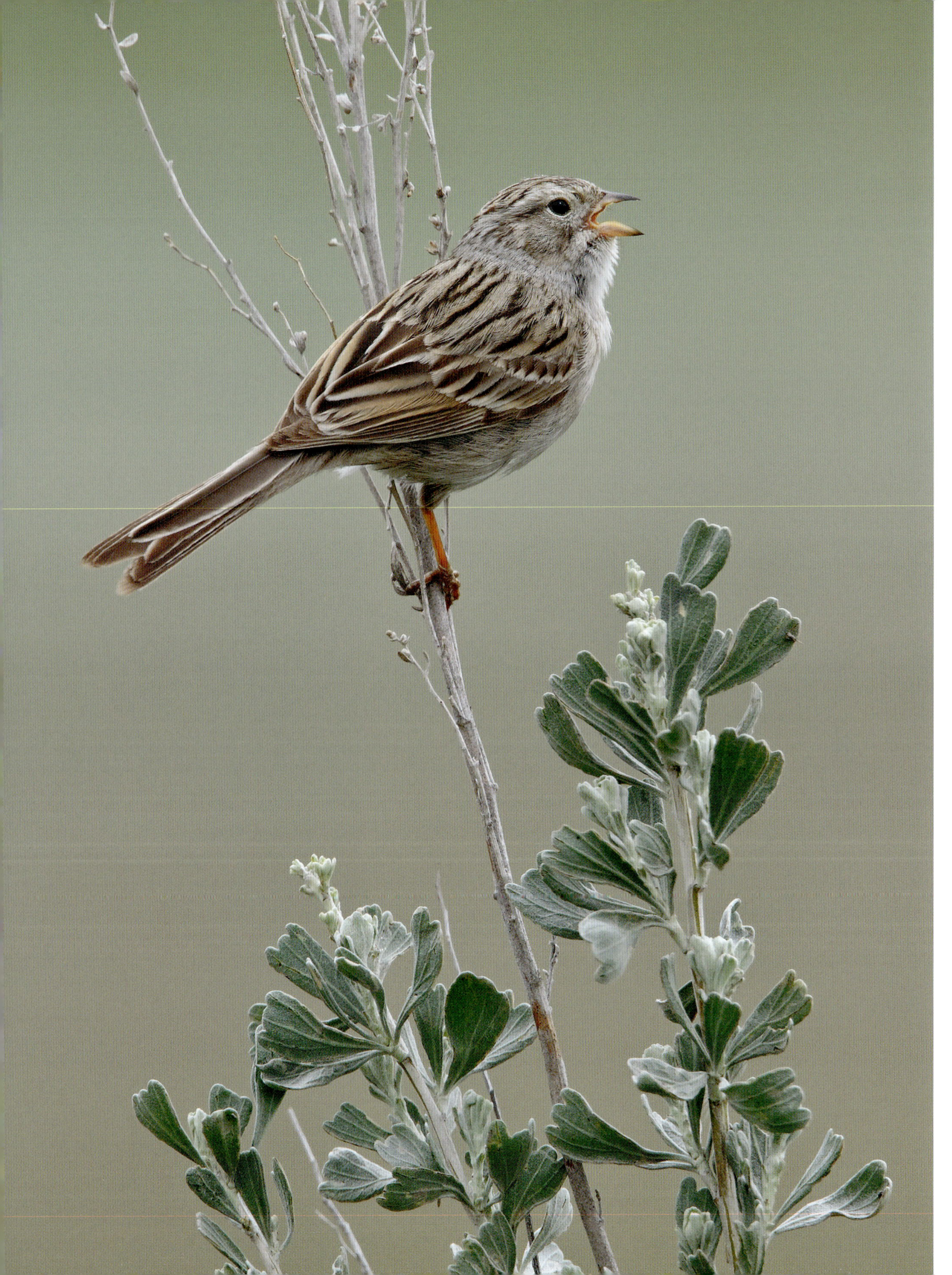

The Brewer's Sparrow is interesting in that it has two distinct nesting zones in BC: one in the alpine habitat of the northern Rocky Mountains and the other in the sagebrush habitat of the southern Interior.

One of BC's more colourful birds, the Bullock's Oriole is commonly found in riparian habitats.

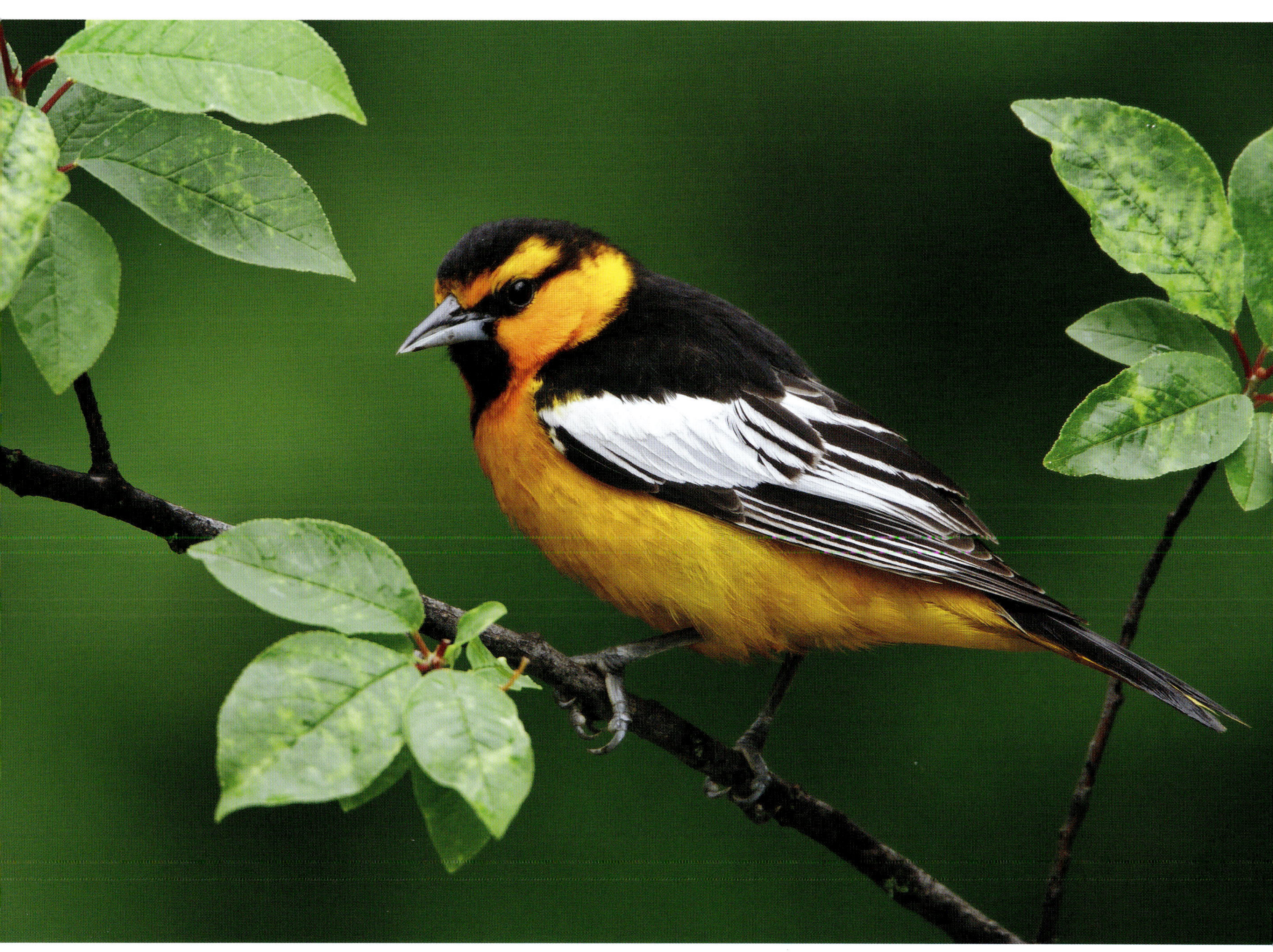

A Sharp-tailed Grouse flies over the grasslands of southern BC. It is quite apparent why this bird earned its name.

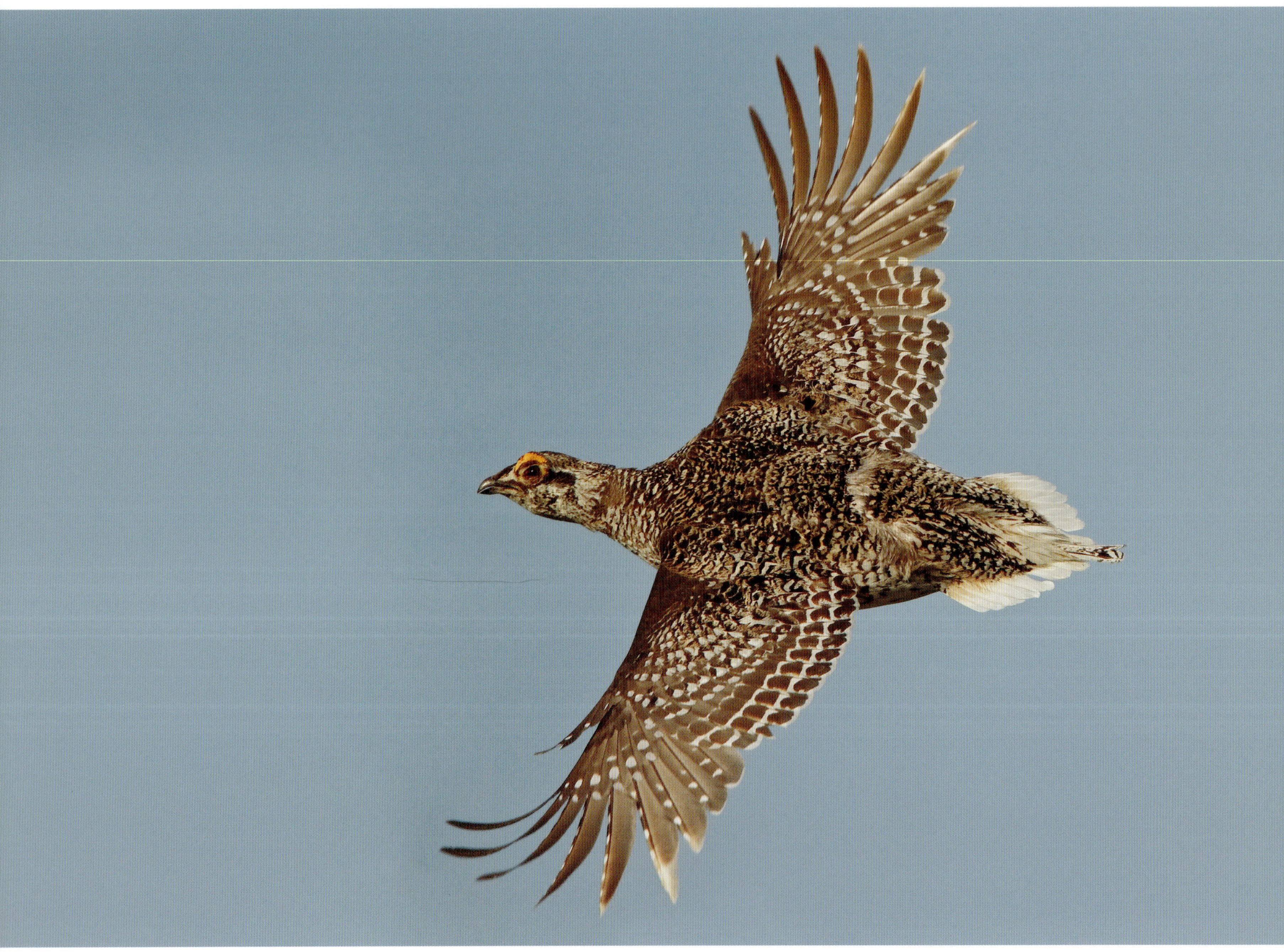

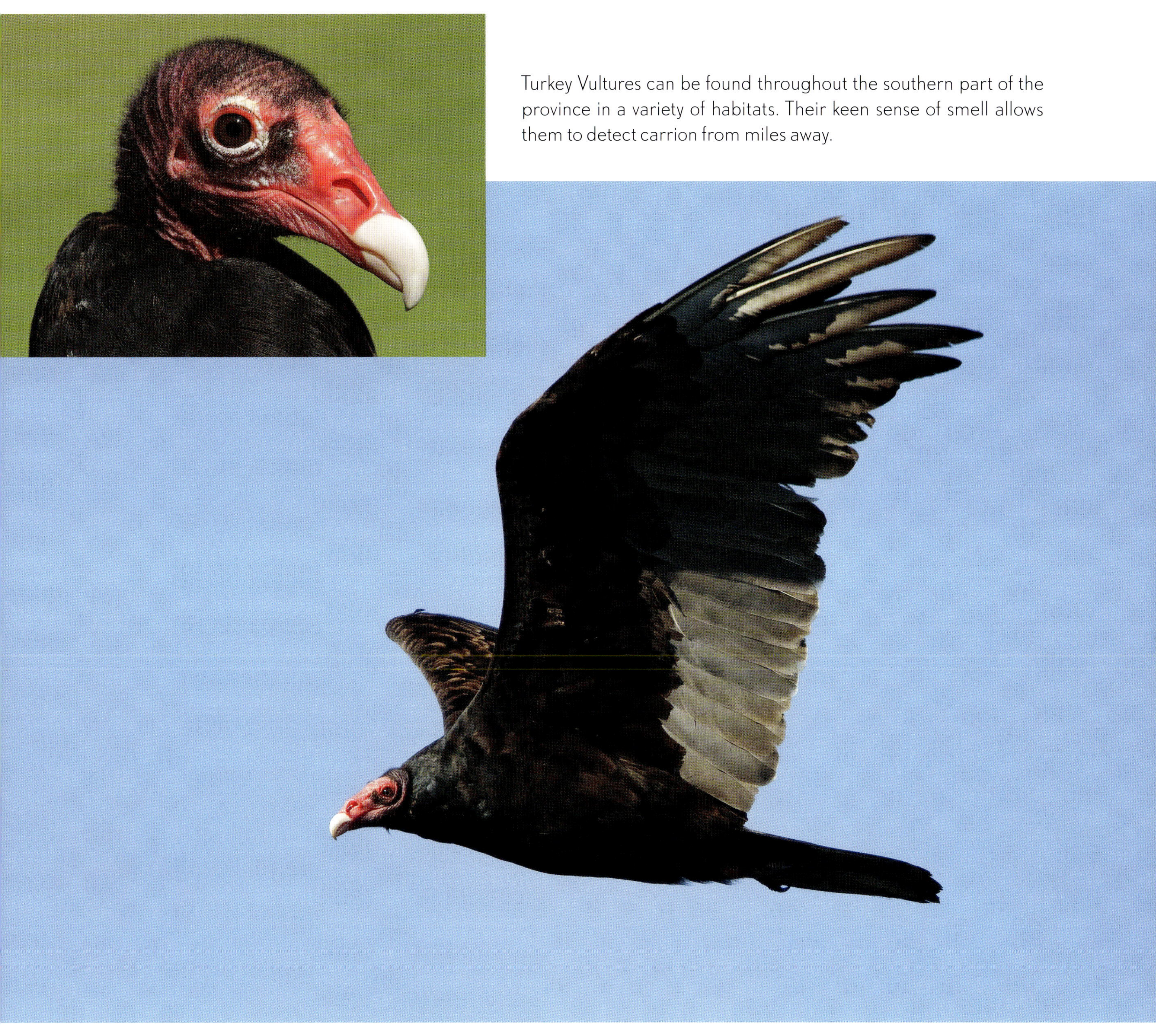

Turkey Vultures can be found throughout the southern part of the province in a variety of habitats. Their keen sense of smell allows them to detect carrion from miles away.

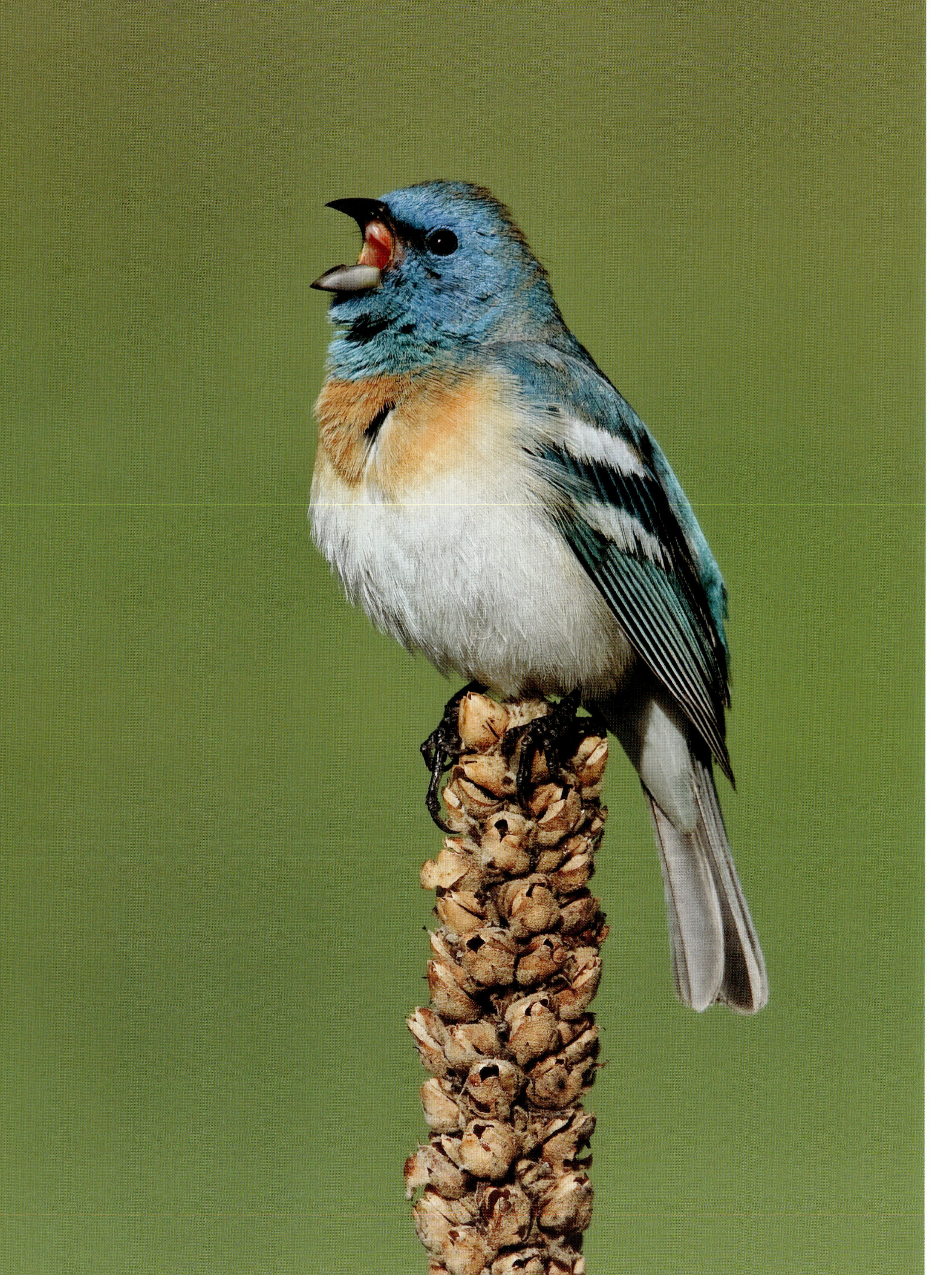

On a sunny spring morning, this male Lazuli Bunting was singing atop an old flower stalk.

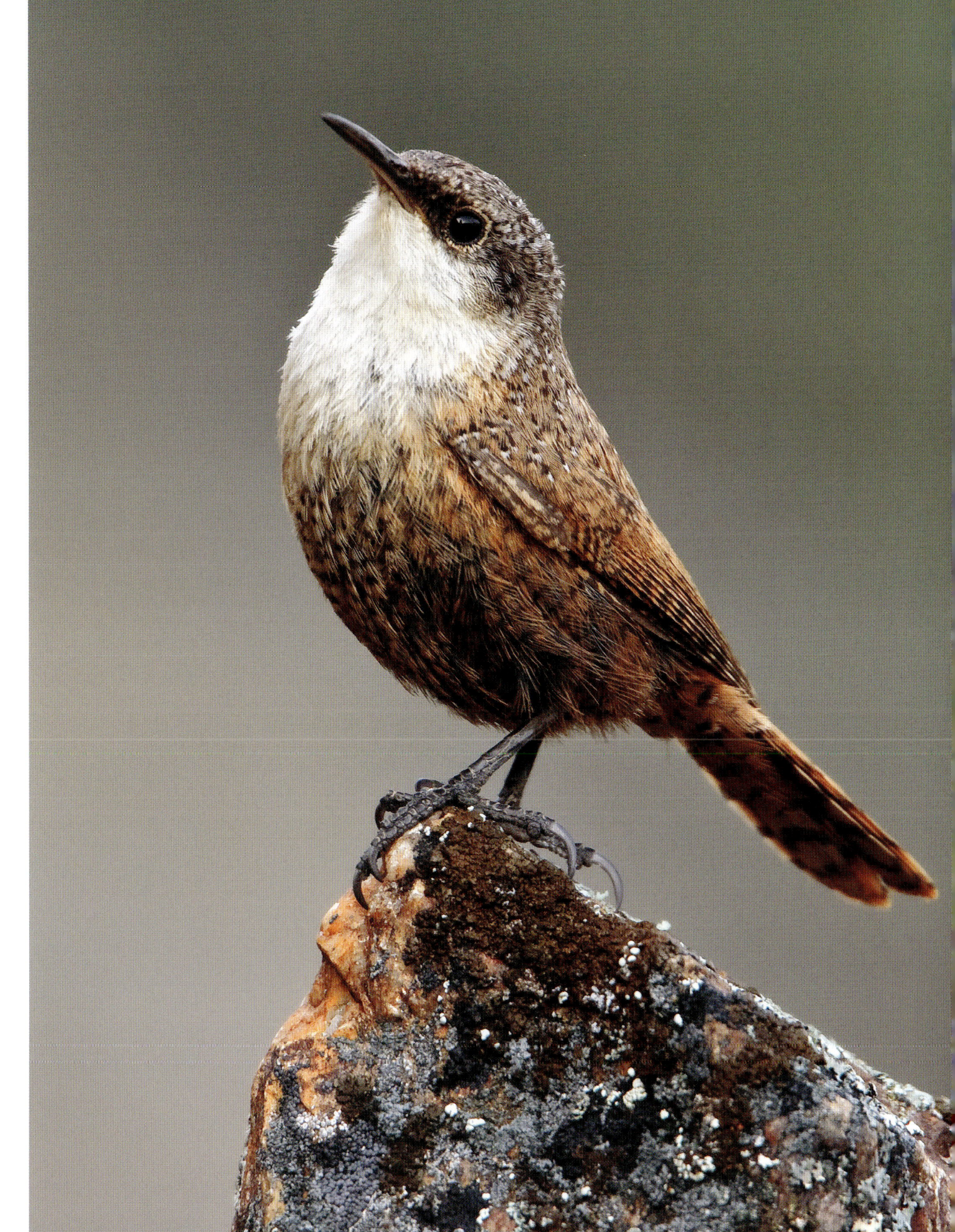

The range of the Canyon Wren barely extends to Canada. It is found only in thc southernmost portion of the BC Interior.

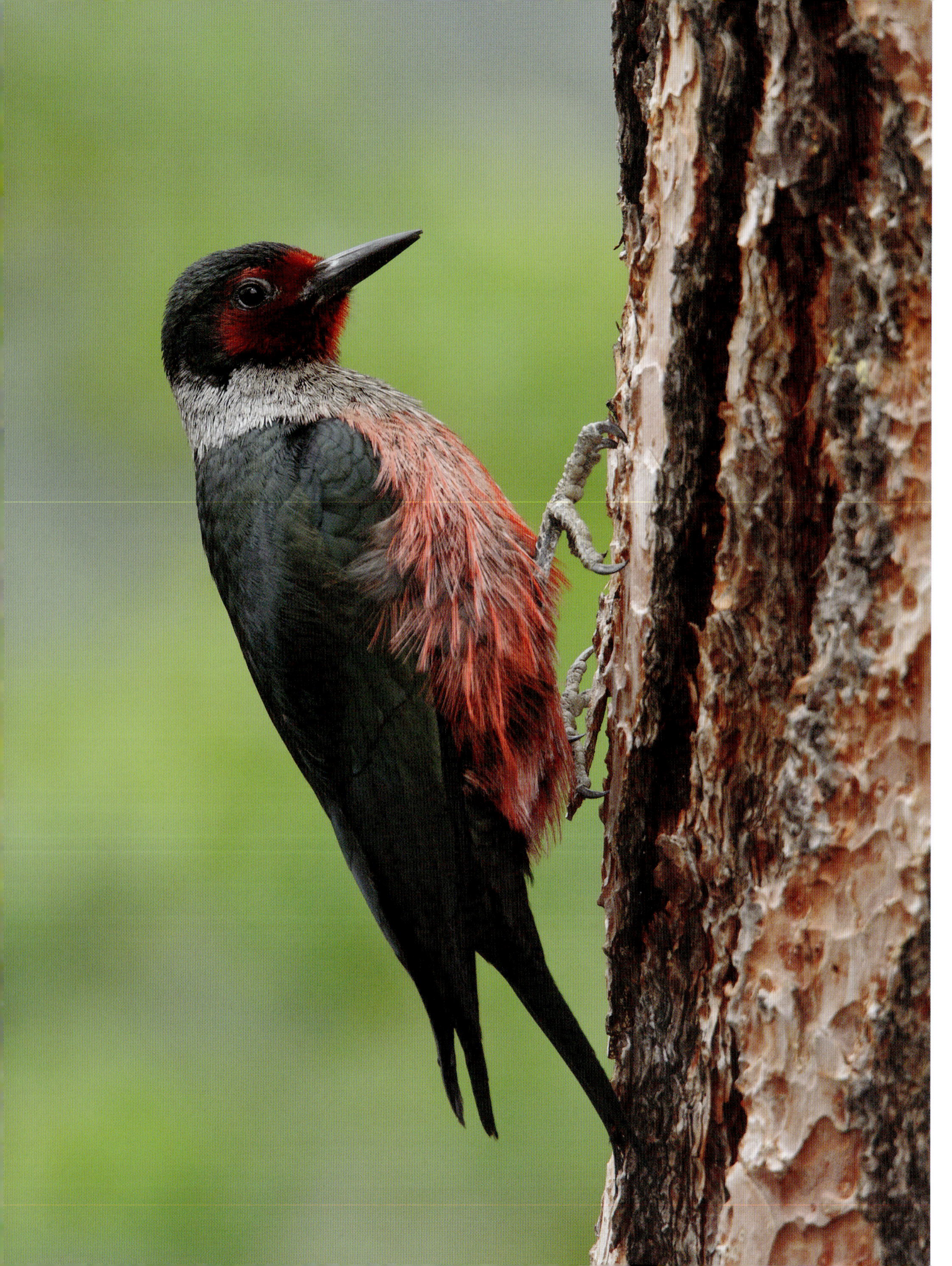

A Lewis's Woodpecker clings to the bark of a Ponderosa Pine. These birds are generally found near riparian areas and particularly in areas where cottonwoods grow.

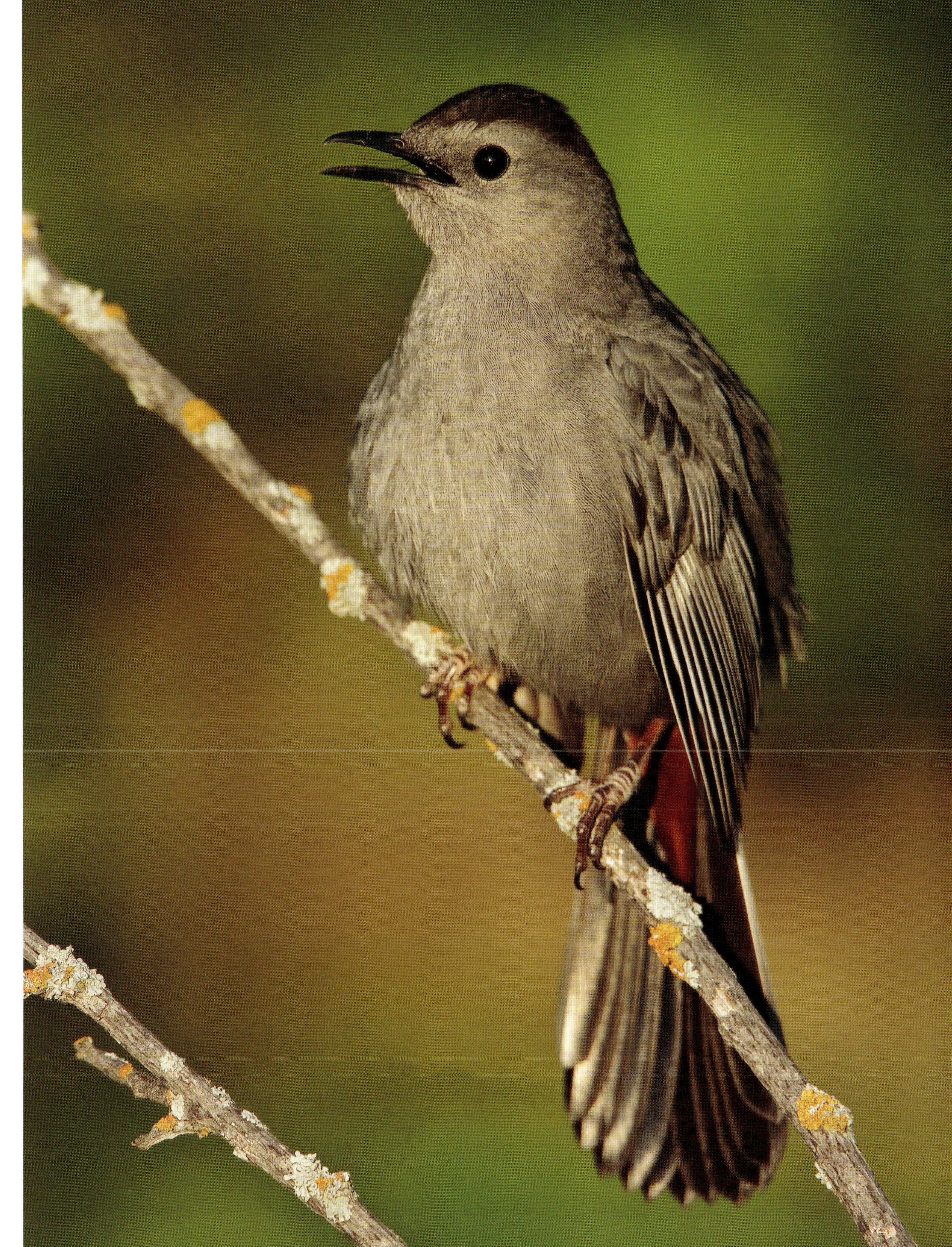

The quirky calls of the Gray Catbird include a catlike "meow," which earned the bird its name.

The Northern Saw-whet Owl is one of the commonest and most widespread owls in BC, found wherever there are tree cavities for nesting and dense vegetation for roosting.

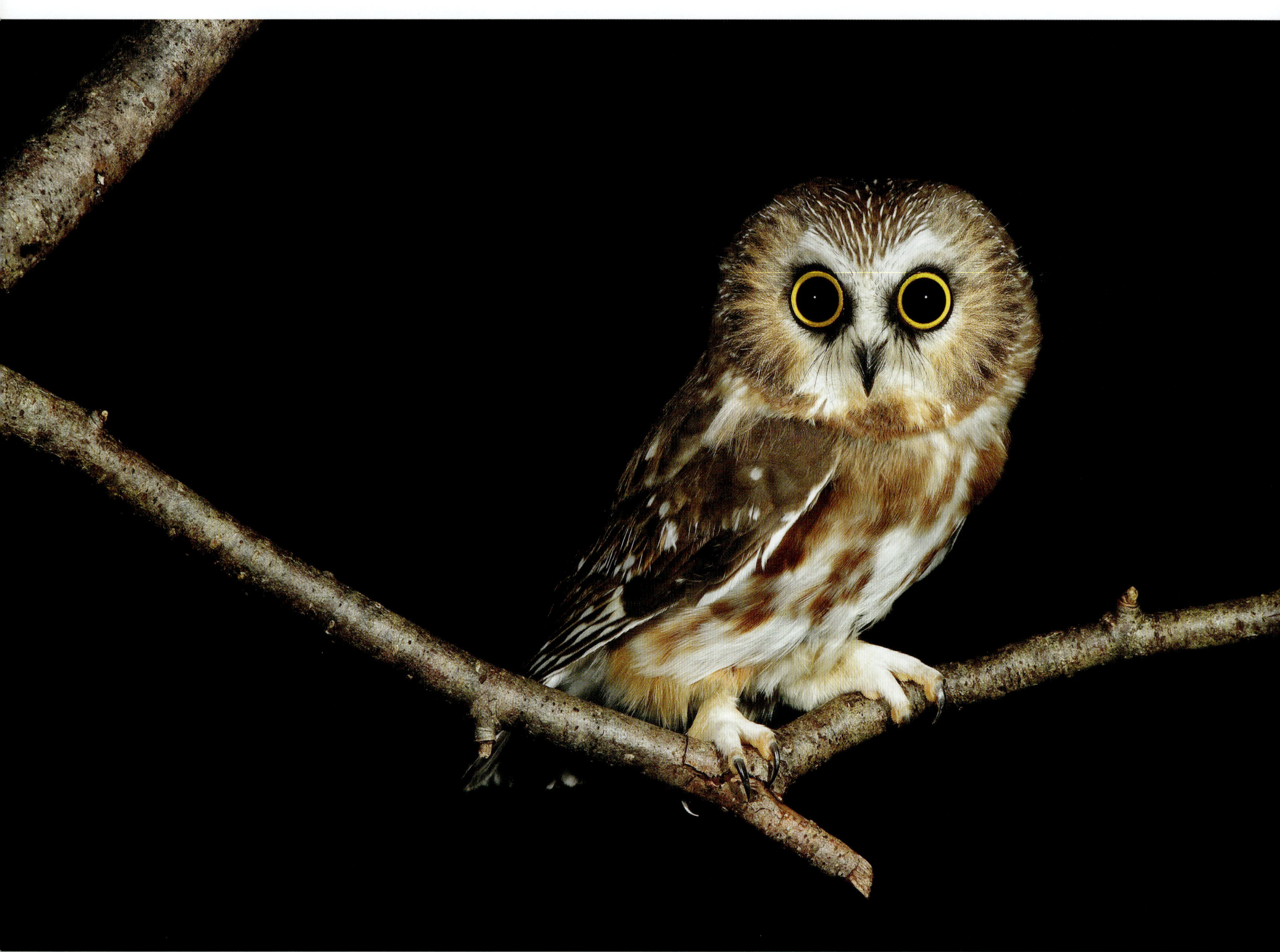

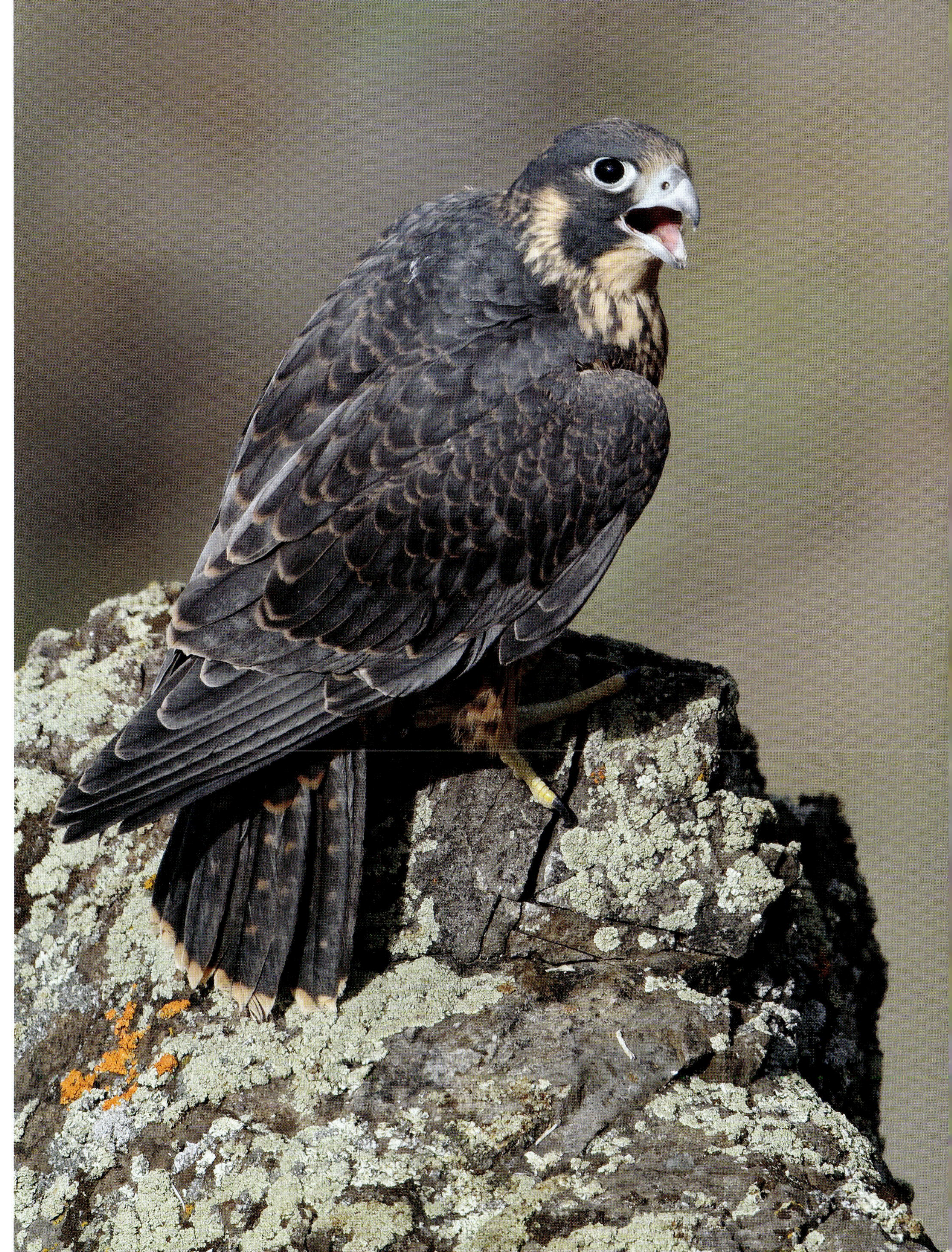

A young Peregrine Falcon calls from a cliff face before taking off to test its wings.

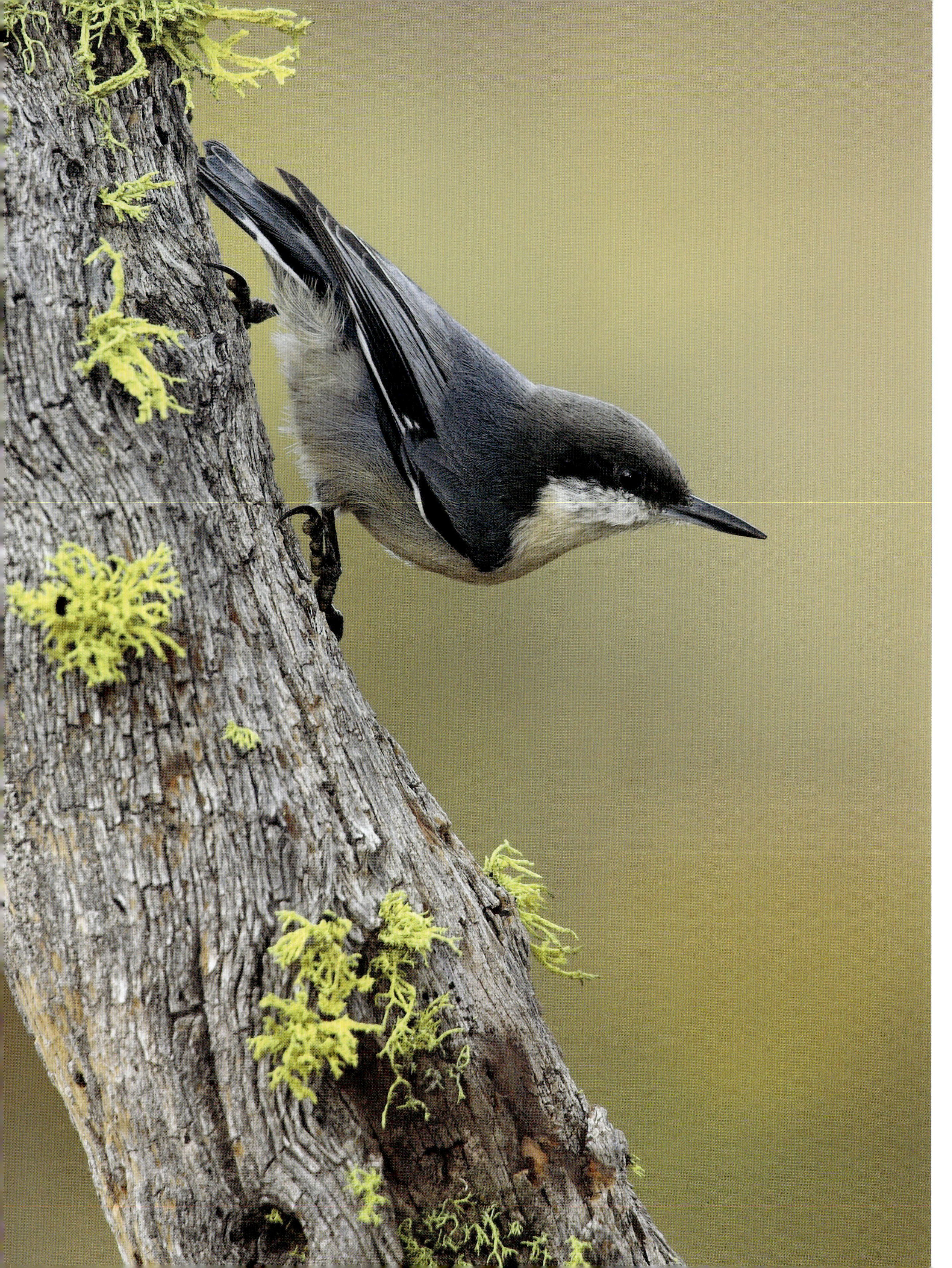

Pygmy Nuthatches are very social birds. They are unique in that they roost communally—sometimes up to 100 birds share a single roost cavity for the night.

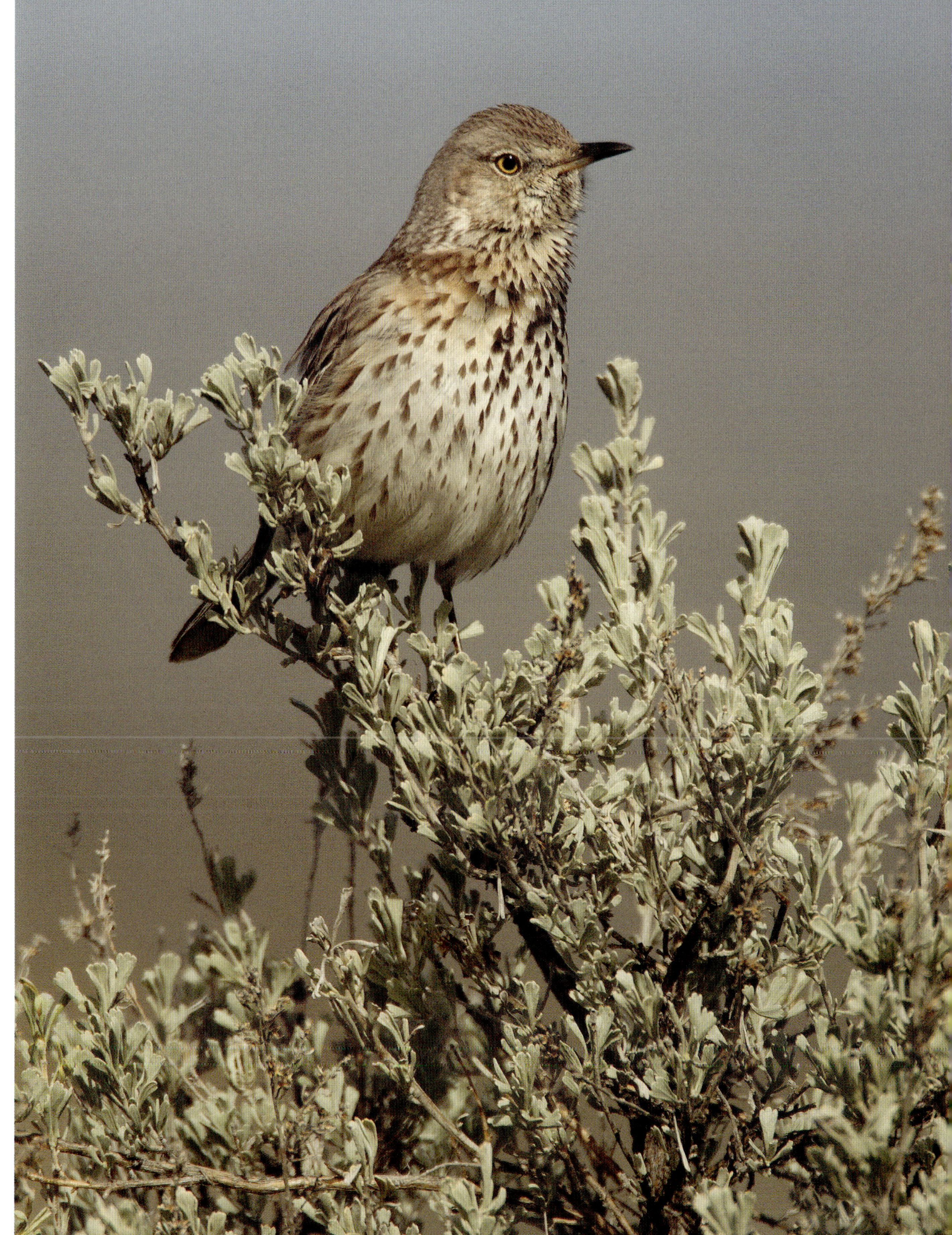

The Sage Thrasher is another species whose range just barely extends into the southernmost regions of BC.

JARED HOBBS

The Dusky Flycatcher is one of many species that belong to the *Empidonax* genus of small insect-eating flycatchers. Any seasoned birdwatcher will tell you that they can present some serious identification challenges in the field.

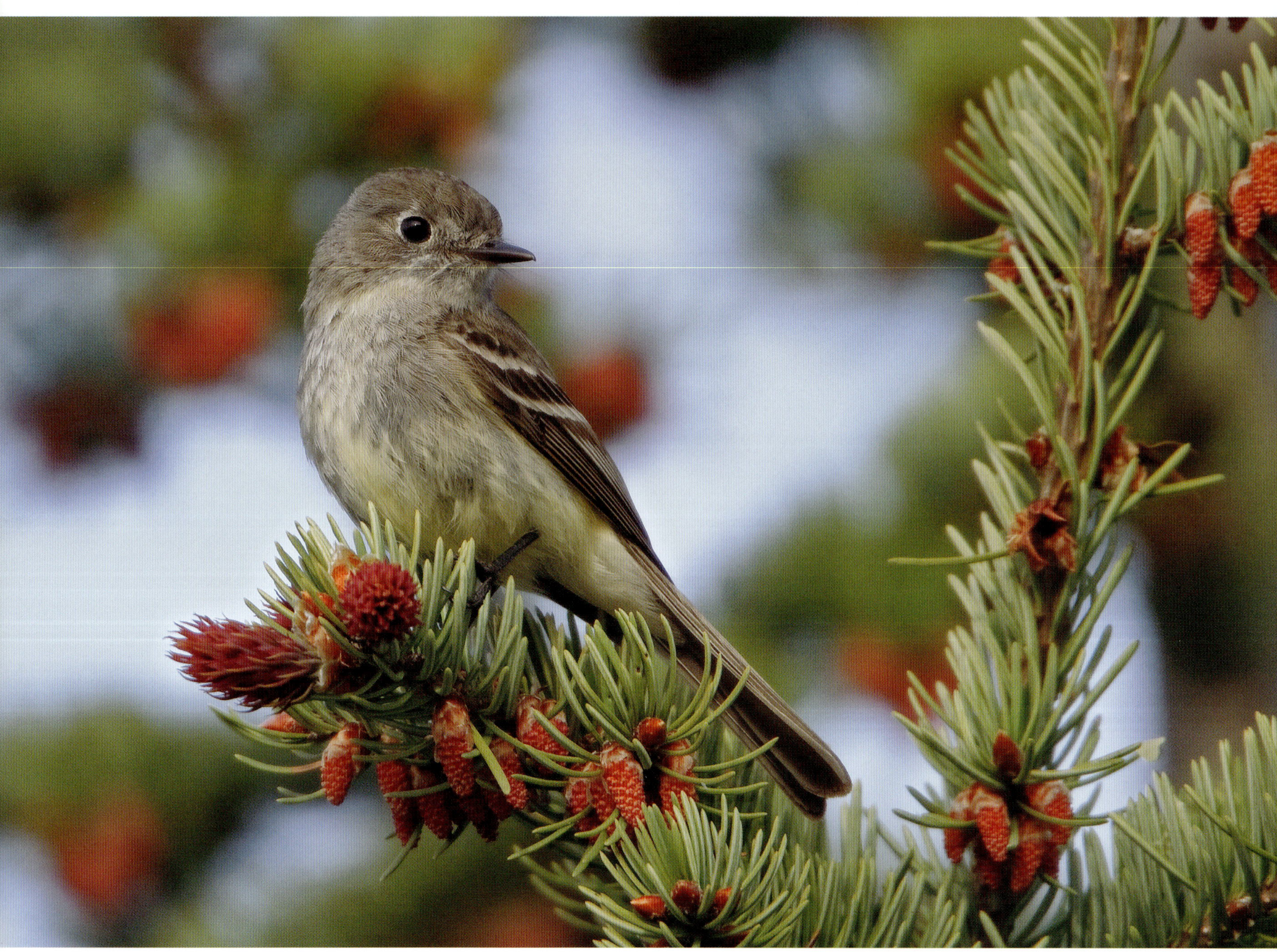

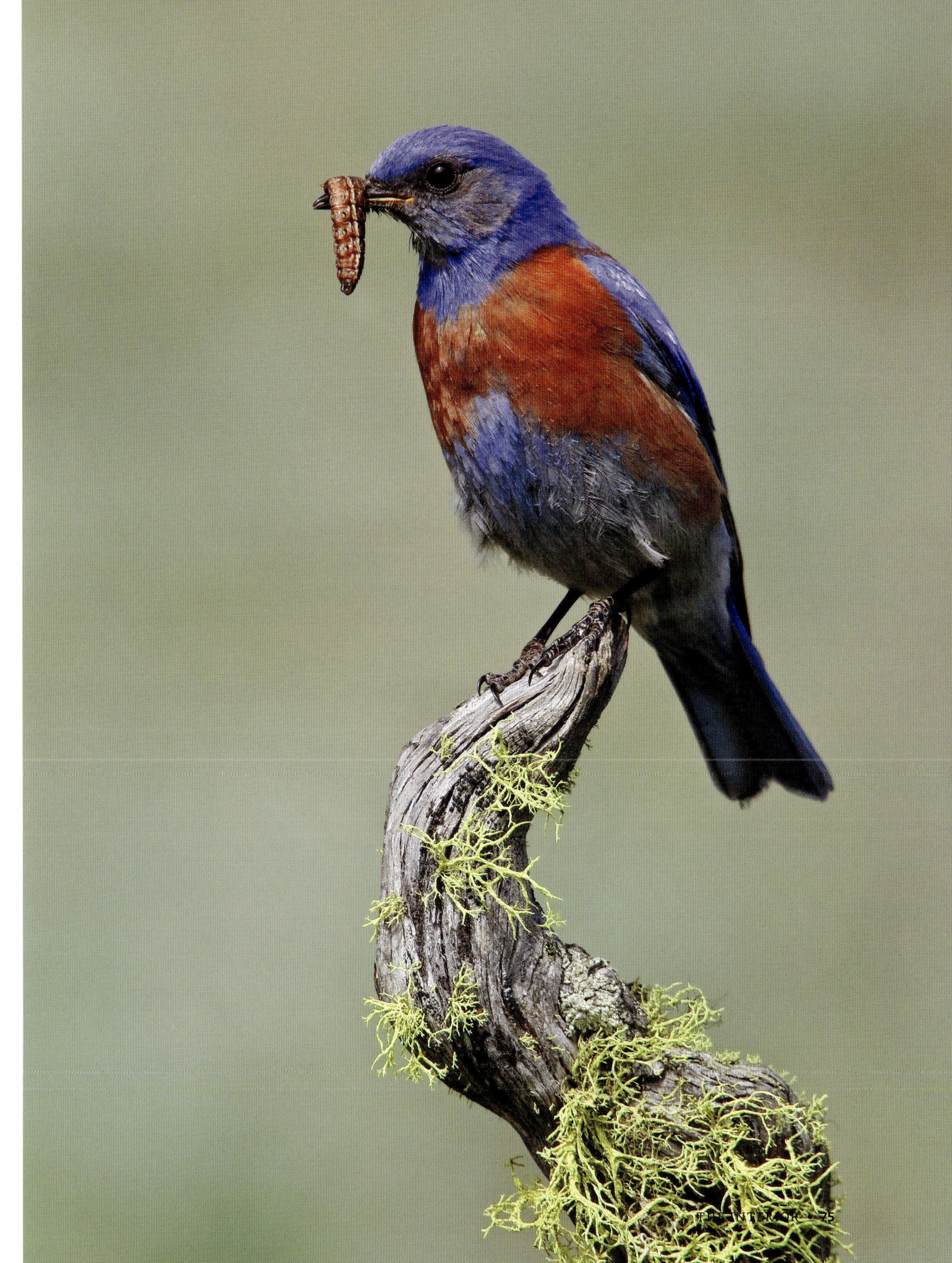

A Western Bluebird momentarily perches on a lichen-covered snag before returning to its nest to feed its young.

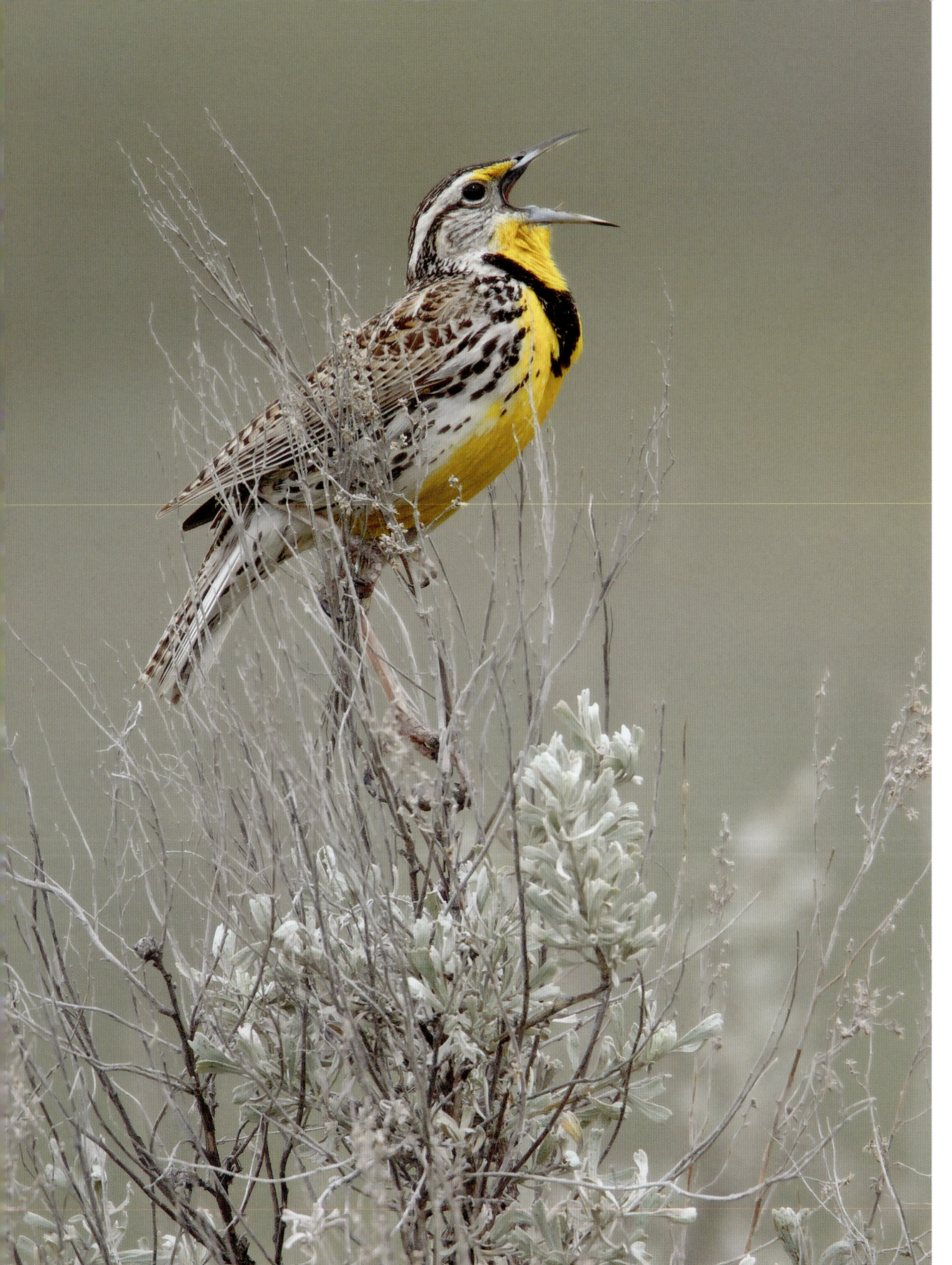

What sound could better signify the arrival of spring than a Western Meadowlark calling from the sagebrush?

A Cedar Waxwing poses on a branch before flying off to join its flock.

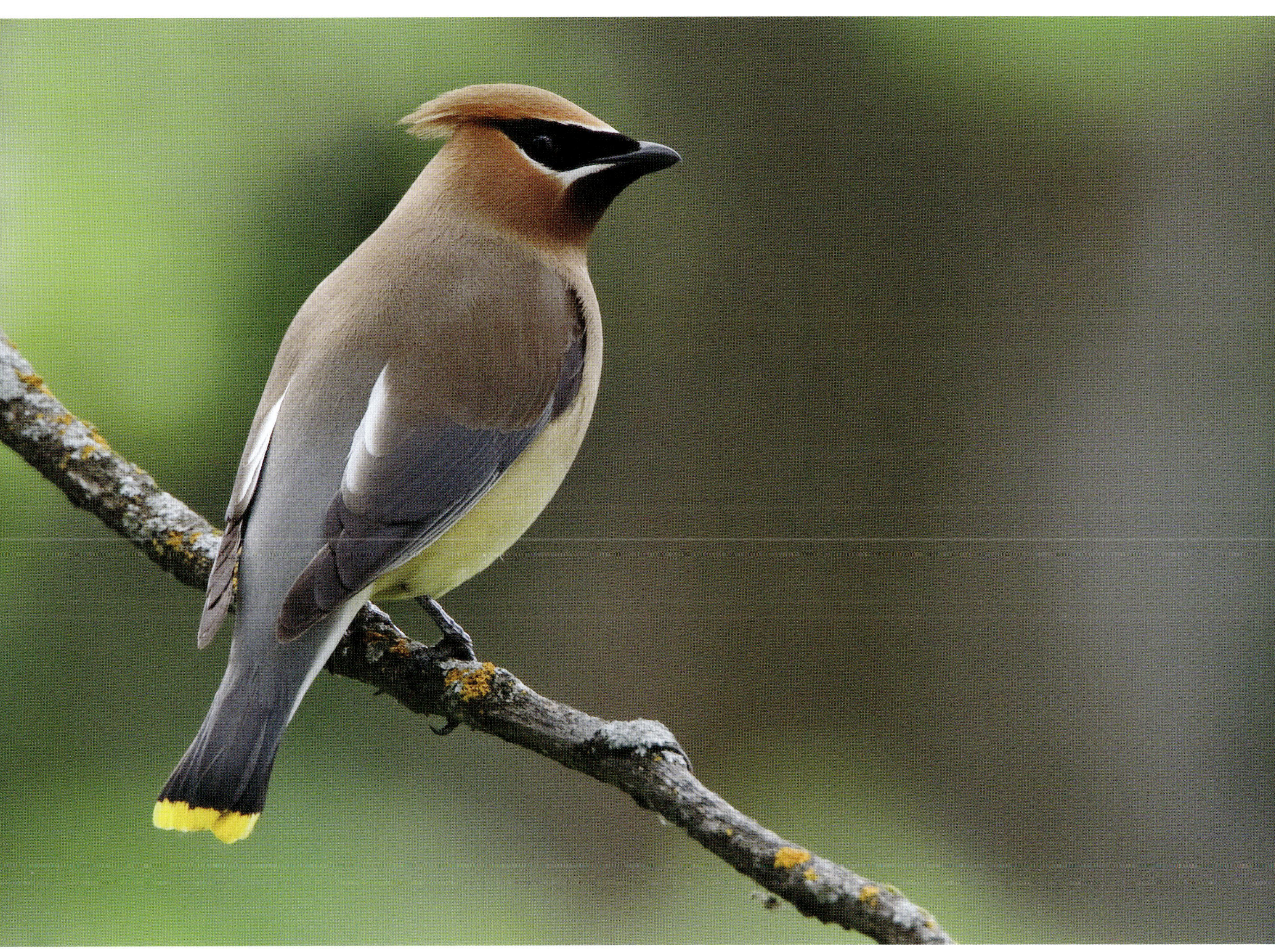

Common Poorwills are most often spotted from the road as their eyes glow red from oncoming headlights.

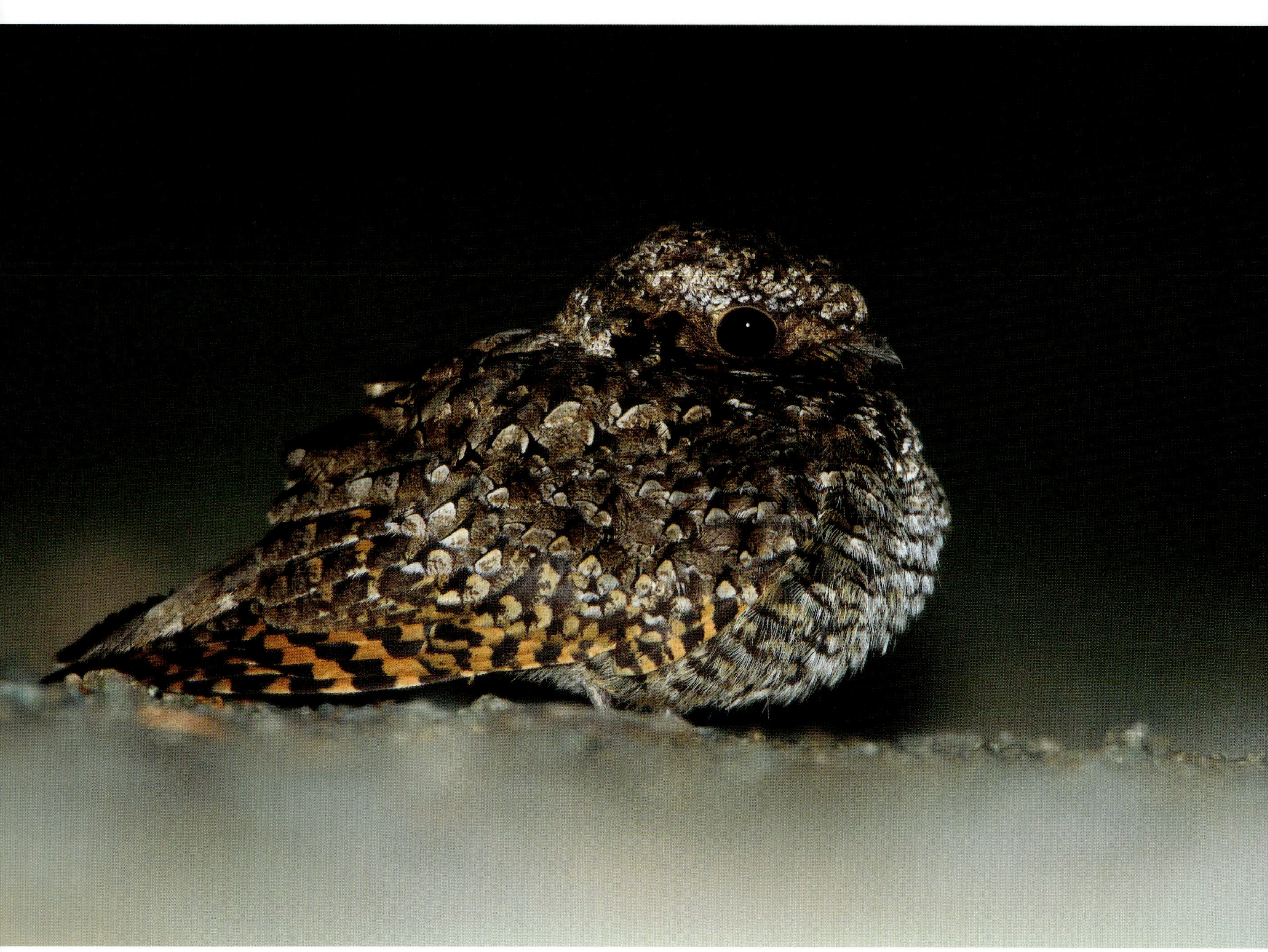

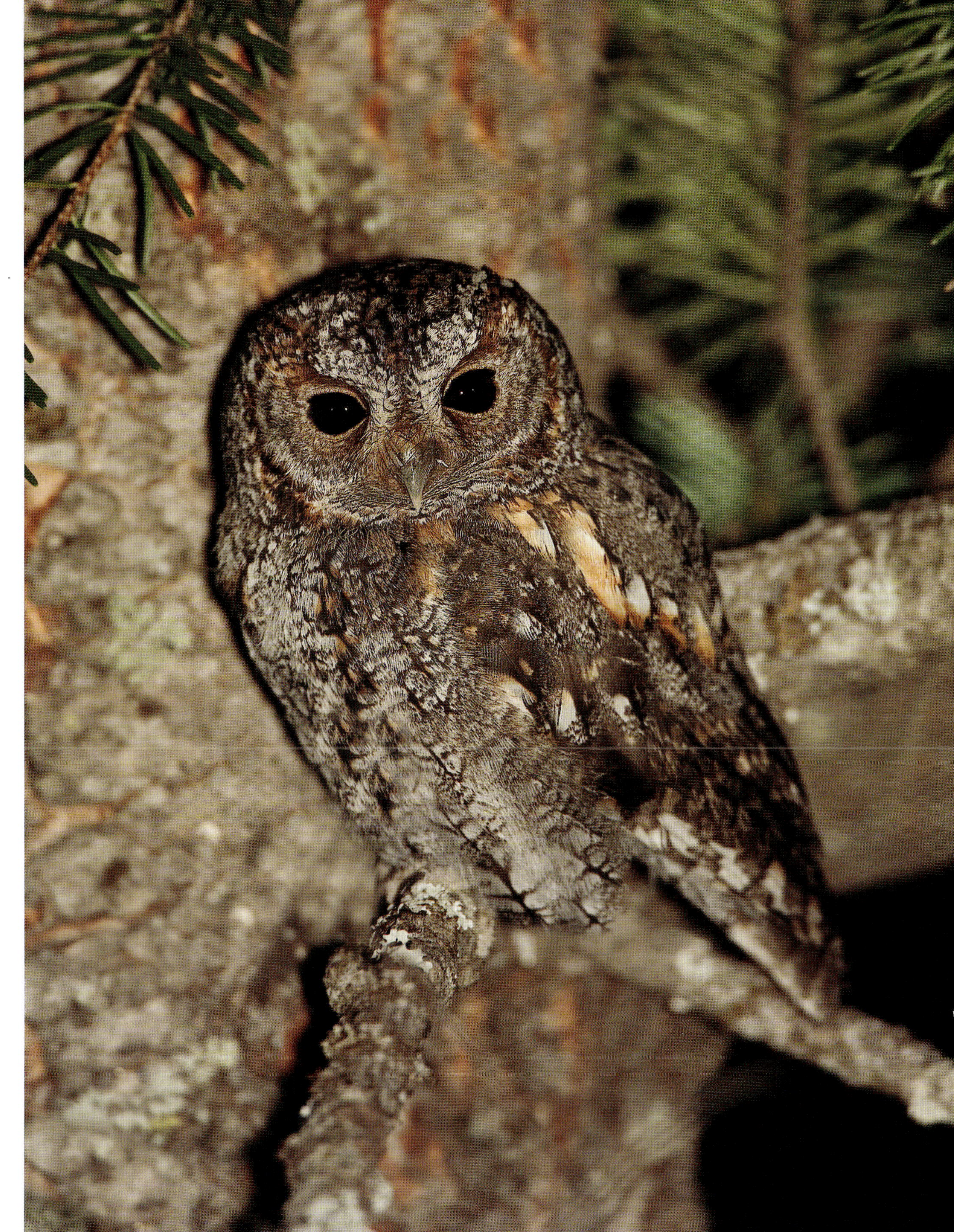

The Flammulated Owl is a small owl that is quite secretive and often difficult to detect. This one blends in with the bark almost seamlessly.
JARED HOBBS

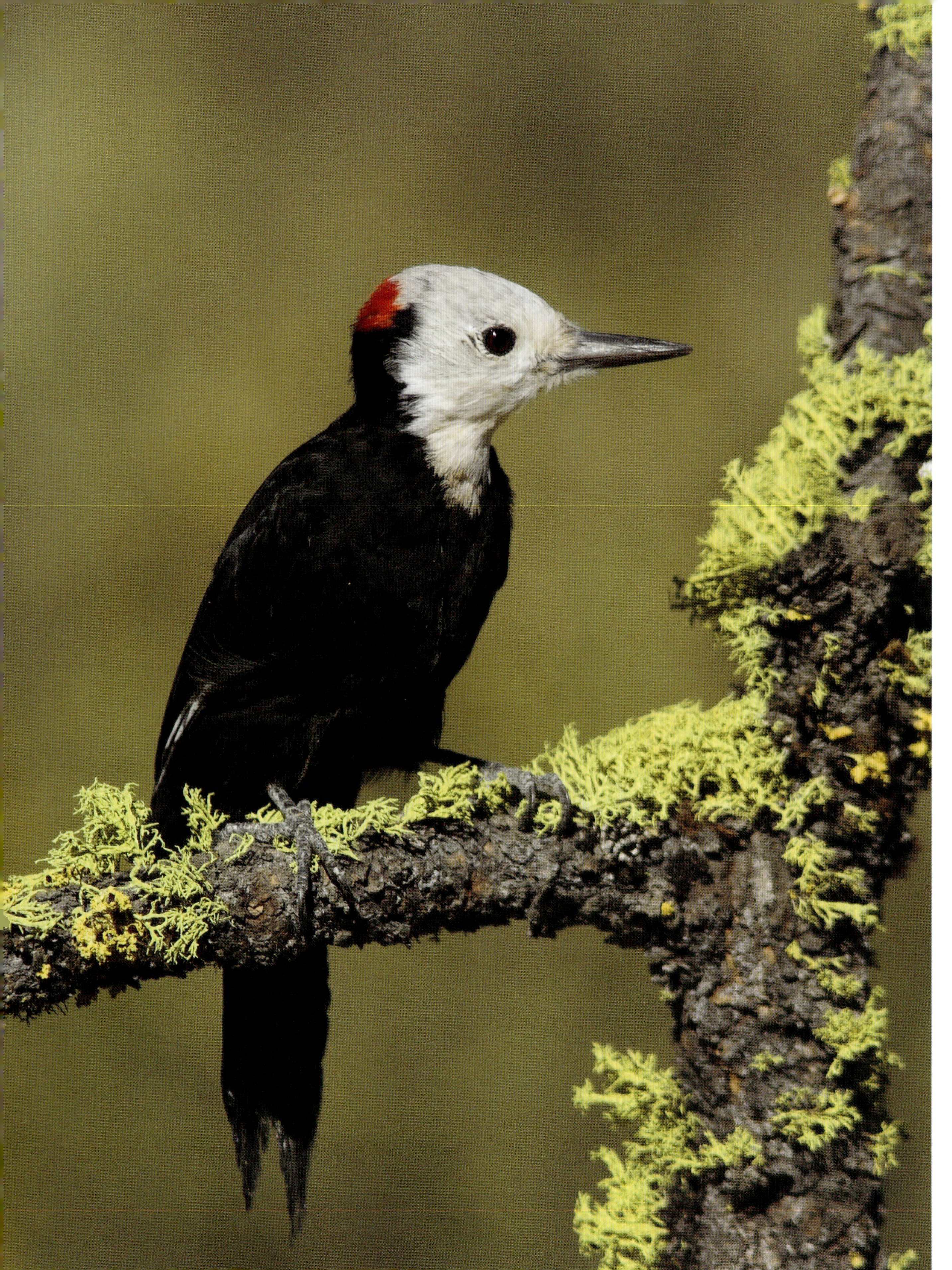

A White-headed Woodpecker perches on a lichen-covered branch. This is another bird whose habitat barely extends into southern BC.

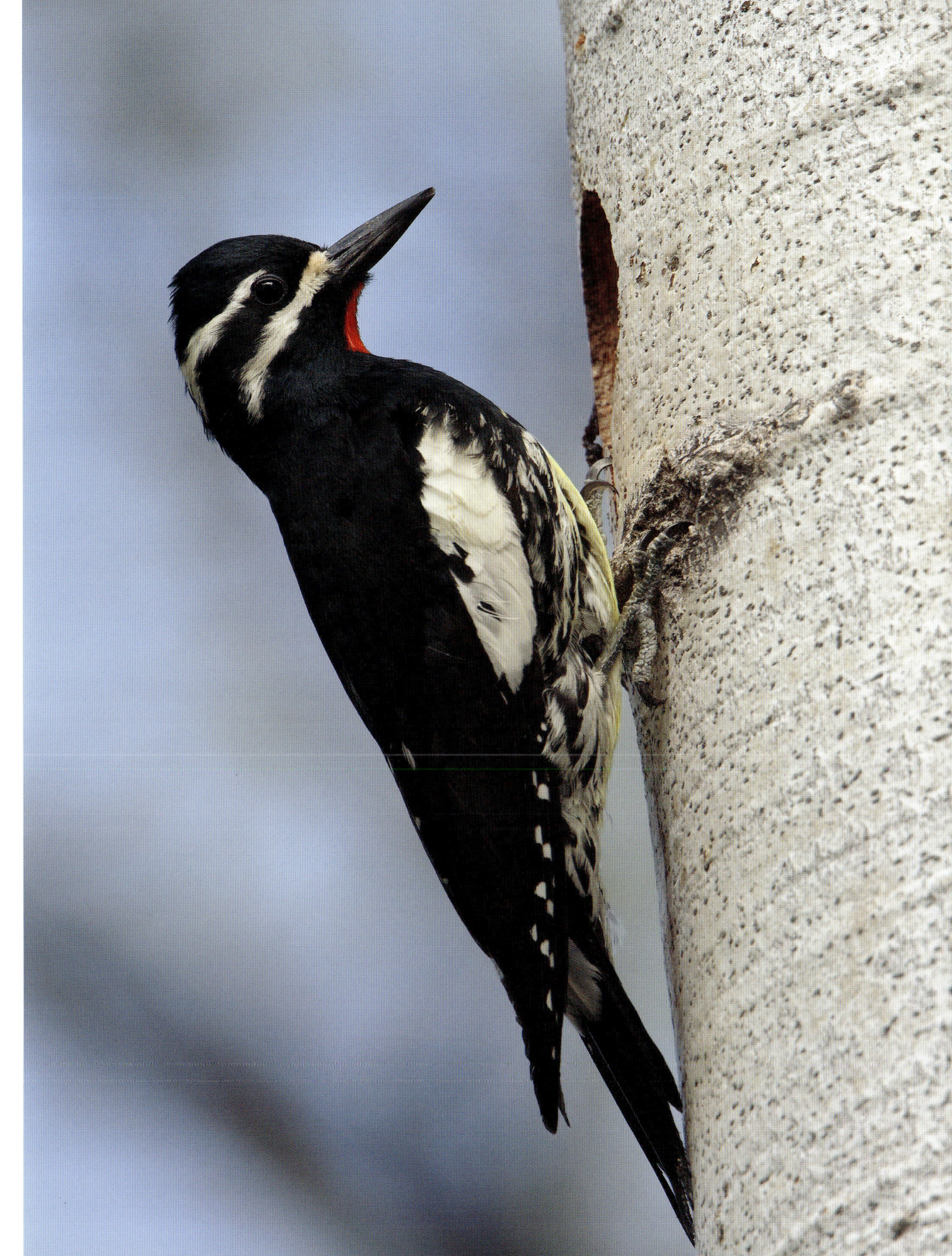

A male Williamson's Sapsucker returns to its nest hole to take over incubation duty from his mate.

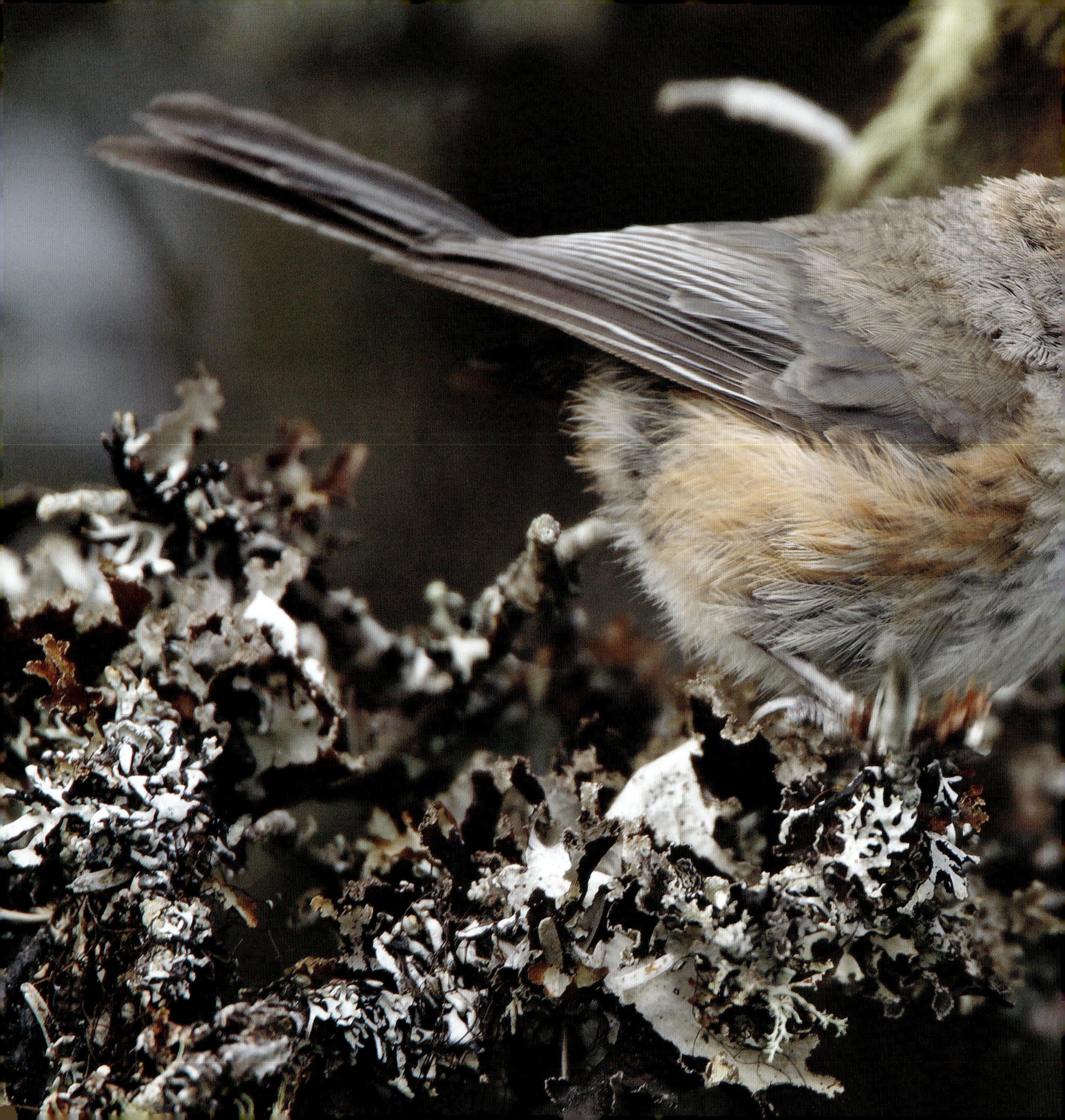

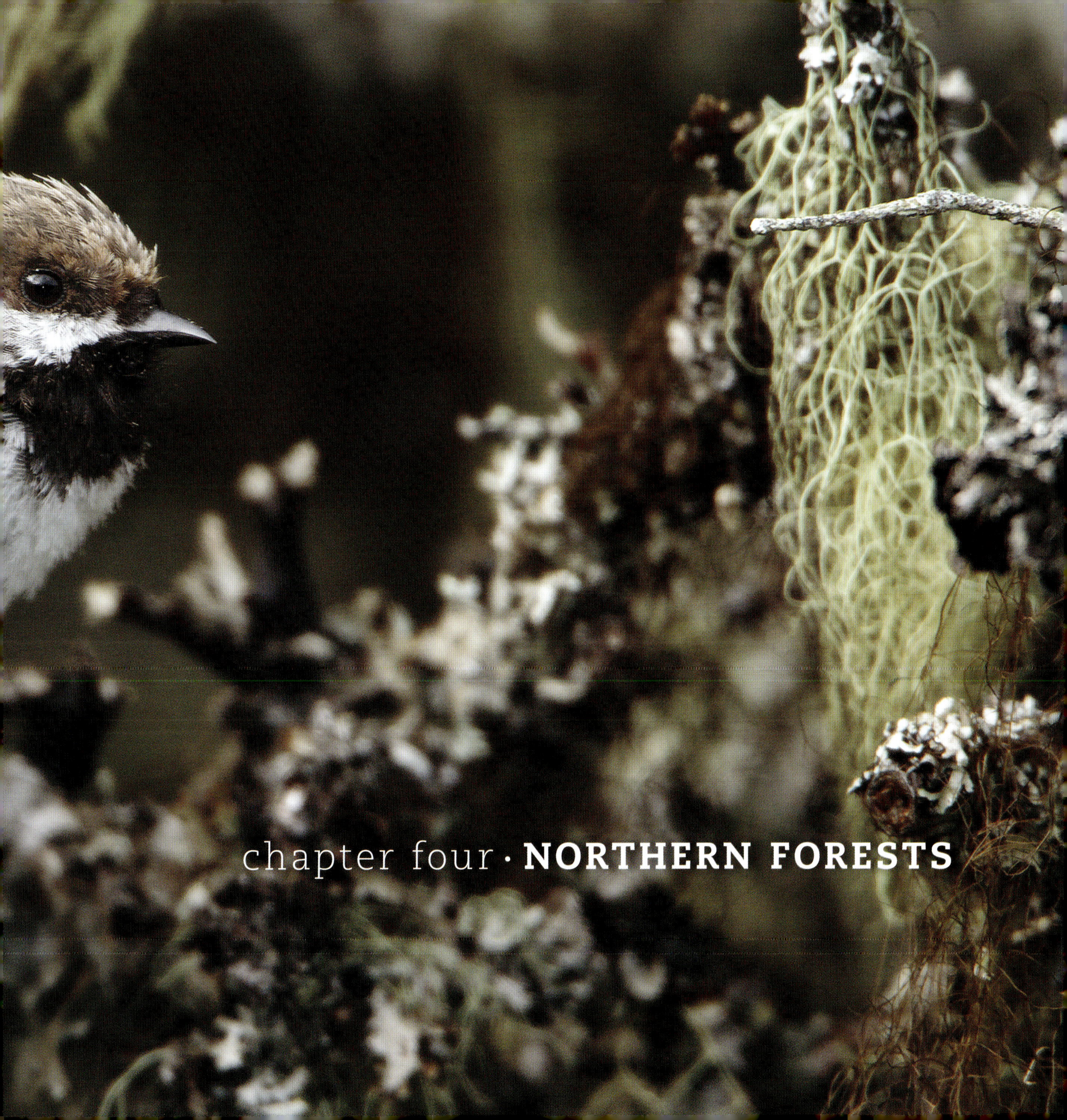

chapter four · NORTHERN FORESTS

Of all the habitat types in Canada, there is none more remote or more untouched than the northern boreal forest. The trees that live in the northern forests are not impressive in their size. They do not inspire awe in the same manner as their magnificent cousins on the coast. In fact, the boreal trees are not even what most people would consider beautiful. These spindly trees, covered in black horsehair lichen and tightly packed together, are noteworthy because of the scale over which they cover the northern realms of the entire northern hemisphere.

Dominated largely by Black and White Spruce trees, the boreal region is an area comprised of dense forests interspersed with sphagnum-lined bogs and crystal-clear lakes—relicts from ice ages of the past. The poor soils, crowded forest canopy and brutally cold winters limit what species are able to grow; as a result, a dense blanket of moss often covers the understorey. While the boreal forest is composed primarily of spruce trees, which are able to thrive in poor soil and moist conditions, it is far from a stagnant or featureless landscape. Trembling Aspen, willow, Lodgepole Pine and Tamarack are mixed in with the plentiful spruce in areas that offer richer soil or receive more sun.

The boreal forest is often called the "bird nursery" of North America because literally *billions* of birds migrate there each year to nest, breed and raise their young. From ducks to warblers, flycatchers to chickadees and gulls to owls, these birds all flock to the northern forests every spring.

THE LAND OF WARBLERS

One family of birds that is much more diverse in the northern forest than elsewhere in the province is the wood warbler family (Parulidae family). This is especially true in the northeast corner of BC that is known as Peace River Country. In BC, this is the only area where you will find several species of these beautiful songbirds, because many eastern birds are isolated from the west by the largely treeless prairie landscape of central Canada. Some species of boreal birds are able to use the northern forest as a gateway to the province but are unable to venture farther west because the Rocky Mountains act as a barrier to migration. Species such as Black-throated Green, Bay-breasted, Blackpoll, Black-and-white, Canada and Cape May Warblers can be found in these northern forests more regularly than anywhere else in BC. These boreal plains also provide the perfect nesting habitat for the Palm Warbler, which seeks out spruce bogs and muskegs that have an open understorey and plentiful sphagnum moss in which to build their nests. The MacGillivray's Warbler of the *Oporornis* genus is common throughout much of the province; however, its cousins, the Connecticut and Mourning Warblers, are normally associated with the forests of eastern Canada and are found in BC only in the northeastern boreal forests.

FOREST FIRES

An inevitable side effect of vast areas of forested land is frequent and, sometimes, very large forest fires. Although often viewed as negative events, these fires are actually rejuvenating and are vital to the long-term health of the forest. Fires also create opportunities for a few specialized woodpecker species that have evolved to become experts at exploiting these freshly burned forests. The Black-backed Woodpecker and the American Three-toed Woodpecker are commonly encountered in forested areas that have been burned or flooded. Walking through a burn scar, you can see the evidence of these two species on the charred black trees that have small orange spots where the bark has been chipped away. Another sure sign is the hollow drumming sound that resonates through the open remains of the forest. These two species are similar looking, with black-and-white plumage. The Black-backed is the larger of the two and can be easily distinguished by its all-black back.

WINTER SURVIVAL FOR BIRDS

Winter in the boreal forest is long and cold, making survival for many species a challenge. Most birds flee to more hospitable areas farther south. To survive in this region, birds must be able to find food and stay warm. This rules out small insect-eating birds such as warblers and flycatchers. Those that remain must be either able to hunt for live prey (hawks and owls); scavenge for scraps (jays); find seeds in the pine cones and in the vertical surfaces that remain uncovered from snow (finches, woodpeckers, chickadees or nuthatches); or live on food that was painstakingly stored throughout the summer and fall.

One of the iconic year-round residents of the northern forests is the Great Gray Owl. Its large size and piercing gaze make it a favourite among birdwatchers who eagerly hope to catch a glimpse of one during their birdwatching career. This can be a frustrating pursuit some years, as the northern forests are remote and often hard to access for many hopeful naturalists. Every few years, however, these owls (as well as other species such as Snowy, Northern Hawk and Boreal Owls) will push farther south in the winter, giving birdwatchers a much better chance of encountering them. These irruptions generally take place during times when prey is scarce and birds are forced to move farther south to feed. Interestingly enough, there can also be irruptions in years when food is bountiful during the breeding season and more young birds survive than normal.

DOWNSIDES, UPSIDES AND SURPRISES

My first visit to the boreal forest came several years ago, when I took part in what has become a rite of passage for many young Canadians: tree planting. Our camp was north of Fort Nelson on the Liard River, one of the remotest areas I had ever been. I have a lot of memories from that summer—perhaps some that I would rather forget, like the relentless mosquitoes and back-breaking work—but even on the most gruelling days, I could always count on the exuberant song of the White-throated Sparrows to keep me company. I will never forget the day I nearly had my head taken off by a Lesser Yellowlegs. There I was, minding my own business reforesting the land, and from out of nowhere this angry little shorebird attacked me! I'm not sure if I was more surprised by its aggressive behaviour or the fact that it was actually perching up in the trees. It was shocking to see a bird that I associated with mud flats and shorelines behaving so differently on its breeding territory.

Exploring the boreal forest is perhaps not something that everyone would enjoy. There are often hordes of mosquitoes and blackflies during the summer months. The ground is often wet and spongy, and the thick forests can at times be utterly impenetrable. During the winter, the temperatures become bitterly cold and the forests appear lifeless. Nevertheless, encountering an incredibly tame Spruce Grouse, spotting a Great Gray Owl hunting at dusk or hearing the fantastic dawn chorus during breeding season make the boreal forest a fantastic and worthwhile place to visit.

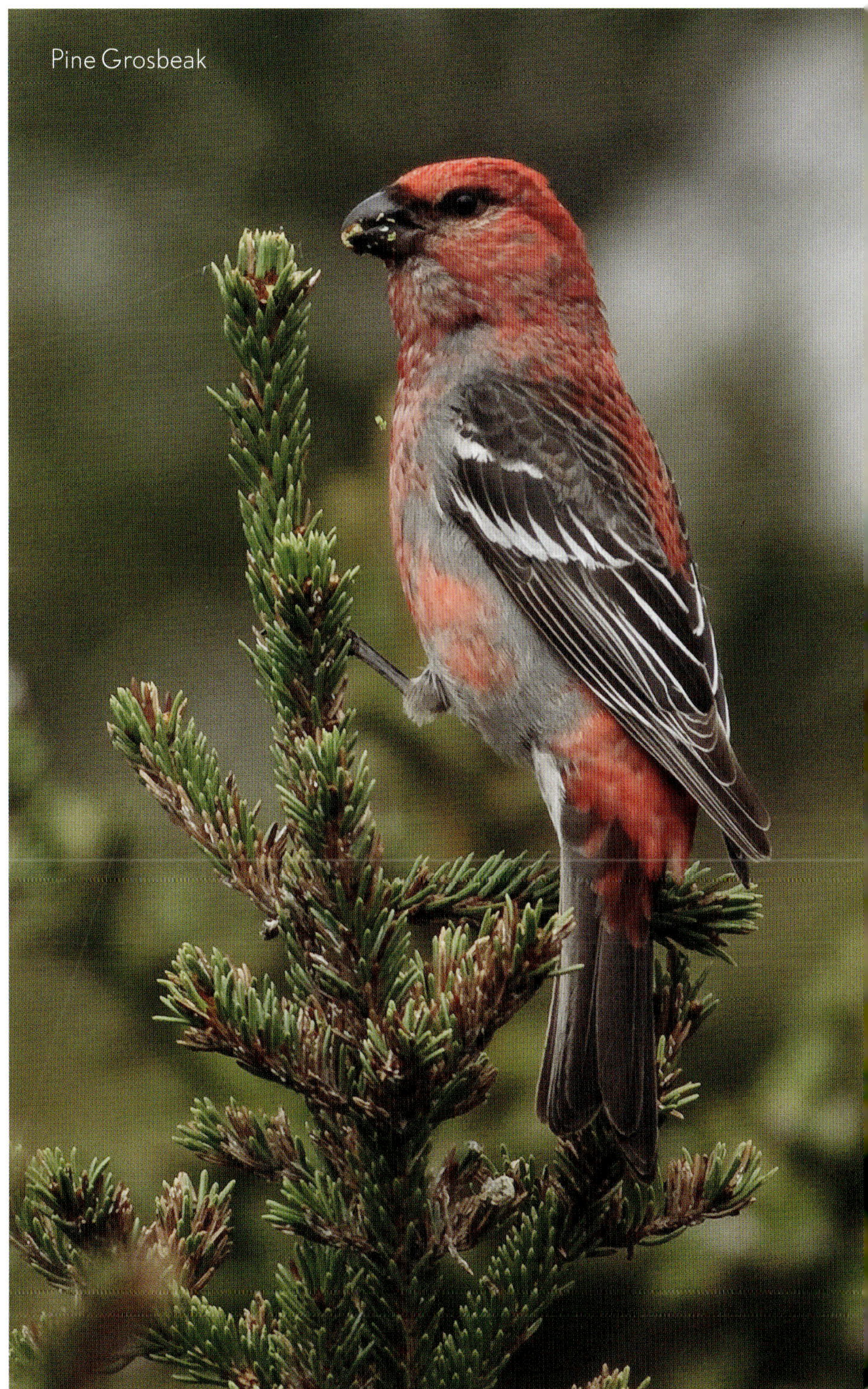
Pine Grosbeak

The Blackpoll Warbler is a classic bird of BC's northern forests. It has an extremely high-pitched call that may not be audible to everyone, making it difficult to spot.

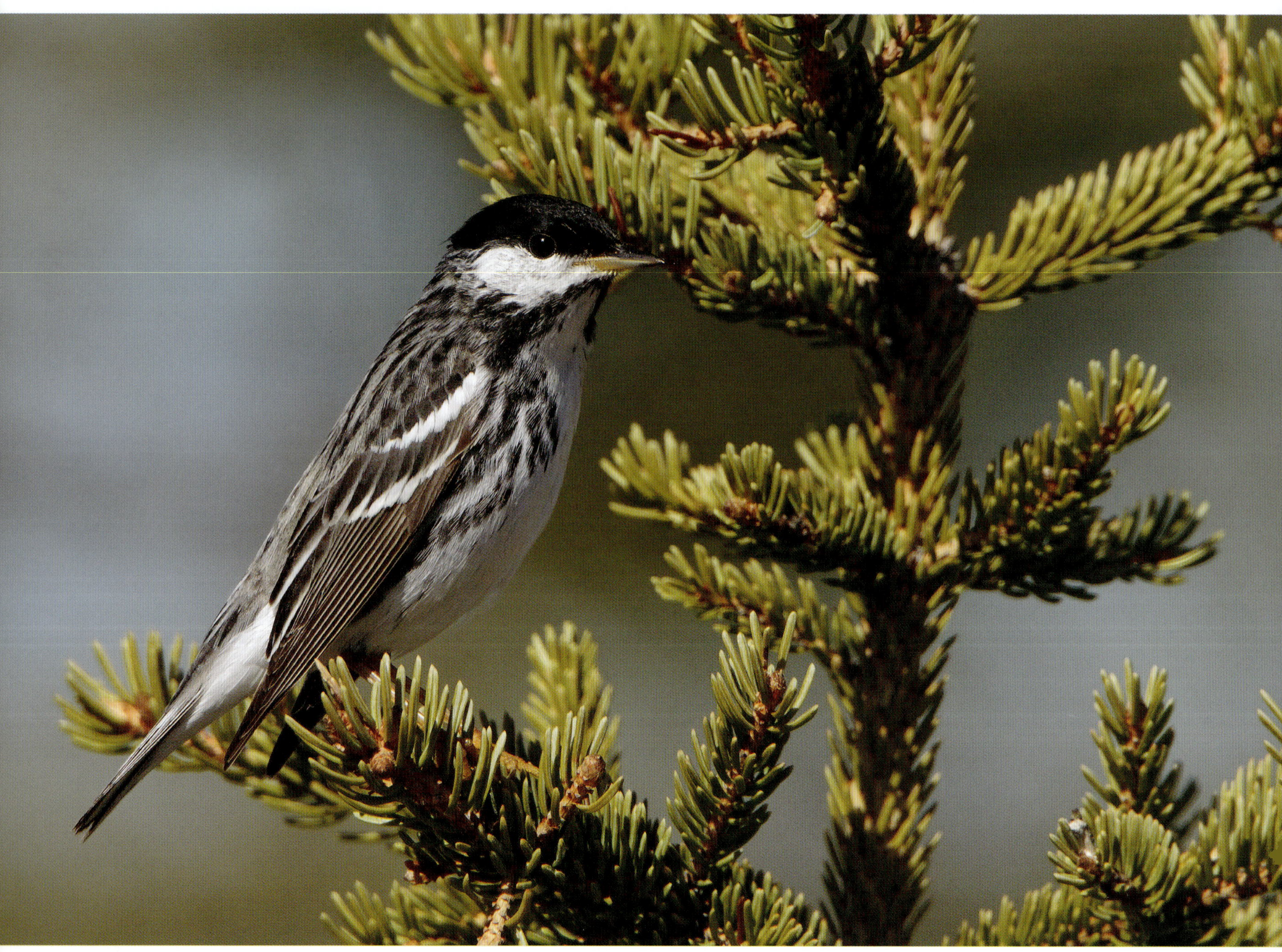

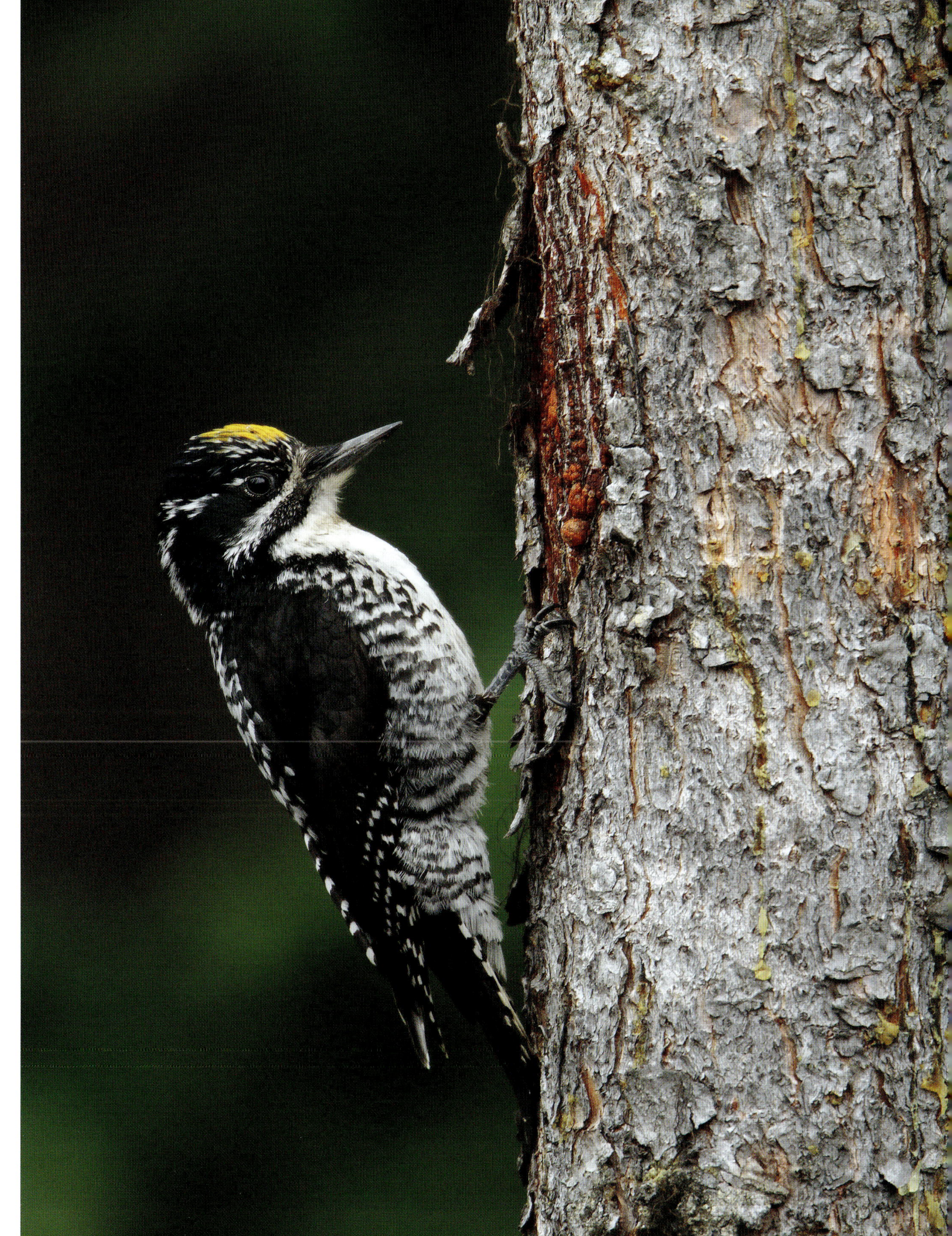

An American Three-toed Woodpecker clings to a pine tree while searching for its next meal.

The Cape May Warbler's scientific name is *Setophaga tigrina* because of the tiger-like stripes on the male birds.

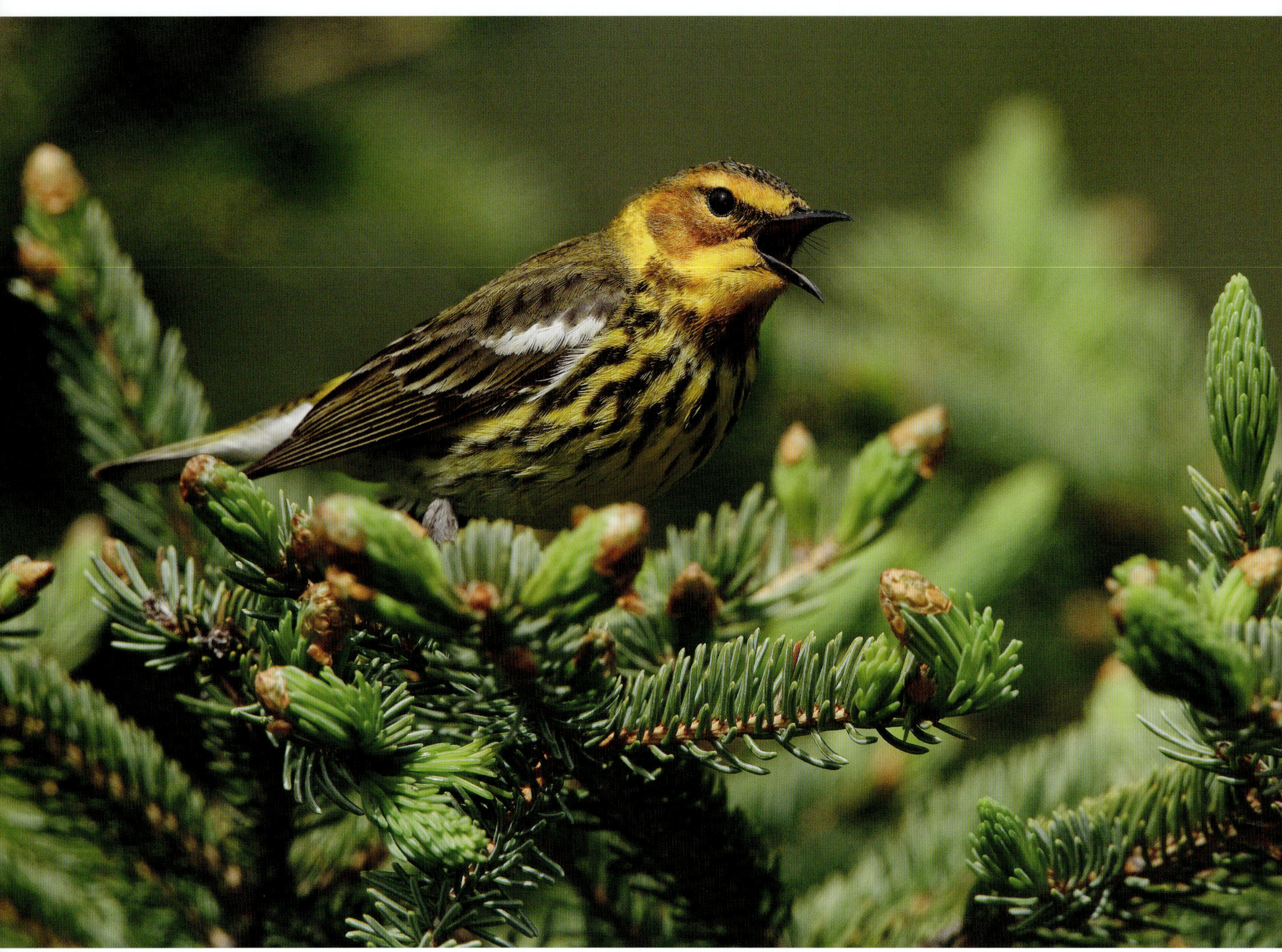

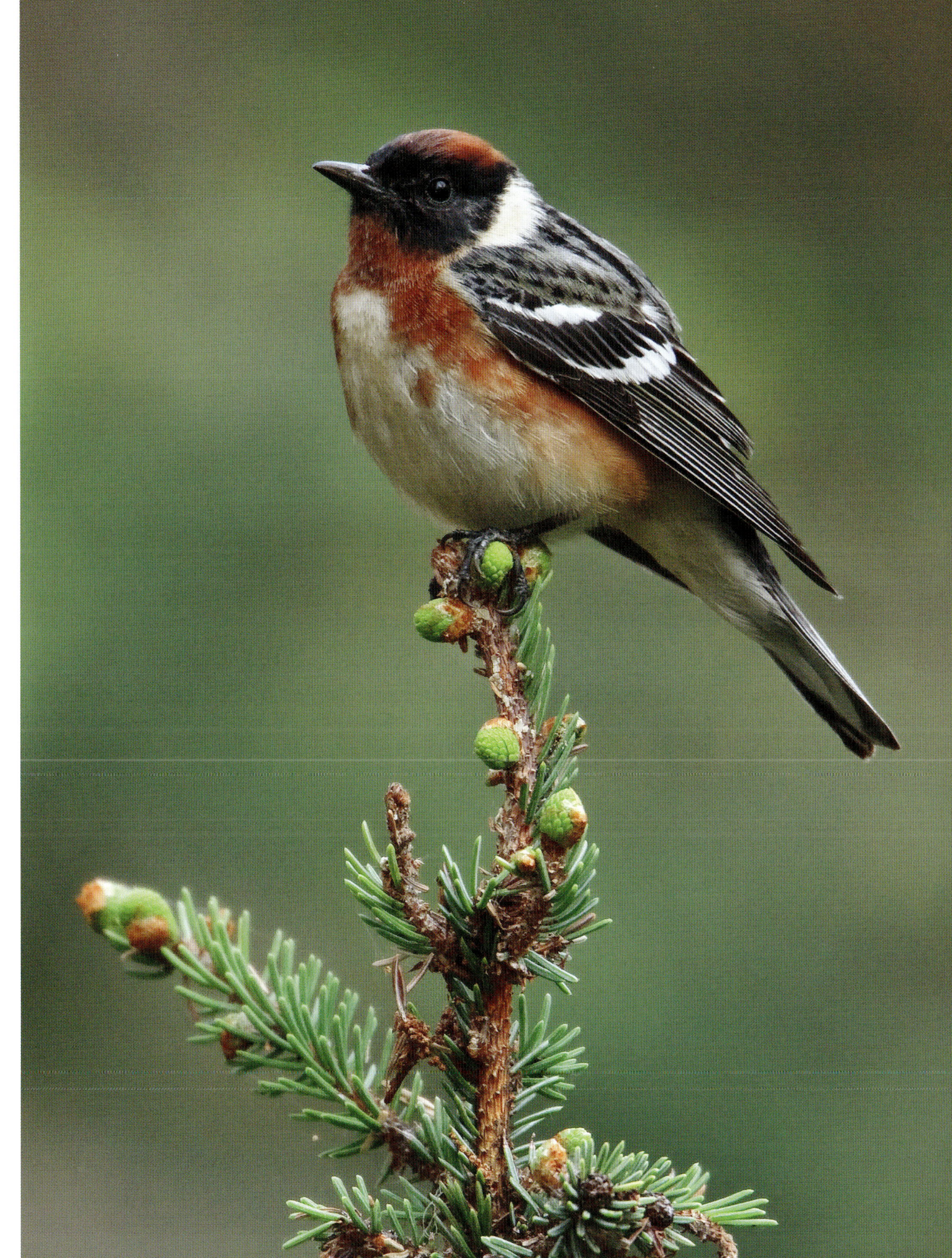

A classic northern songbird, the Bay-breasted Warbler breeds almost exclusively within the boreal forest.

Generally considered an eastern bird, the Canada Warbler is a creature of moist forests with abundant undergrowth. In BC they are found only in small pockets of the northeast.

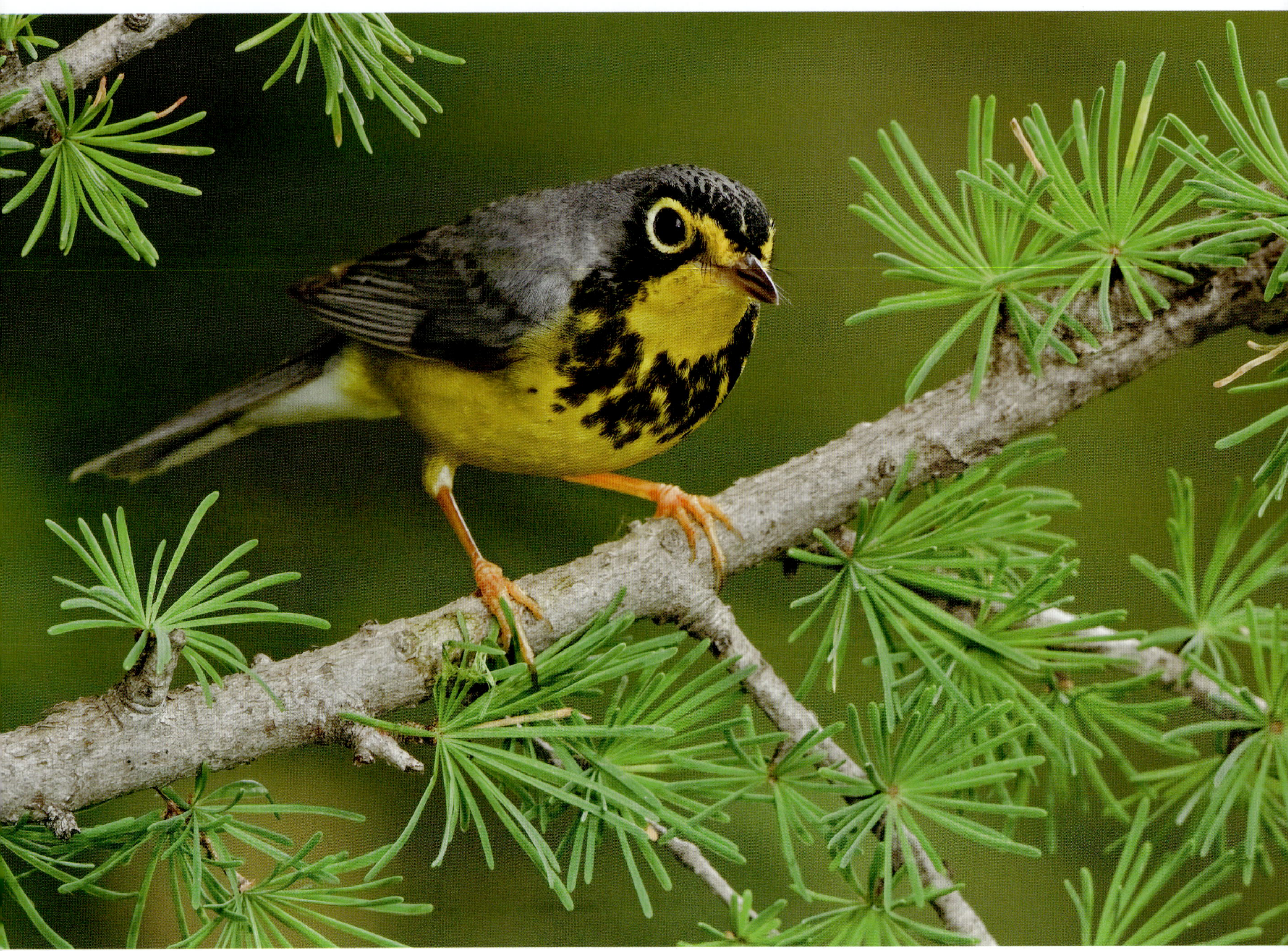

The Black-and-white Warbler is found only in the boreal and taiga plains of northeastern BC. This species has been classified with its own genus because it has an unusually long rear toe and claw, allowing it to grip the bark of trees.

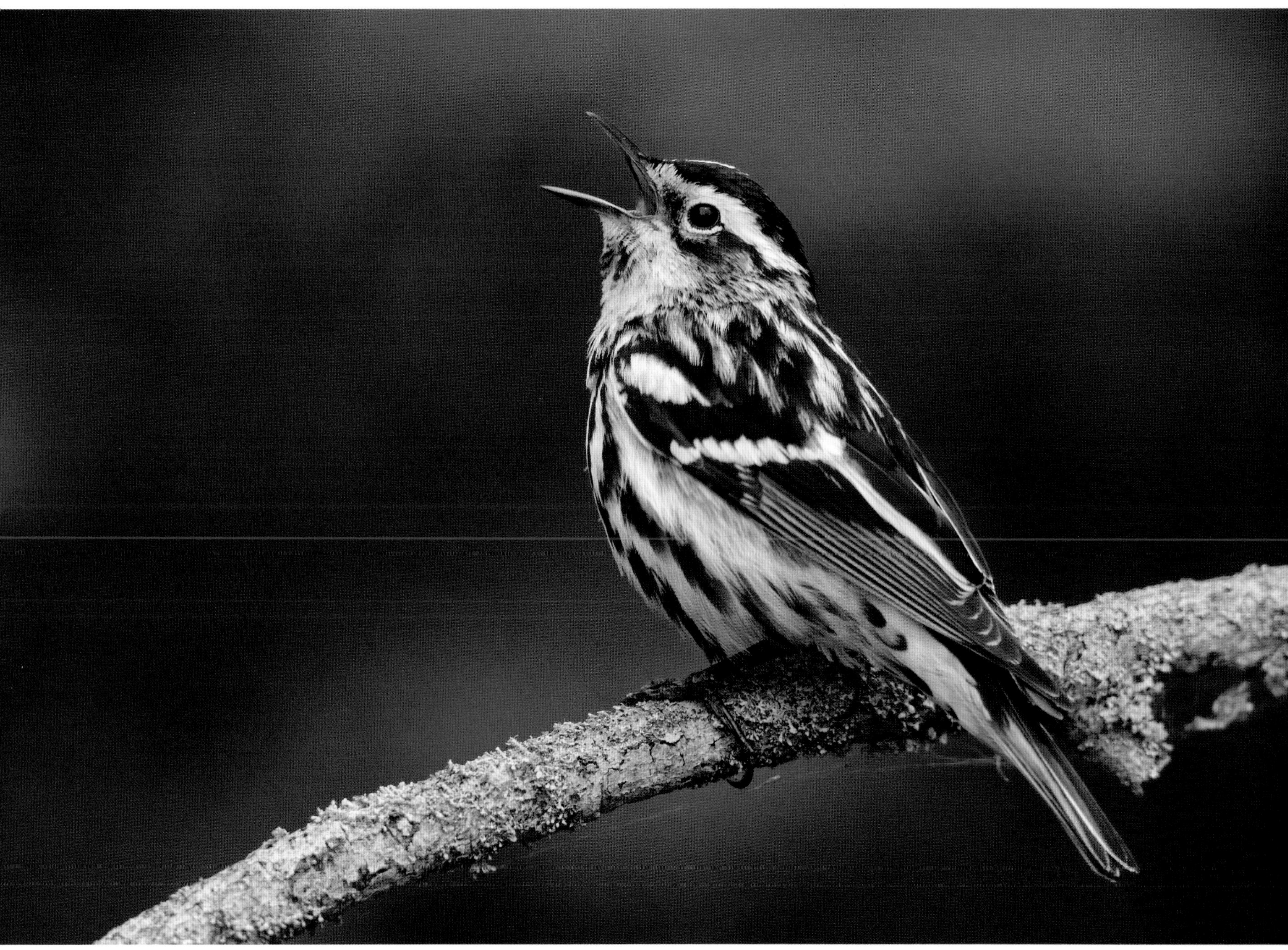

On a cold winter's day, a Boreal Owl searches for its next meal. HAROLD STIVER

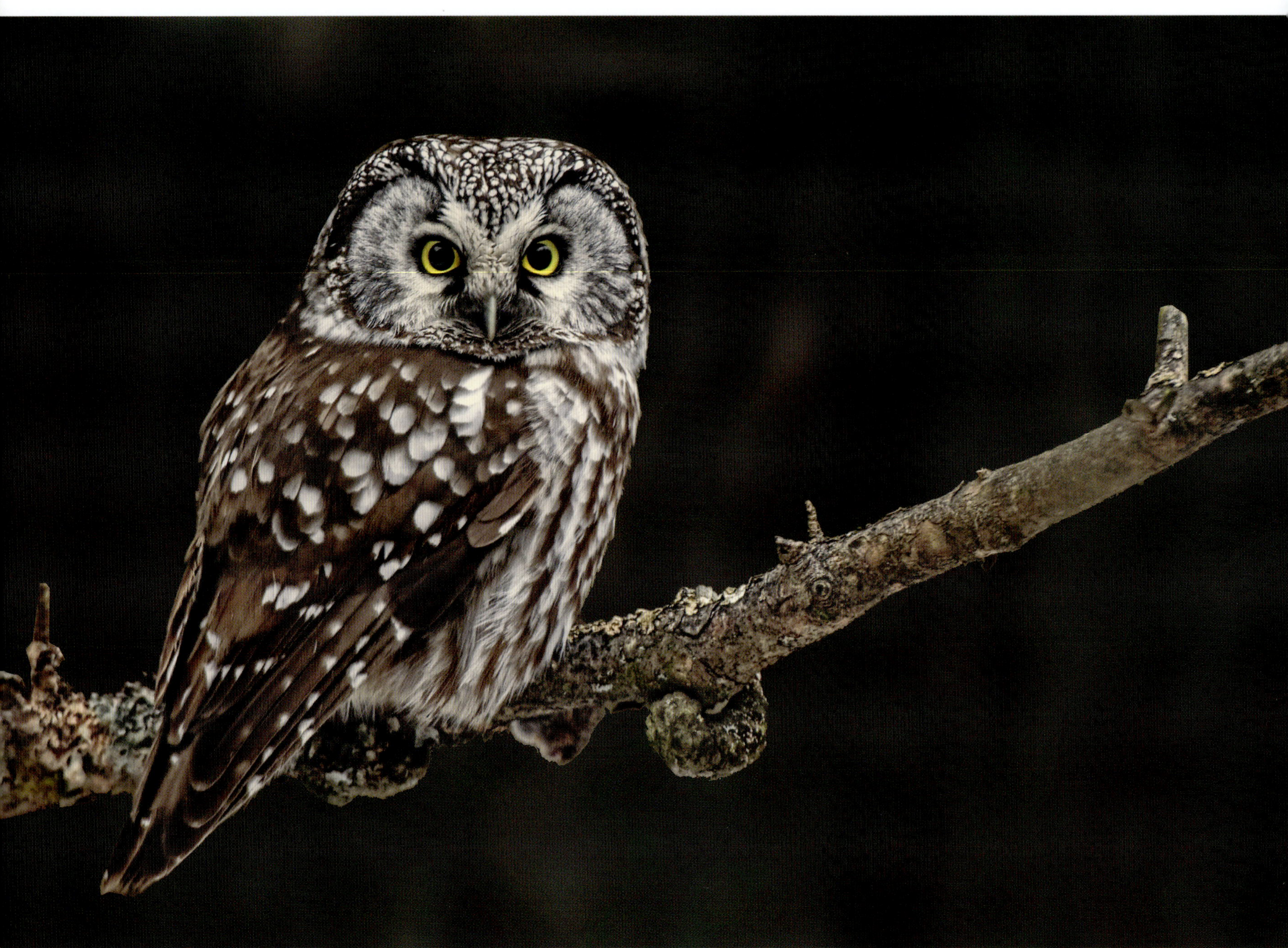

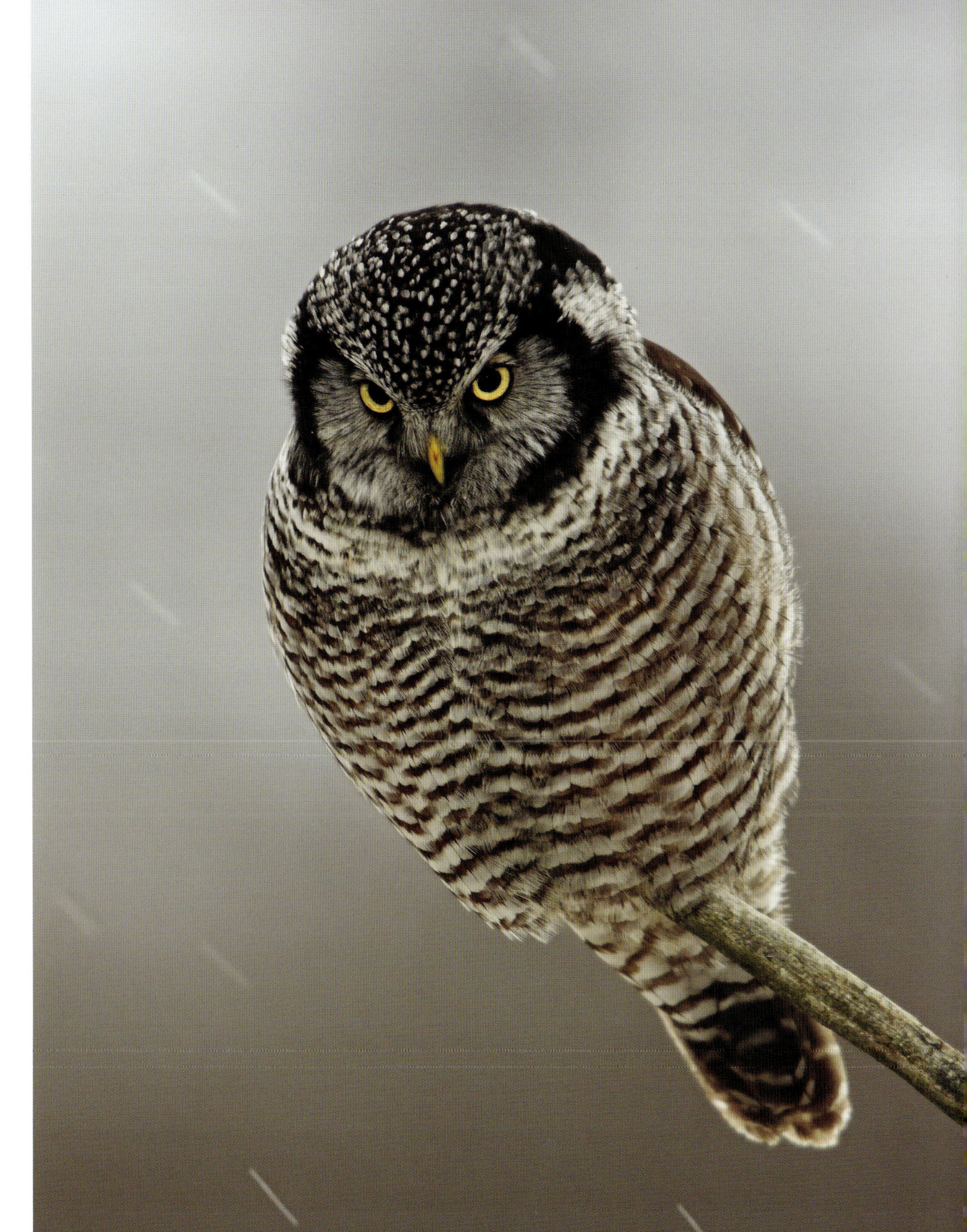

Driving snow and wind cannot interrupt the intense stare of this Northern Hawk Owl.

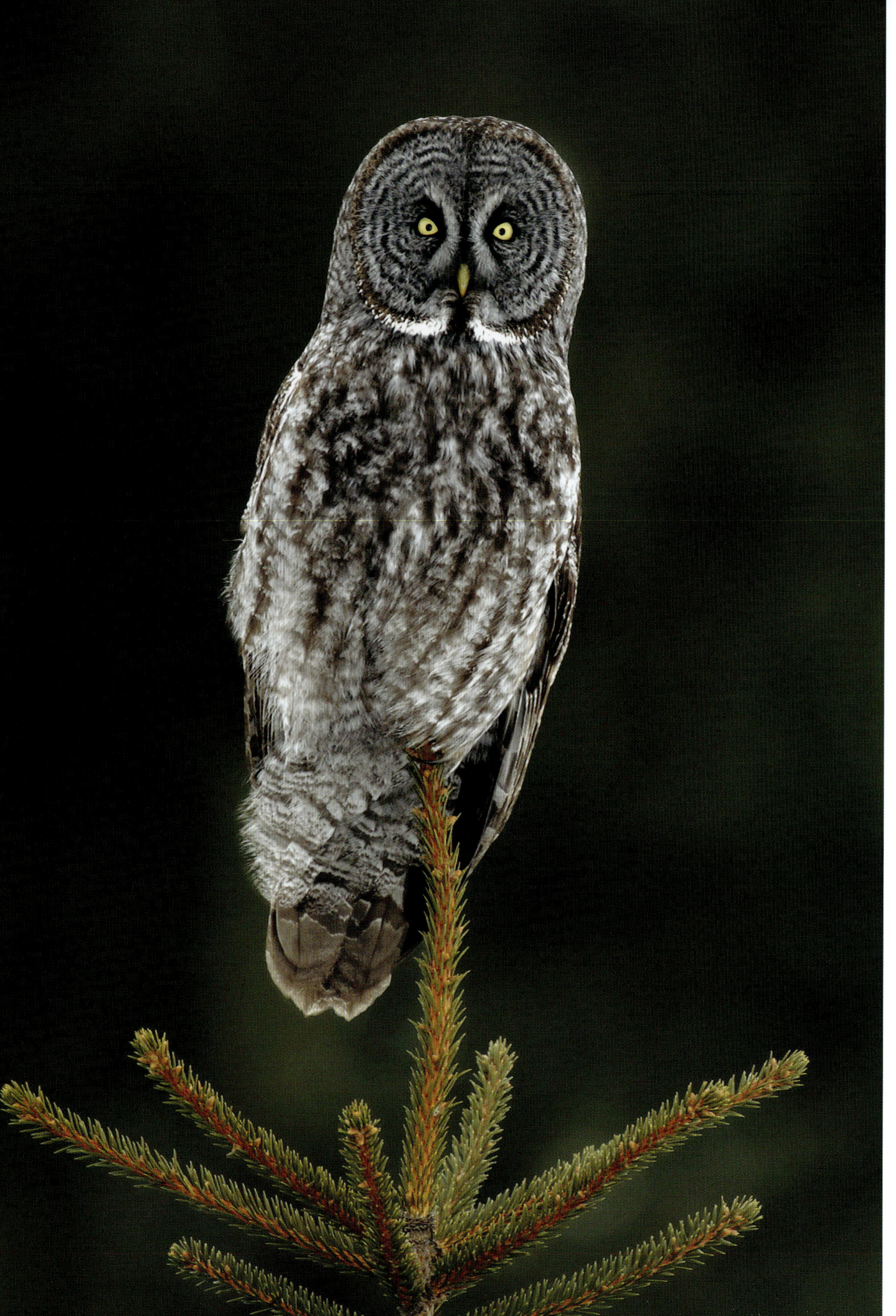

The Great Gray Owl is the largest species of owl in North America. They have enormous facial disks that allow them to hear their prey from great distances and even beneath heavy snow. ALAN MURPHY

A true symbol of the north, the Snowy Owl breeds in the high Arctic each summer. Depending upon food supply and nesting success, they may travel farther south during the winter months to find suitable feeding grounds.

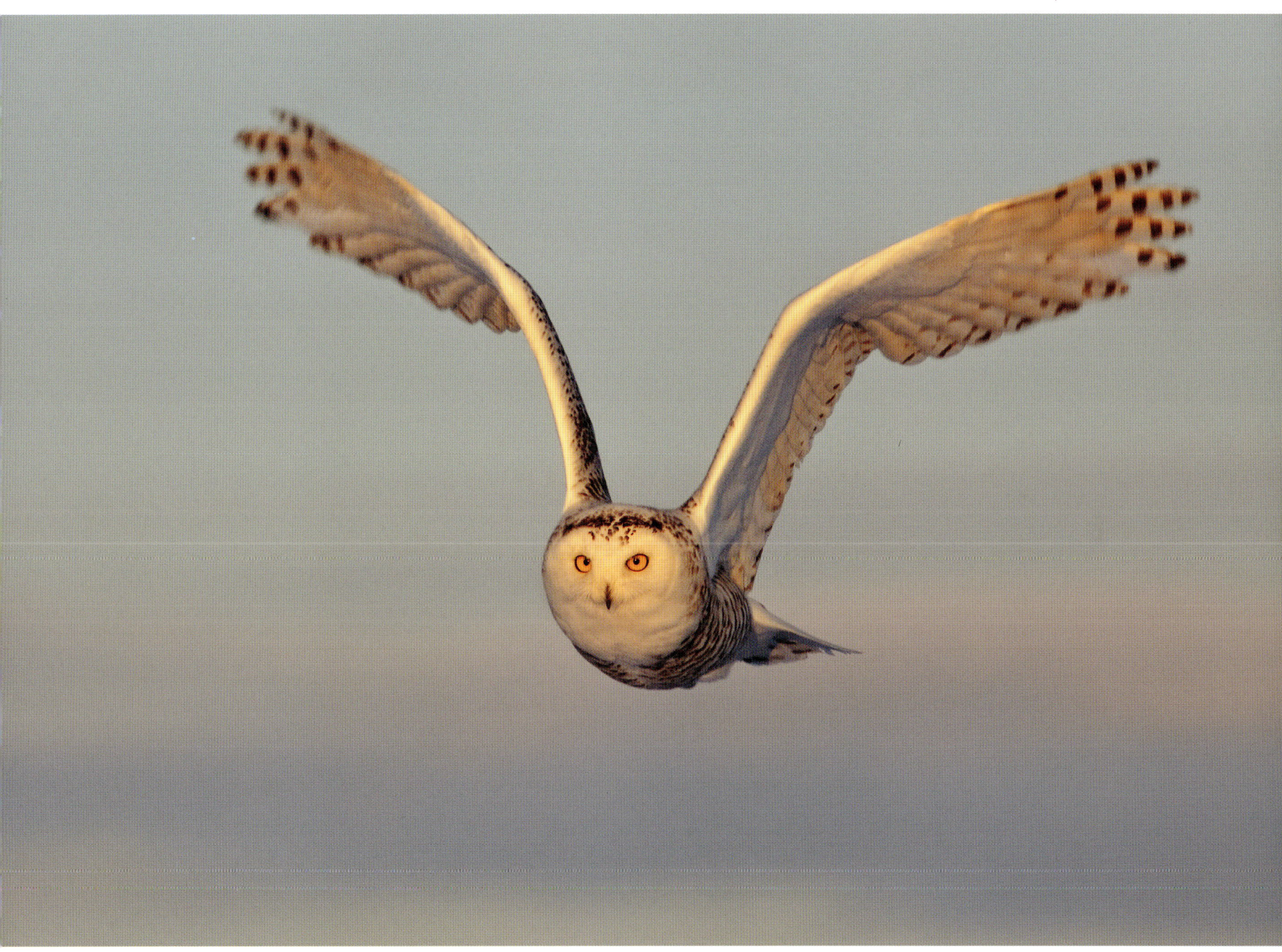

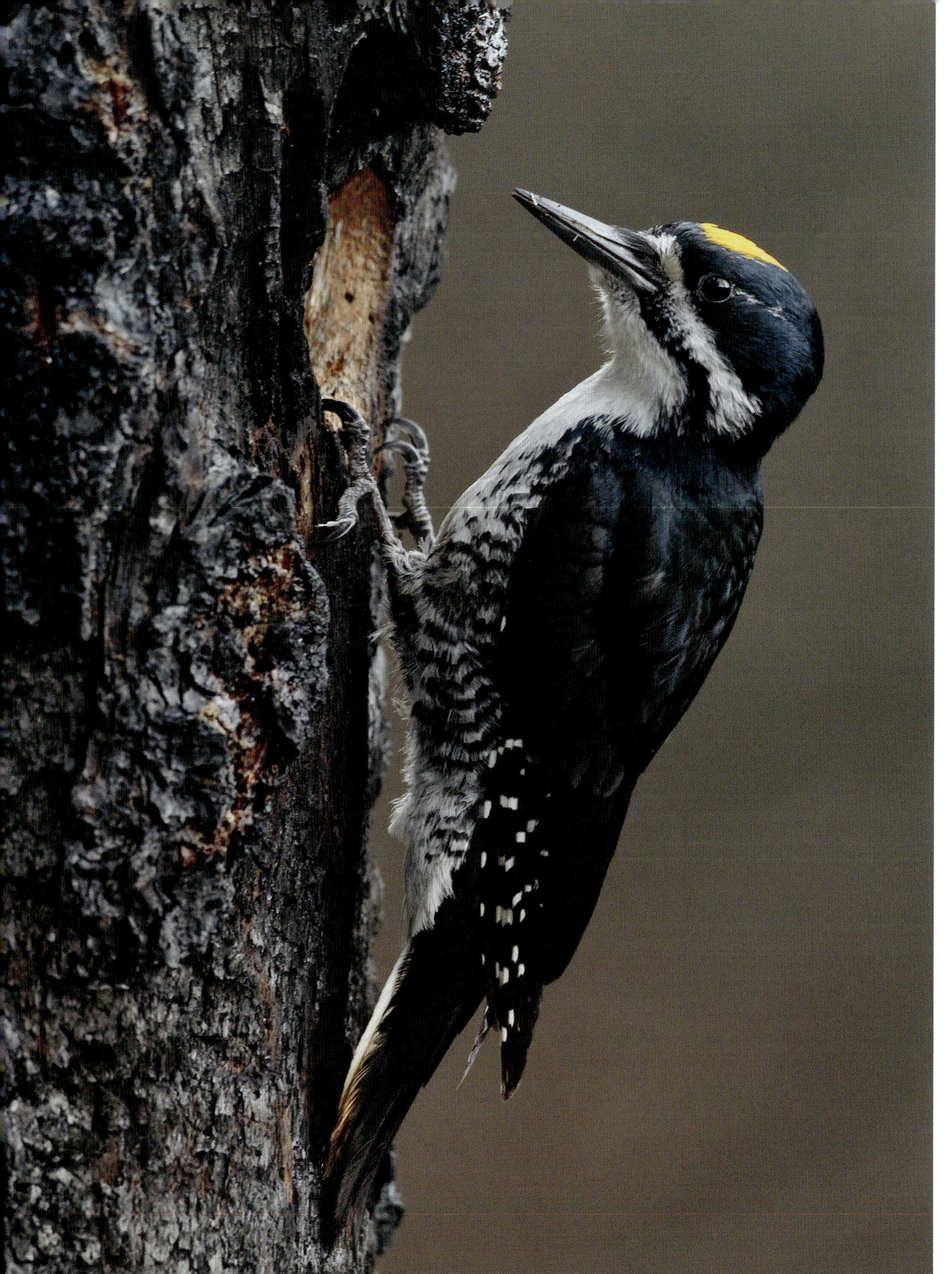

The Black-backed Woodpecker is often found in areas that have experienced disturbances such as forest fires.

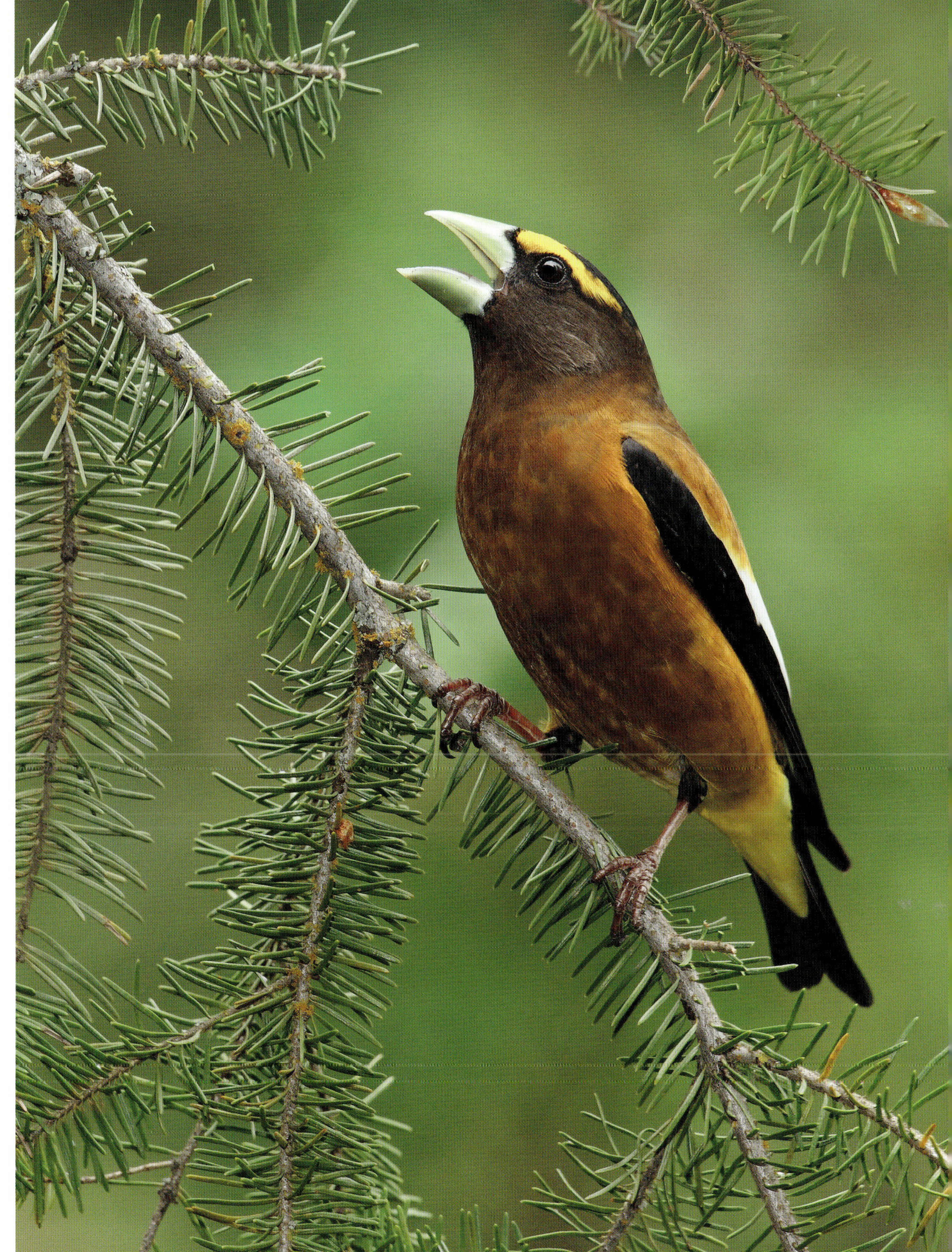

An Evening Grosbeak sings from its perch. This bird is common in many areas of North America.

There can be no mistaking how the Golden-crowned Kinglet earned its name. These tiny birds are found throughout the province, although they mainly breed in the forest. MATTHEW STUDEBAKER

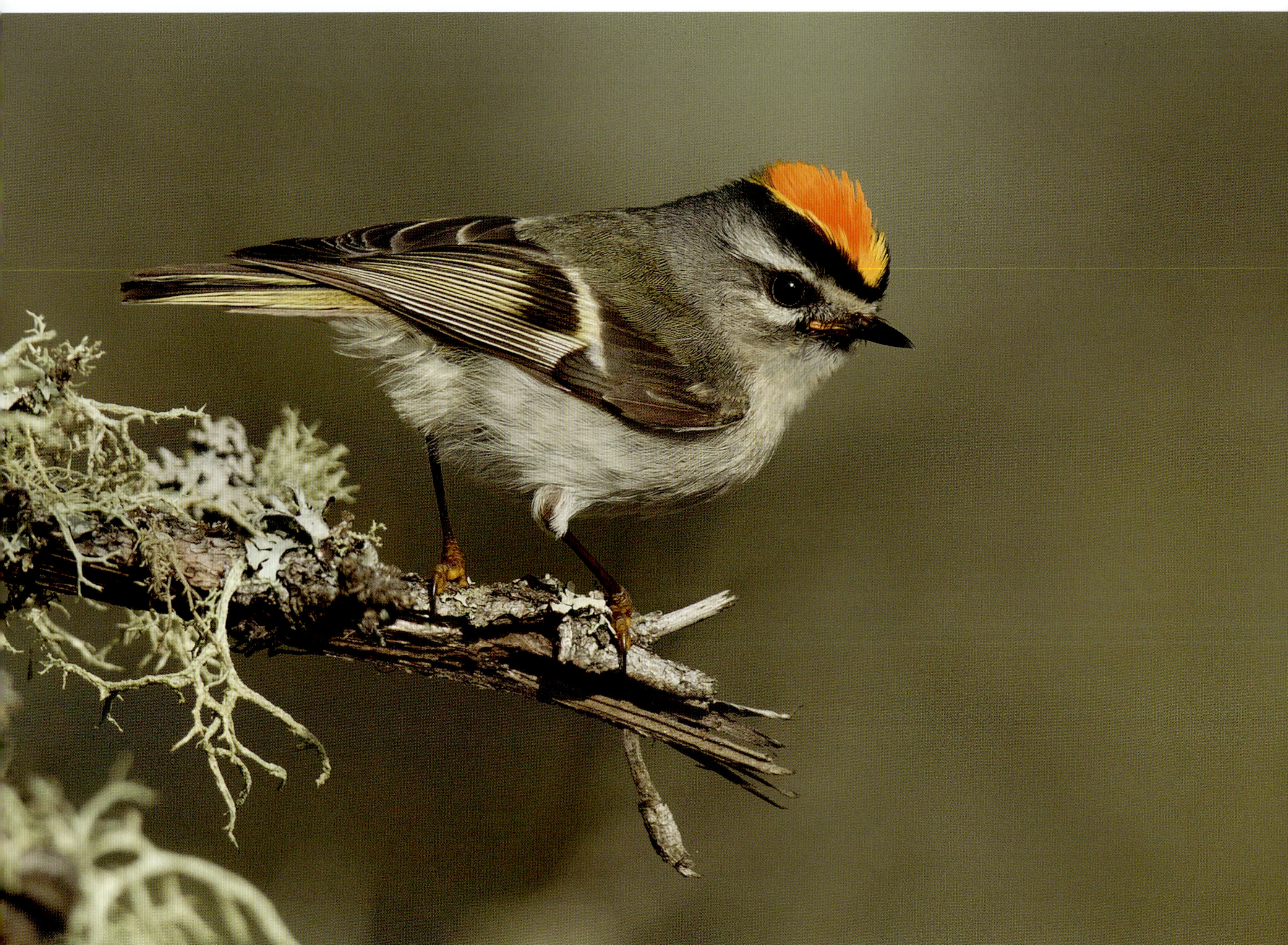

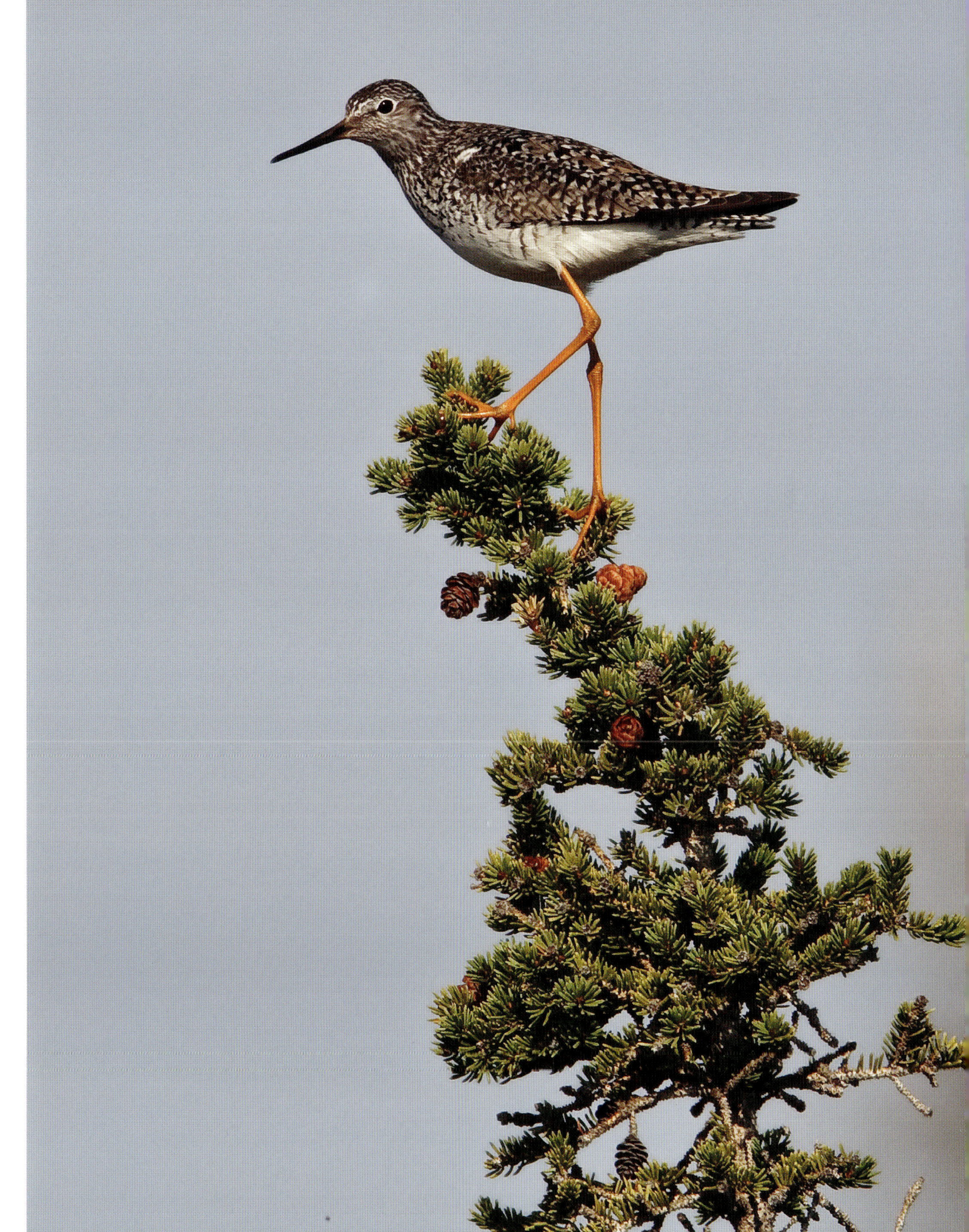

Most often thought of as a quiet bird of coastal areas, the Lesser Yellowlegs, like many shorebirds, changes its behaviour—and habitat—completely when breeding season arrives.

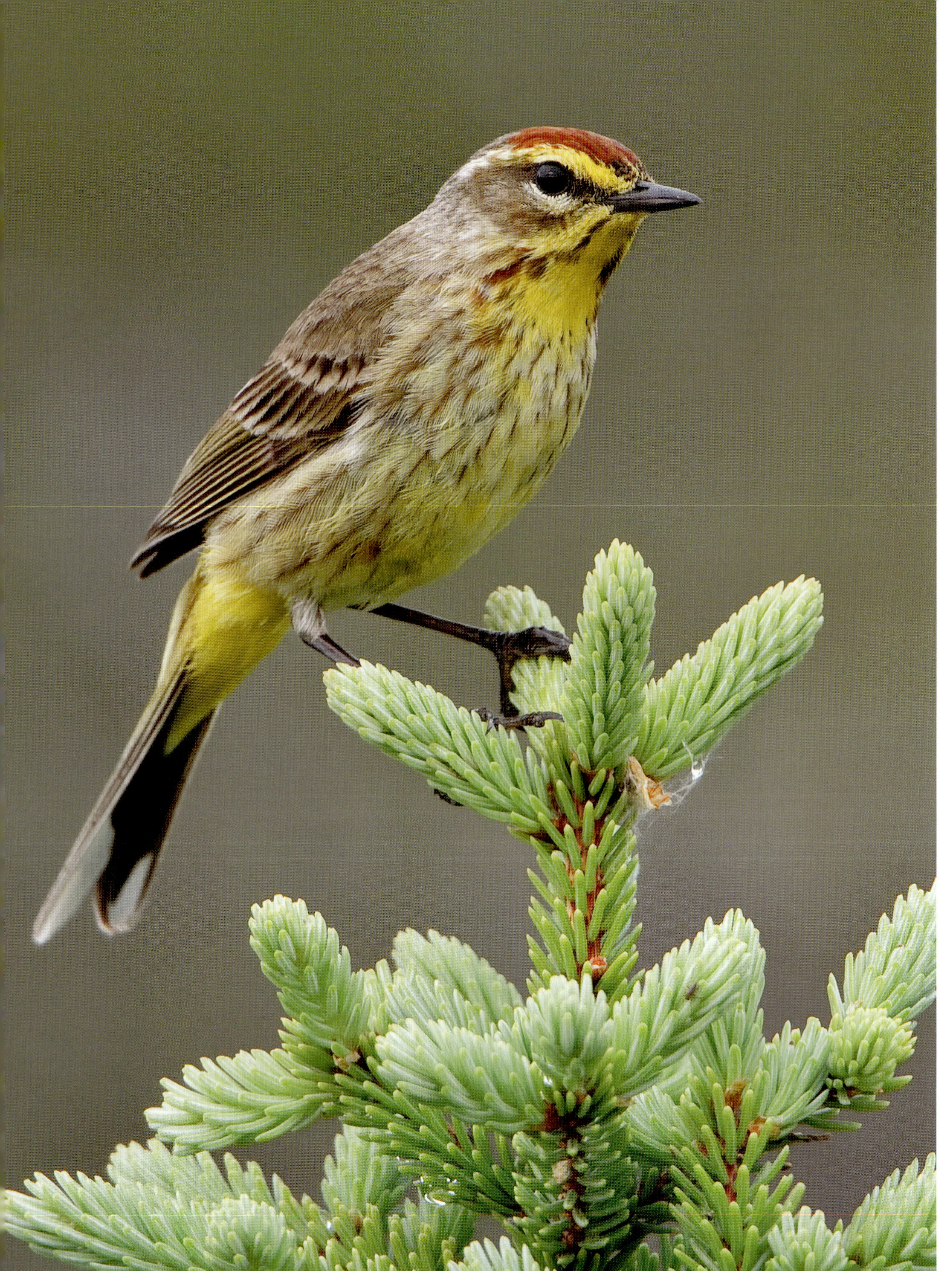

Palm Warblers prefer to breed in the Black Spruce bogs and muskegs of the northeastern portion of BC.

The Northern Waterthrush inhabits swamps, bogs and the perimeter of lakes in the northern part of BC, where it spends much of its time on the ground.

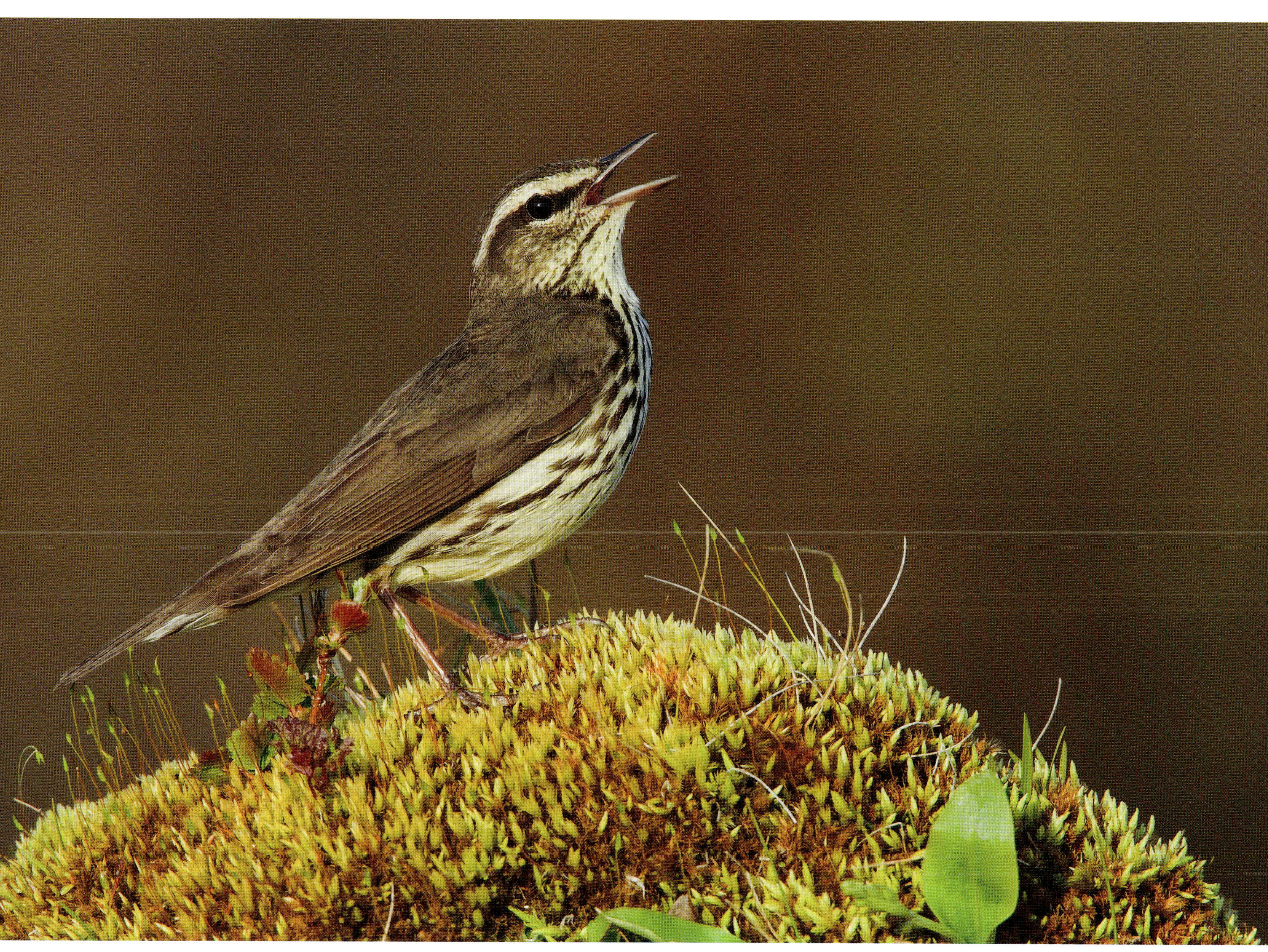

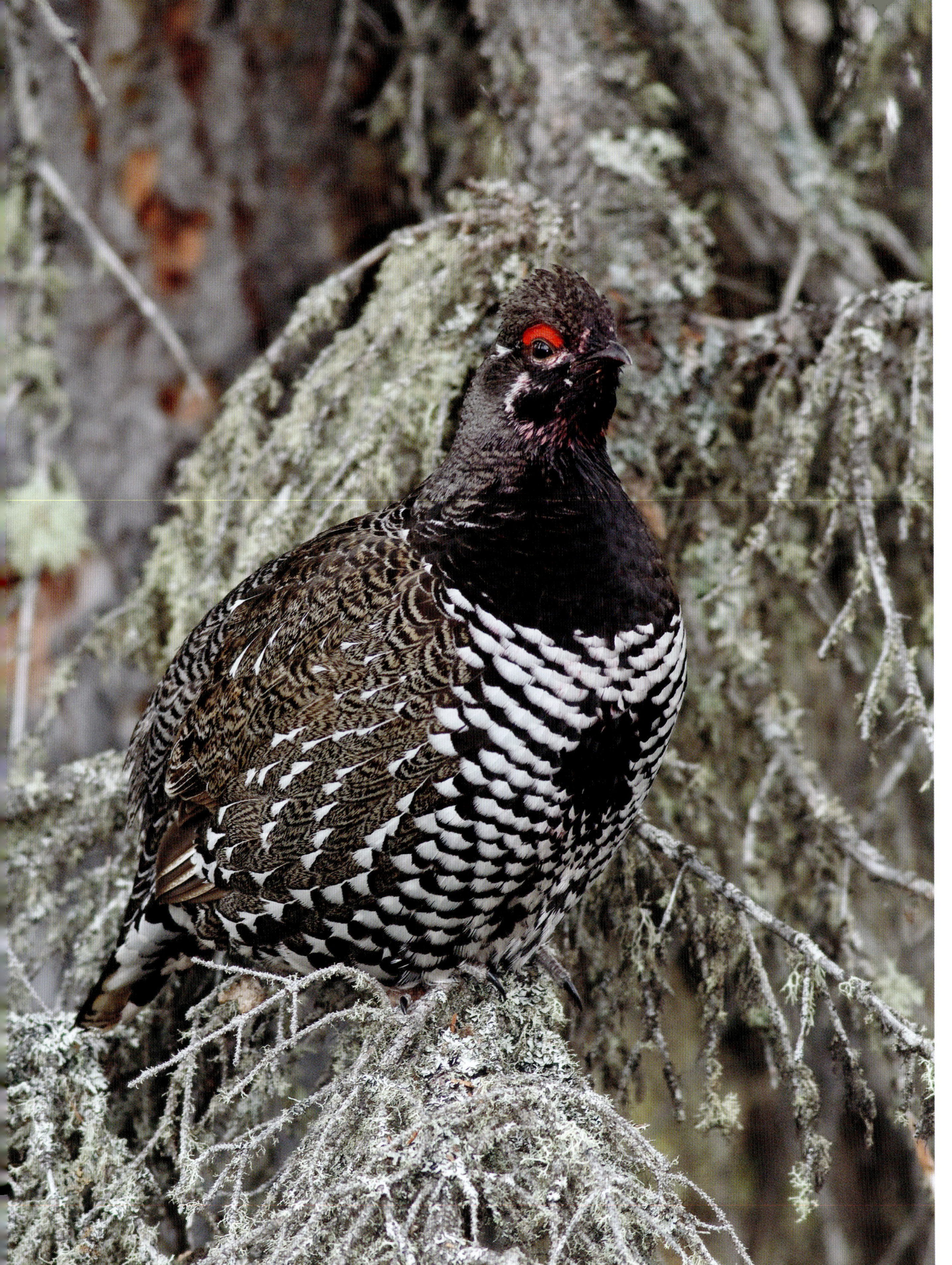

The Spruce Grouse is an extremely tame bird of the northern forest. They seem to have supreme confidence in their camouflage and are more likely to sit still than take flight.

The intense red eyes and conspicuous golden tufts of the Horned Grebe have earned it the nickname "hell diver."

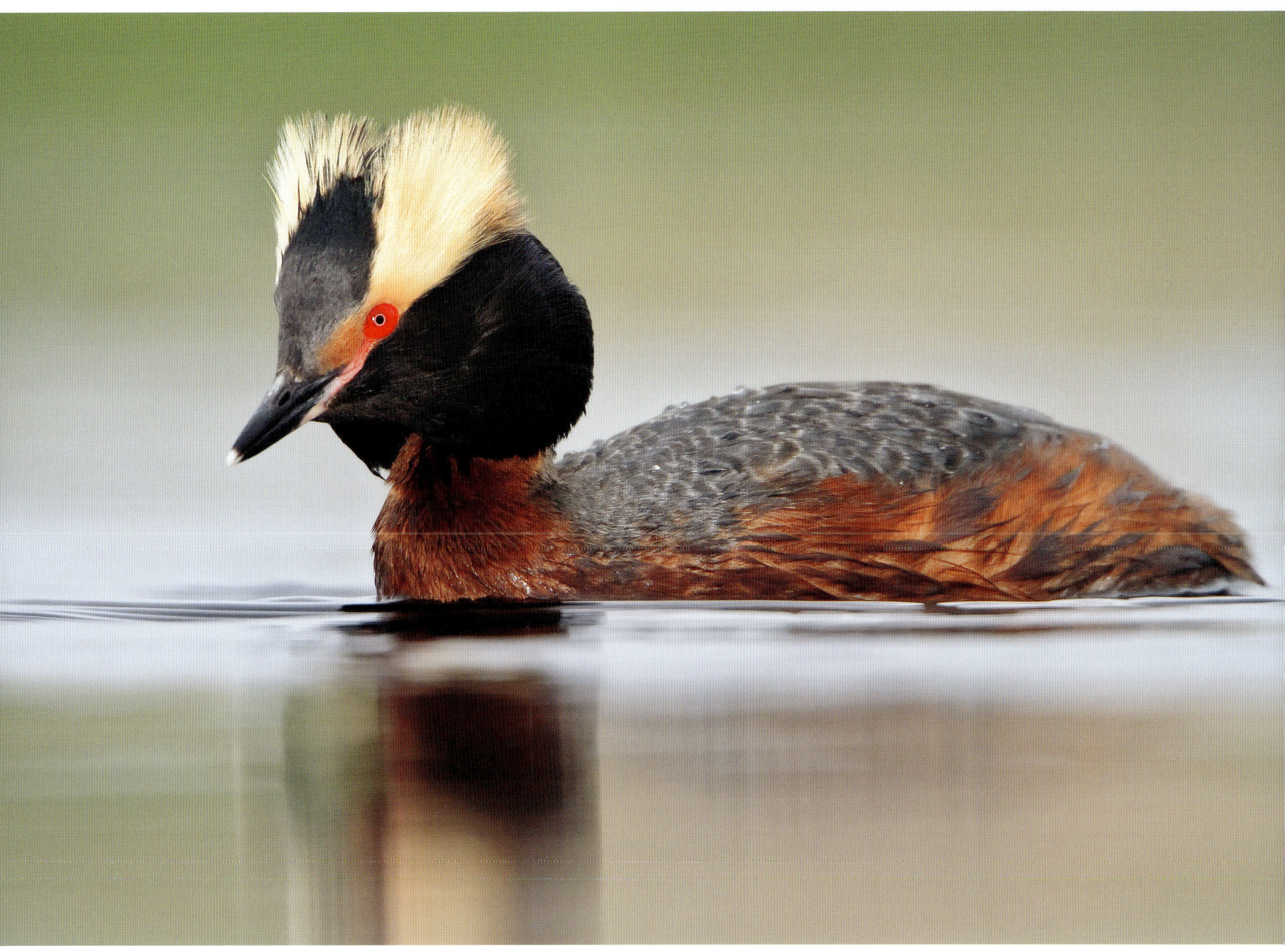

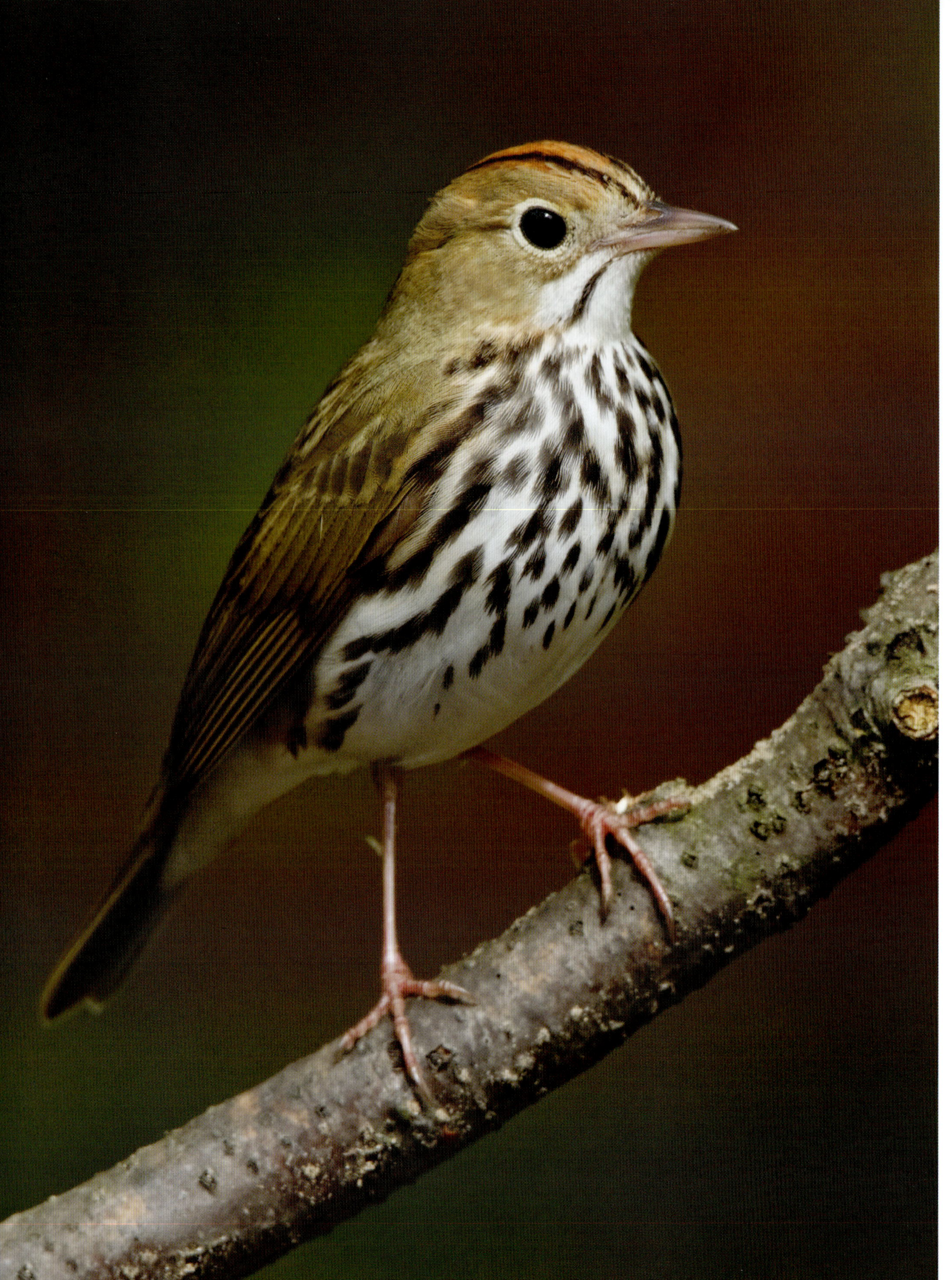

Normally a ground-dwelling species, an Ovenbird perches temporarily on a branch to show off its beautiful striped breast and orange crown.

The Lincoln's Sparrow is another bird that inhabits swampy regions. They are more often heard than seen.

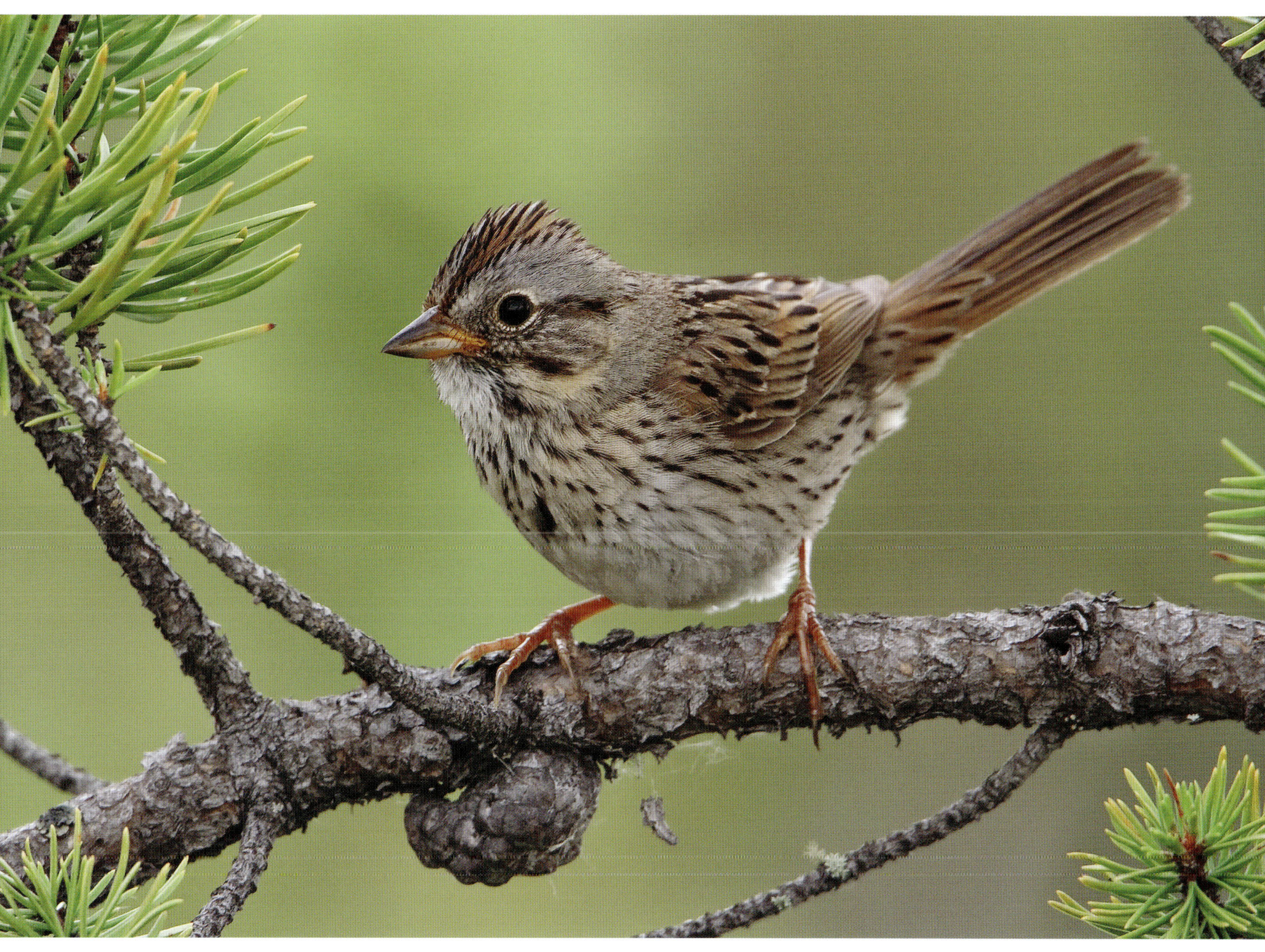

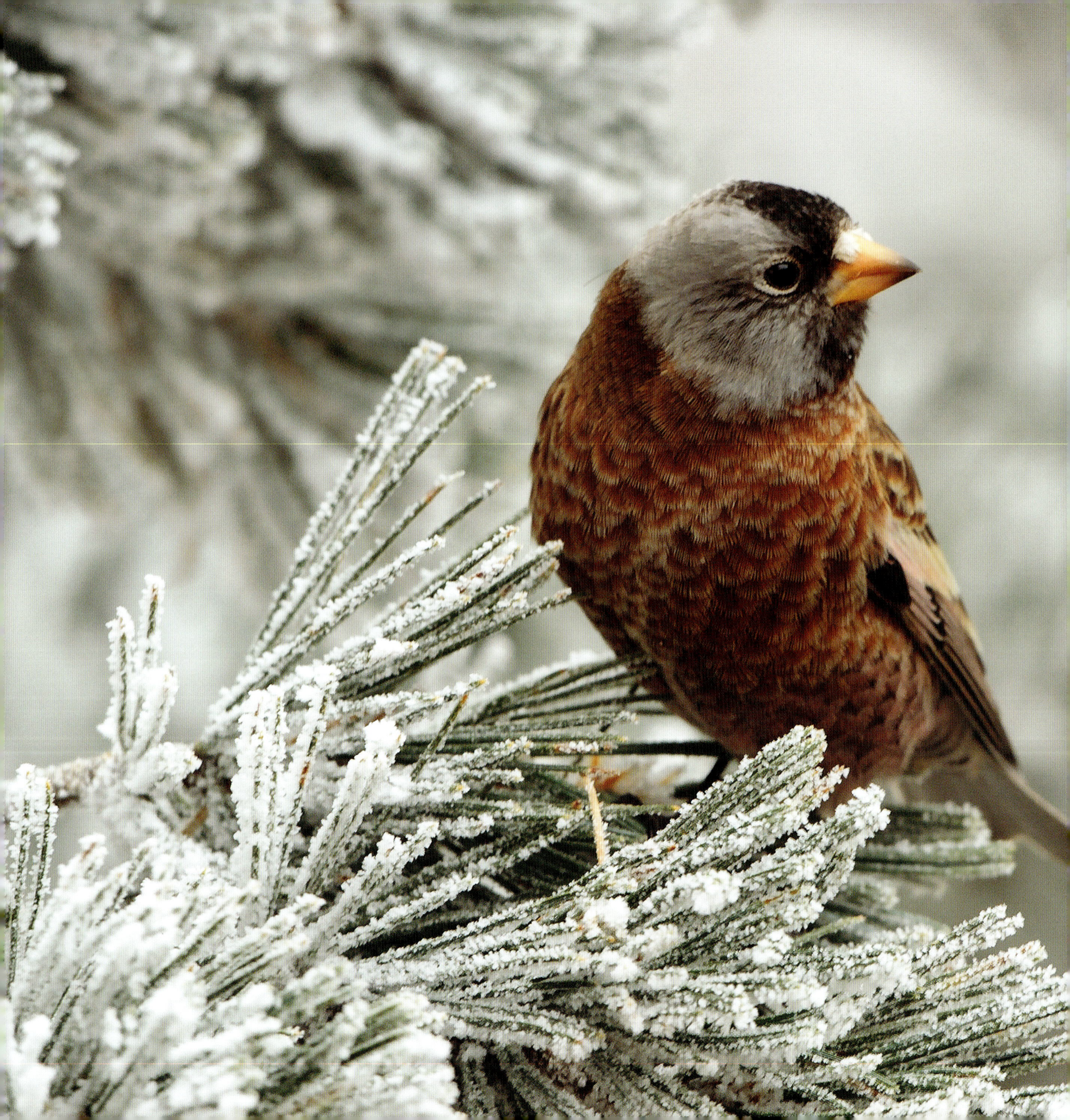

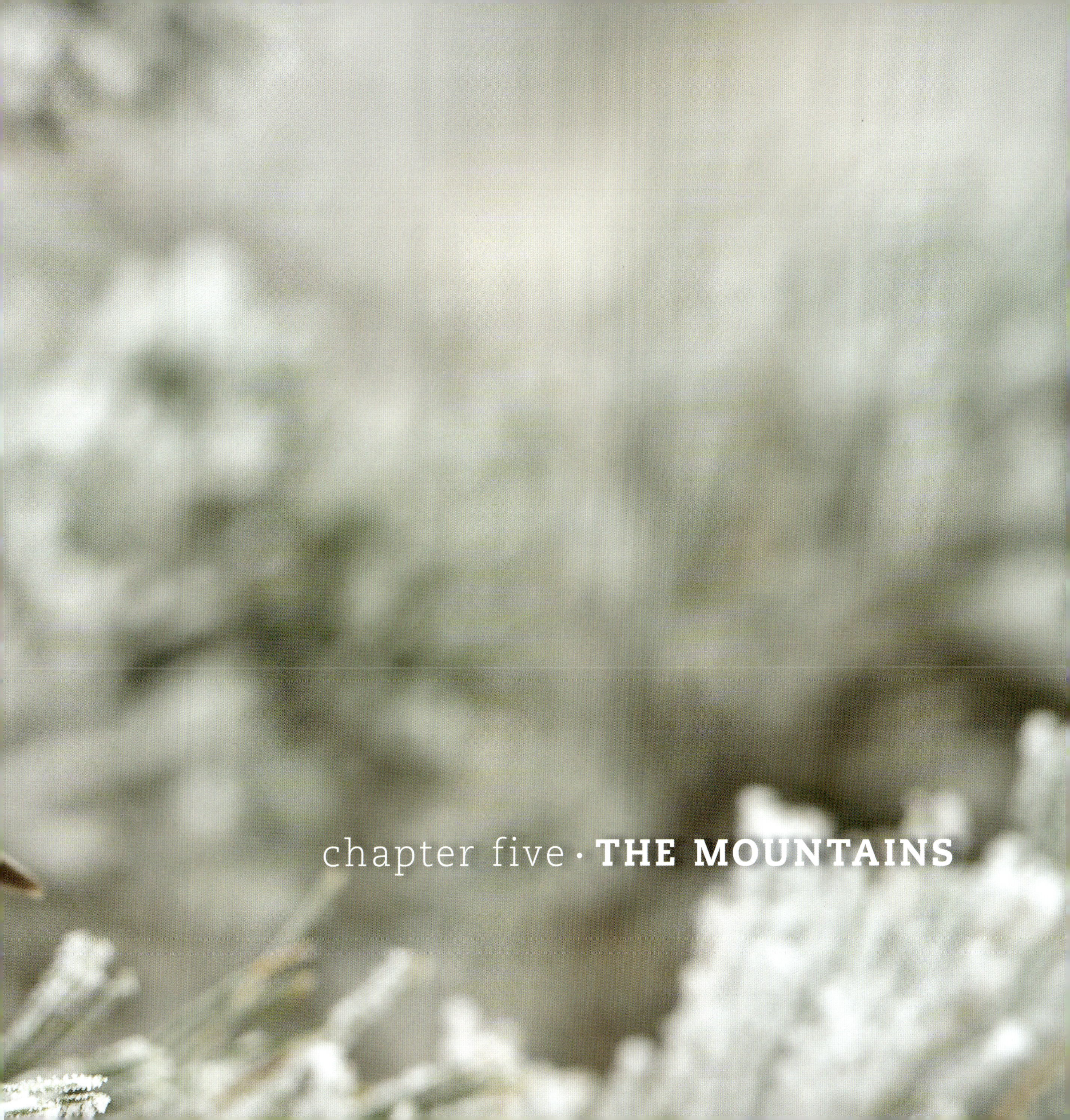

chapter five · **THE MOUNTAINS**

Few places on this planet are as rich as British Columbia when it comes to spectacular mountain ranges. In fact, aside from the interior plains of the northeast portion of BC, the various ranges that make up the Western Cordillera of North America dominate the rest of the province. From the Golden Hinde on Vancouver Island to Mount Waddington, the highest mountain entirely within BC, and the expansive chain of the Rocky Mountains, these epic spikes of jagged rock emerge from the earth to give this province its shape and its character. The immensity of these geologic landforms affects all life around them: climate, types of forests and, of course, the types of bird that exist within the region. The incredible forces and lengthy geological timelines that we must contemplate each time we look upon the mountains remind us of the patient persistence of Mother Nature.

While mountains are timeless symbols of eternity, their climate is anything but. Weather varies wildly and can change almost momentarily from sunny and beautiful to cold and miserable. Any animal that lives in the mountains must be incredibly adaptable, and the birds that call these peaks home are no exception.

Throughout the world, mountain ranges act as barriers to animal migration. Many animals, including birds, are simply unwilling to move over such hostile and unsheltered terrain. In South America, the Andes range has even been one of the causes of speciation, meaning animal species are separated for such extended periods of time that they evolve into entirely new species. And yet, despite the extreme conditions, some birds have been able to adapt and thrive in mountain areas.

Relatively few birds are able to live and breed exclusively in the mountains; the birds that do have developed unique traits in order to thrive. Birds like the White-tailed Ptarmigan have heavily feathered feet to insulate them from the bitter cold. Their plumage changes with the seasons from a brilliant white in the winter to a mottled brown in the summer. This ensures they are able to stay hidden from potential predators in a wide-open landscape.

Most birds do not live in the high mountain areas for the entire year. Instead, they migrate into the alpine areas when there is a seasonal abundance of food. Some come in June to build nests, breed and raise their young. Other birds use mountains primarily during late summer and during fall migration. During this time, lower elevations have often passed their peak production period and there is a plentiful supply of food in the higher elevations. American Robins are attracted to the alpine areas for the rich supply of berries. Rufous Hummingbirds travel upslope for the bountiful nectar in the flowering alpine meadows. Insect eaters like Townsend's Solitaires and Yellow-rumped Warblers are also attracted to the high country, where there is often a surge in insect life in late summer. Conveniently, the mountain chains of North America run primarily north to south. Therefore, many birds can use these food-rich habitats as effective migration corridors when returning to their winter homes farther south.

FROM THE FOOTHILLS TO THE MOUNTAINS

Like most Canadians, I will never forget the first time I saw the Rocky Mountains. I was driving from Ontario to BC and had just spent a week or so exploring the Prairies. After a few days of flat land, the Rocky Mountains appeared like a mirage on the horizon. The grasslands gave way to rolling hills, and before I knew it I was surrounded by a landscape unlike any that I had ever encountered.

As I drove, I stopped often to take in the breathtaking views. Escaping the car also introduced me to some of the new bird species that were starting to appear. At one stop, a flash of blue alerted me to the presence of a Mountain Bluebird as it emerged from the grass to land on a fence post. Another stop allowed me to get my first glimpses of a tiny Mountain Chickadee. It would have been next to impossible to miss the Clark's Nutcracker that hopped down onto the picnic table as I stopped for lunch. And this was just the beginning. Before long, I had spotted a beautiful Western Tanager, several species of woodpeckers and a flock of Red Crossbills, and heard a Ruffed Grouse drumming away off in the distance.

MOUNTAIN LAKES

Thinking of mountain ecosystems, our minds tend to immediately envision barren places where rock and ice dominate the landscape and stunted alpine plants comprise much of the ecosystem. Shifting our perception of the mountain realm to include the highland forests allows us to include a whole host of new species. For example, the mountain forests are dotted with pristine lakes, and these lakes are often home to one of the most identifiable symbols of the Canadian wilderness—the Common Loon. Some birds, like the loon, are true Canadian symbols, and their presence adds greatly to the special feeling that comes from spending time in nature. Watching these birds perform their duets and mating dances is magical. Even routine tasks like diving for fish are a joy to watch as these elegant birds gracefully cut through the water. I imagine I am not the only Canadian for whom the loon's mournful call evokes many sentimental memories. I am brought back to canoe rides at dusk and camping trips with my father and brother.

Many of these same lakes are also home to another species of waterfowl, the Barrow's Goldeneye. In fact, the vast majority of all Barrow's Goldeneyes breed in BC. Each year, these birds return from the coast to their breeding territories in the mountains and central aspen parklands. The stakes are high among these beautiful black-and-white ducks, and testosterone levels among the male birds are often overflowing. Their mating display is a hilarious sight to behold; to impress the female birds, these strange little ducks kick their feet out of the water, throwing a splash high into the air. At the same time, they throw their head back and shout out a call that sounds like it belongs to a rubber ducky.

In addition to the Barrow's Goldeneye, other ducks, like the Ruddy and Harlequin, find their way into the mountains to breed. Other birds that spend their summer in the mountain lakes in forests include Spotted Sandpipers, Ospreys and Hooded Mergansers.

ALPINE MEADOWS AND FORESTS

Bird life in the alpine realms and above the treeline is never as abundant as it is in some of the other regions of British Columbia. The unforgiving forces of cold and snow make this an inhospitable place for much of the year. Yet there are always new discoveries to be made for naturalists who keeps their eyes and ears open. I discovered this the summer I was hired to be the lead photographer for a project that was documenting landscape change in the Canadian Rockies. My job was simple—to hike up mountains and try to recreate historical survey images that had been taken at the turn of the century.

But even though the landscape may have been unforgiving, what struck me the most was how unbelievably tame some of the birds were up in the mountains. One day, while hiking up to a peak, I almost stepped on a White-tailed Ptarmigan without even seeing it. I could not believe how well camouflaged this bird was or just how oblivious it seemed to be to my presence. Studying this bird strutting its stuff, I could really appreciate its adaptations to life in the mountains. Aside from its natural camouflage, the other obvious advantage that this bird has when it comes to living in the snowy realm is its densely feathered feet. This trait and all-white winter plumage are defining characteristics of the White-tailed, Willow and Rock Ptarmigans—three species of Ptarmigan that call BC home.

Later that same summer, I had another incredibly close encounter with a group of birds. It was on a hot day in July, and I was just reaching the peak of a mountain when I immediately noticed there were flying ants everywhere. I am not certain if they were breeding or had just hatched, but I do know that they were swarming all over the place and made taking pictures very frustrating. In nature though, such an abundance of food rarely goes unnoticed. Sure enough, a flock of Gray-crowned Rosy Finches had discovered this bounty and were happily gobbling up the easy insect meals. It was quite a treat to see so many of these beautiful finches at such close range. These finches are able to breed and thrive in the high mountain environments precisely because they have learned to take advantage of such seasonal abundances in prey. For example, they can often be seen walking out on the snowfields to feed on the insects that have been caught in updrafts and then frozen. They are also quite accomplished at navigating the often-windy mountain air. Despite the gusts of wind, these finches effortlessly navigate the skies and rocky terrain—in large part due to their long, pointed wings.

Confronted with powers and landscapes of this magnitude, one could easily become so absorbed in the beauty of the mountains that it would be possible to miss some of the birds. This, however, would be a shame, because the birds that make their homes in these special places are unique and beautiful additions to the avifauna of BC.

As its name suggests, the Common Loon can be found throughout a variety of habitats. Mountain lakes ringed with forest provide ideal nesting conditions.

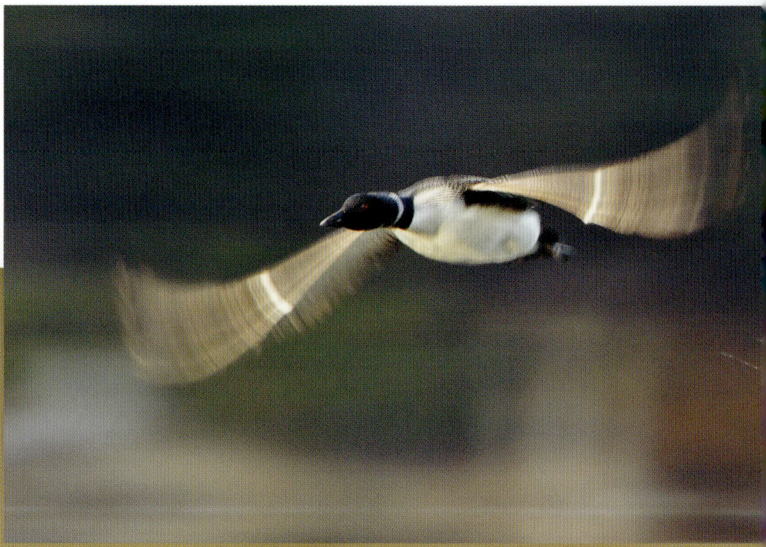

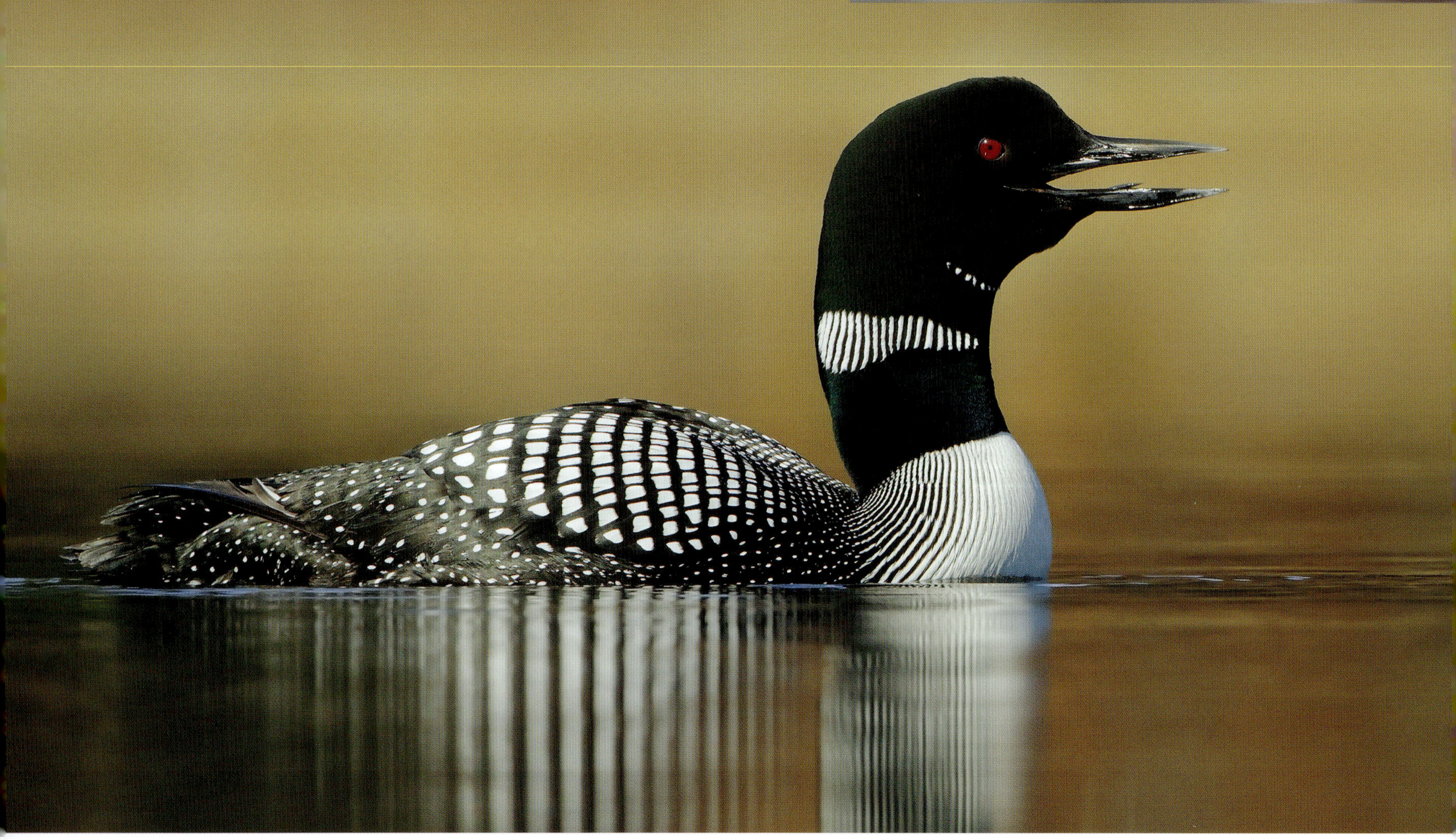

A Barrow's Goldeneye performs his courtship display. British Columbia is home to more than half the world's Barrow's Goldeneyes.

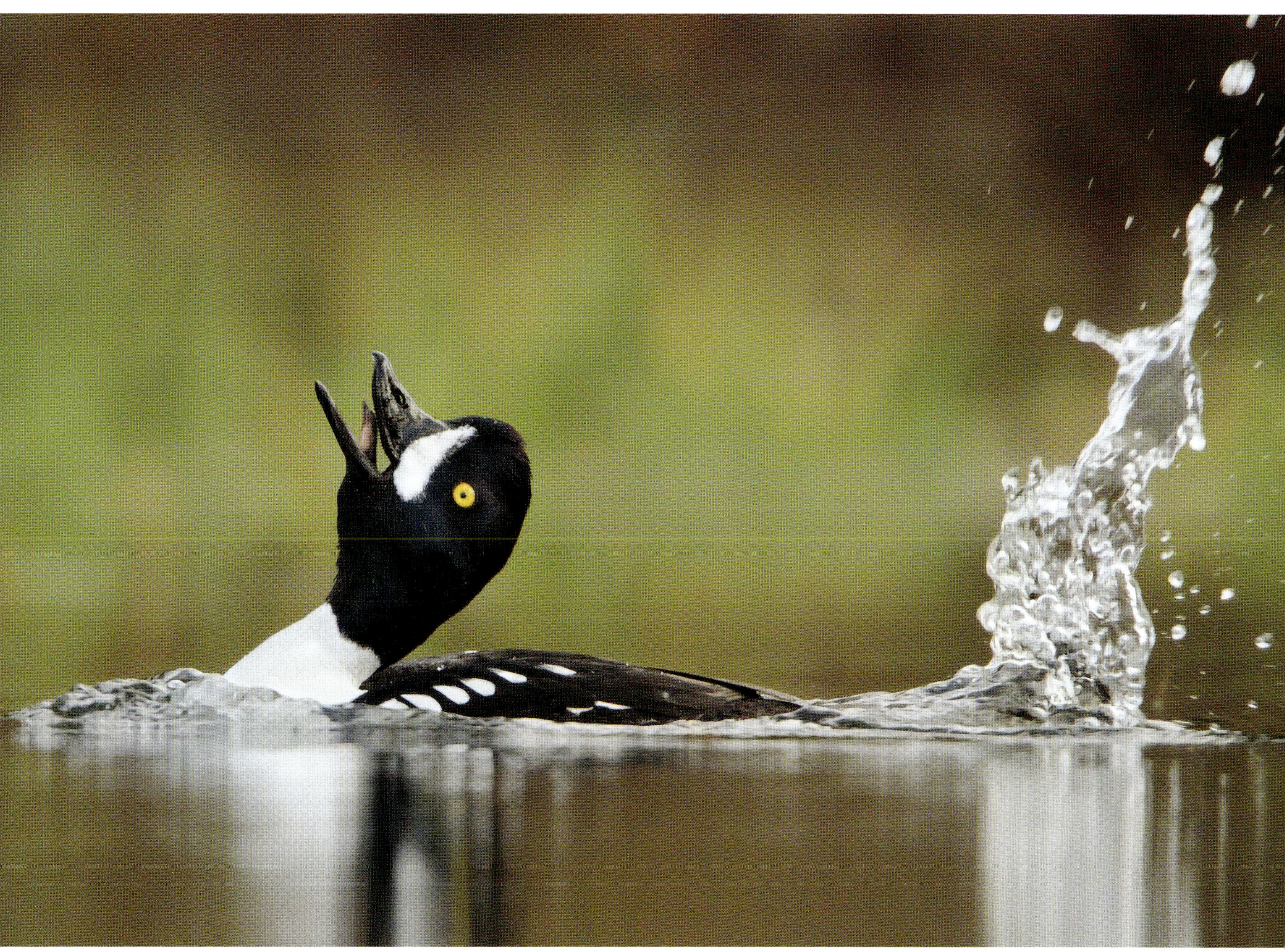

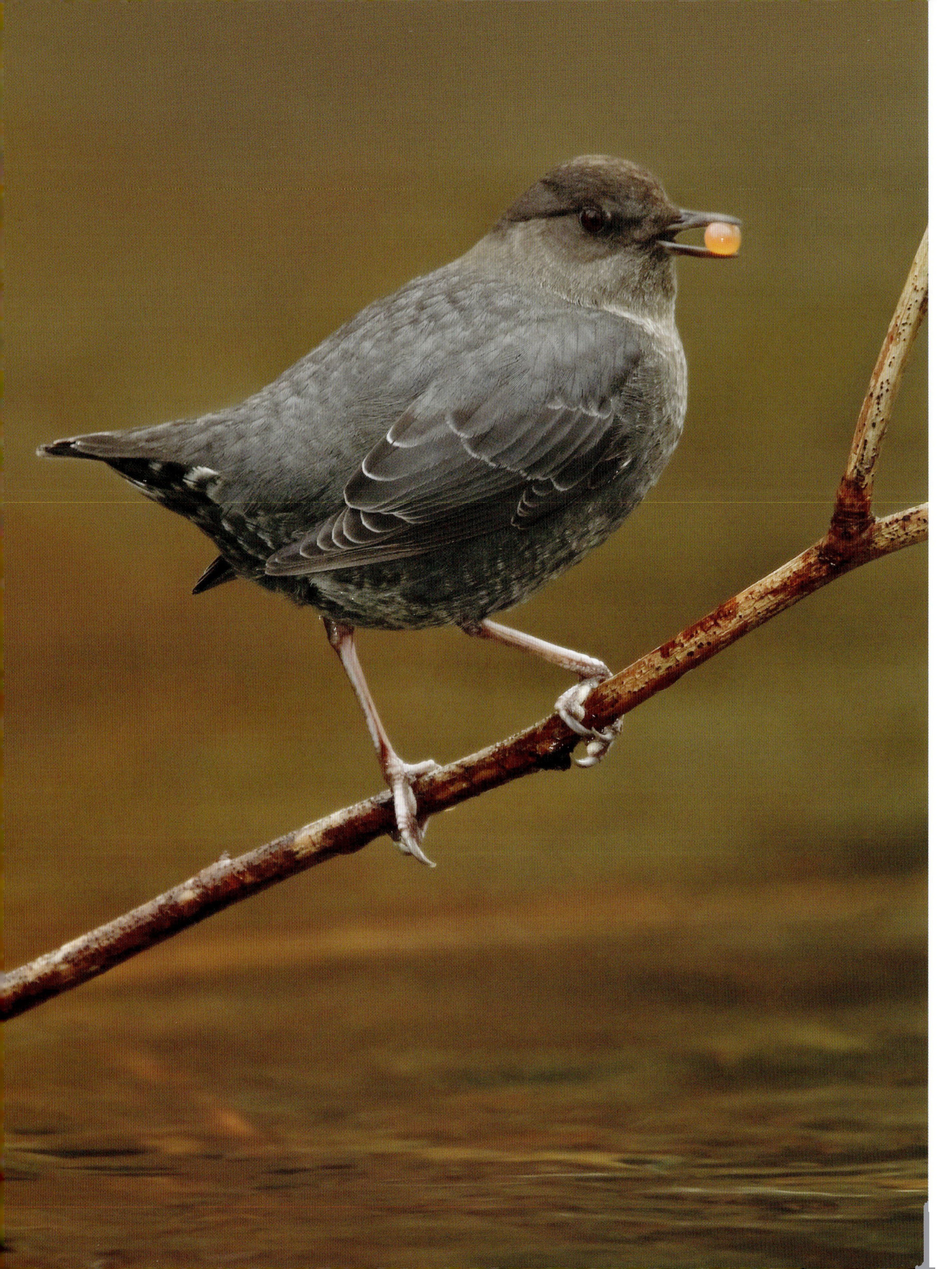

American Dippers love to live near fast-flowing mountain streams. These aquatic birds are adept at venturing underwater to find their next meal.

The Clark's Nutcracker lives in mountains near the treeline in stands of pine trees. Using specialized pouches in their mouth, these birds are able to store large numbers of pine seeds, which they cache throughout the summer months. Many of these seeds are never retrieved and will grow into new trees.

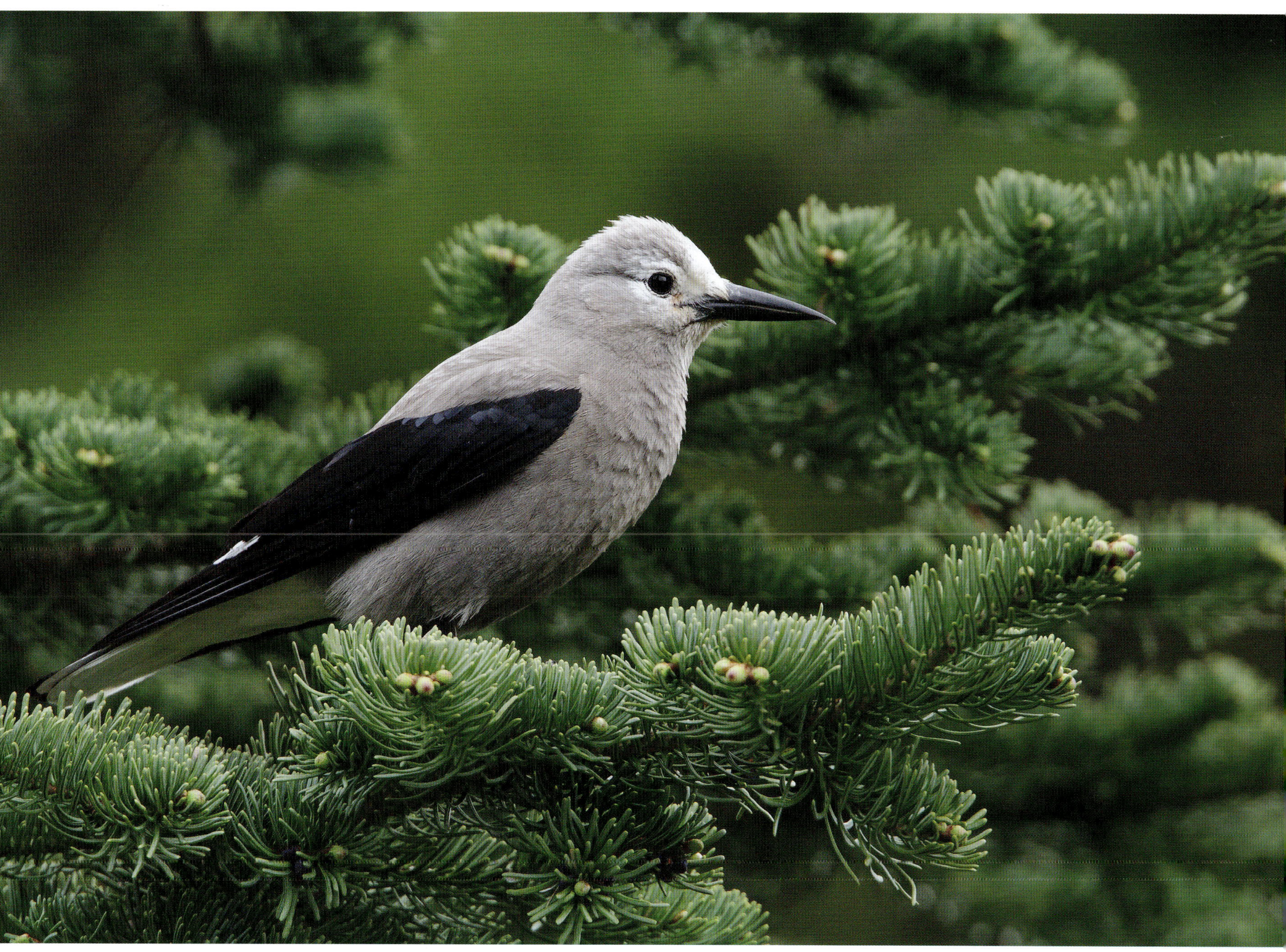

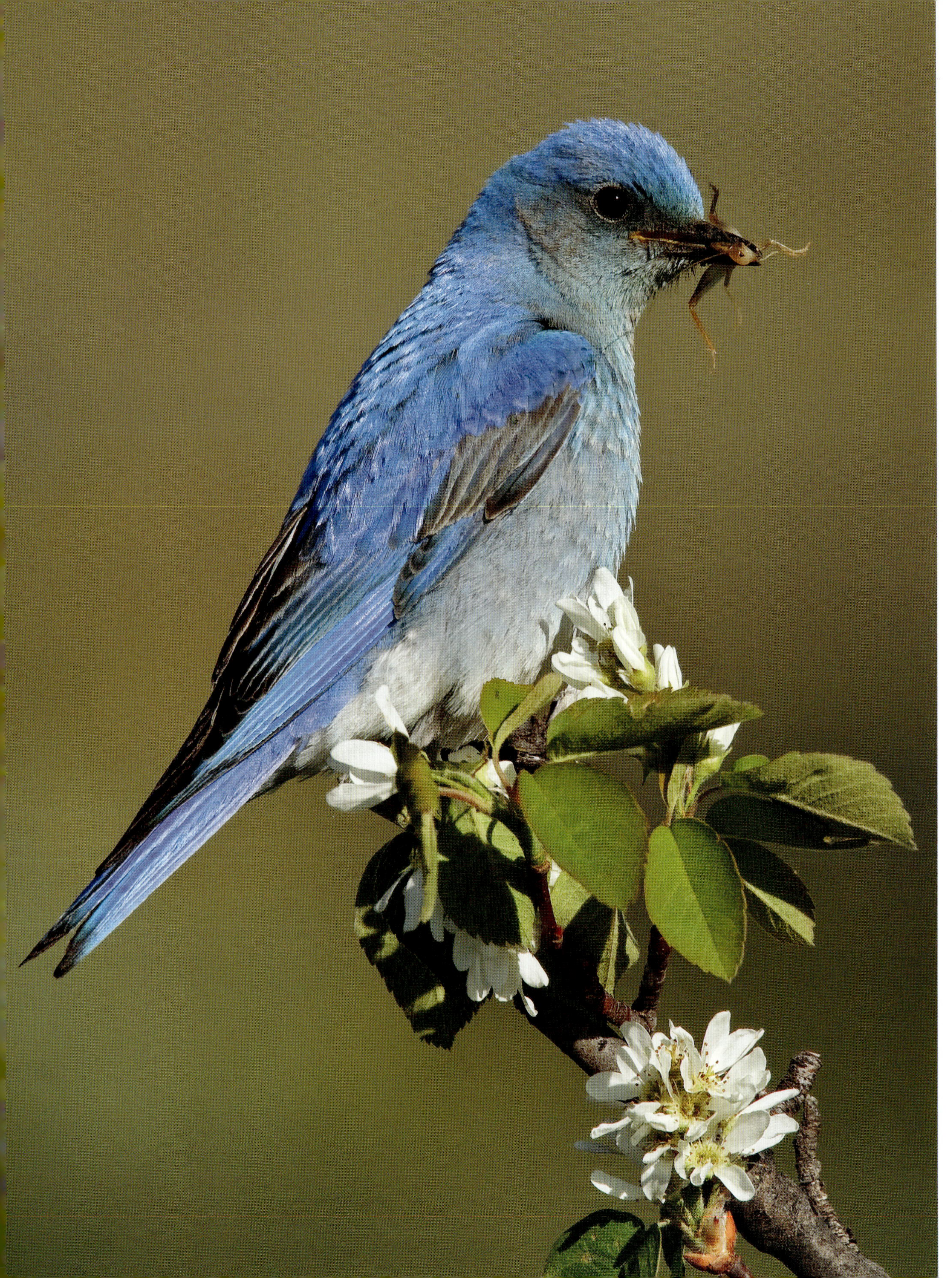

The brilliant colour of the male Mountain Bluebird makes it one of the most distinct birds in the province.

A Mountain Chickadee perches on a frozen limb on a frosty morning.

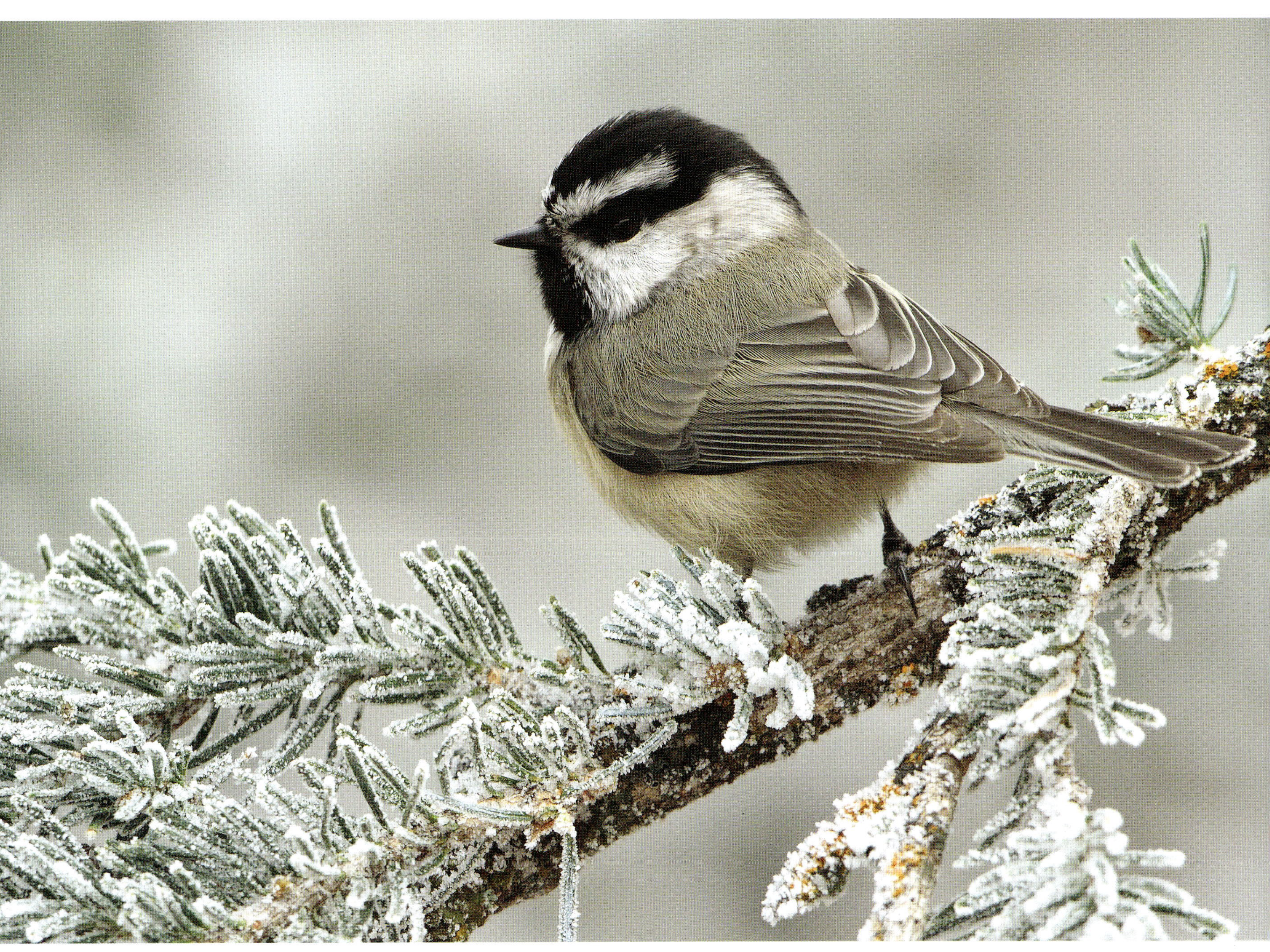

Like all members of its genus, the Rock Ptarmigan has heavily feathered feet to keep it warm during the winter.

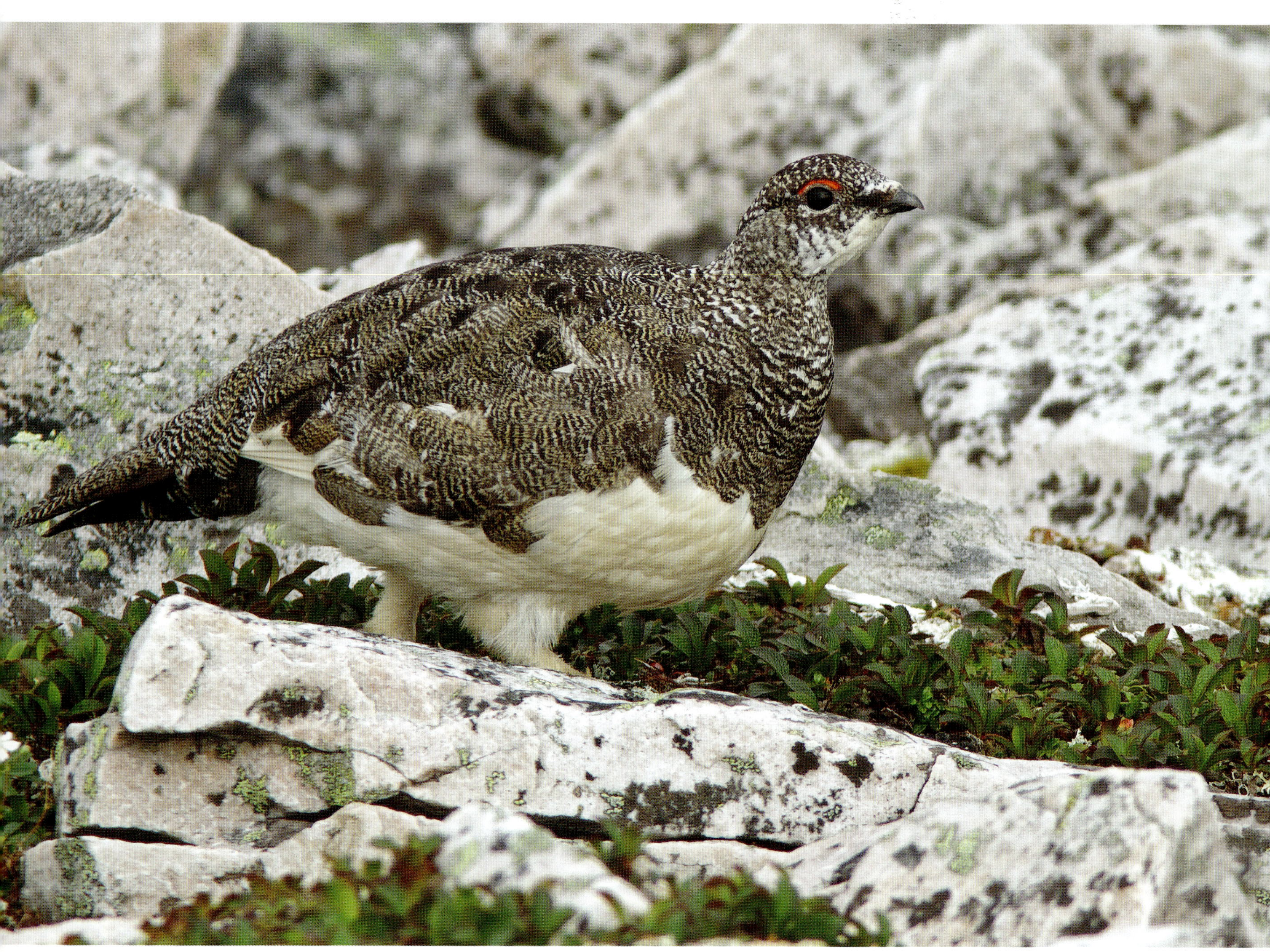

This White-tailed Ptarmigan knows where to find a great view. JESS FINDLAY

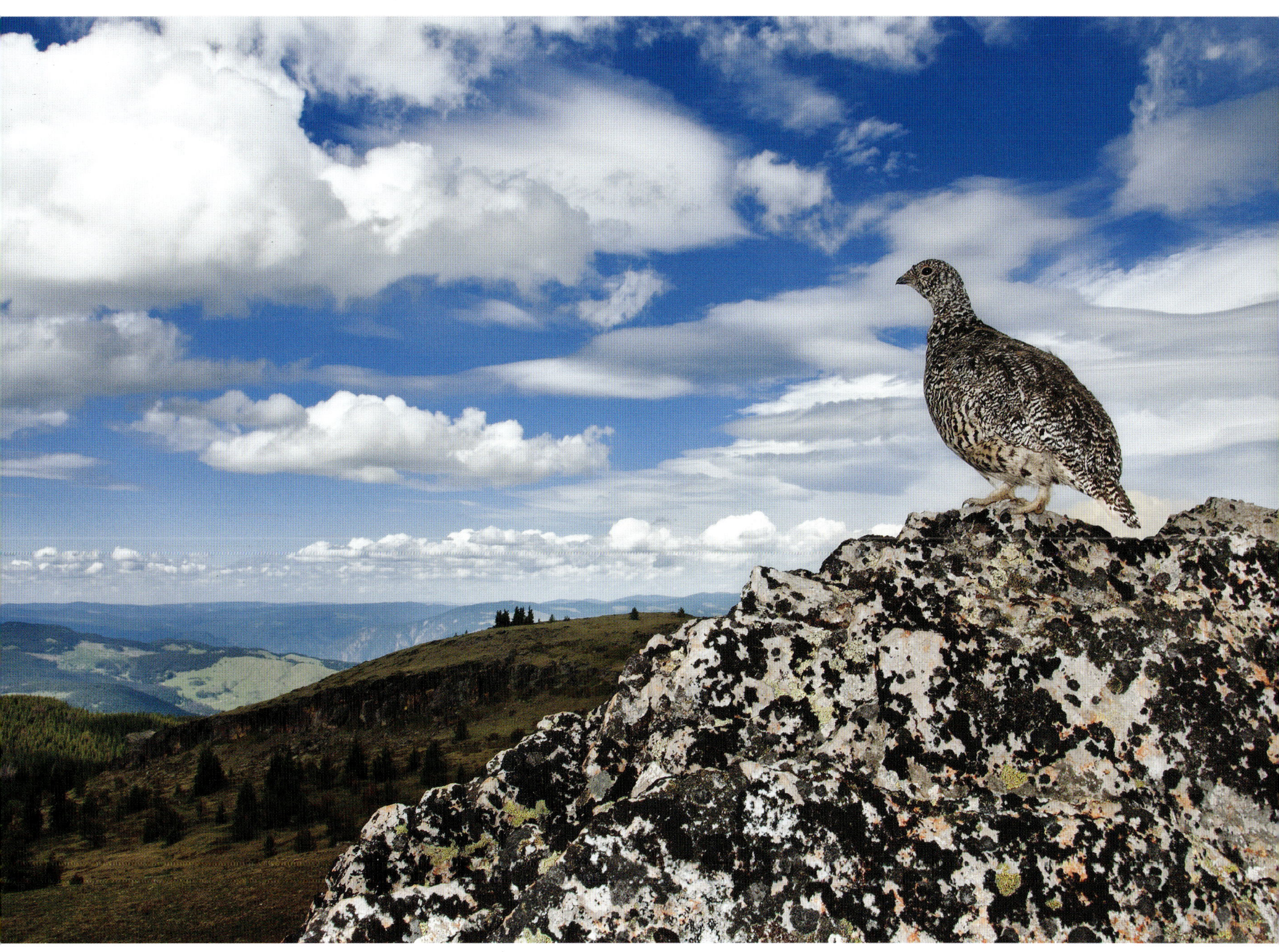

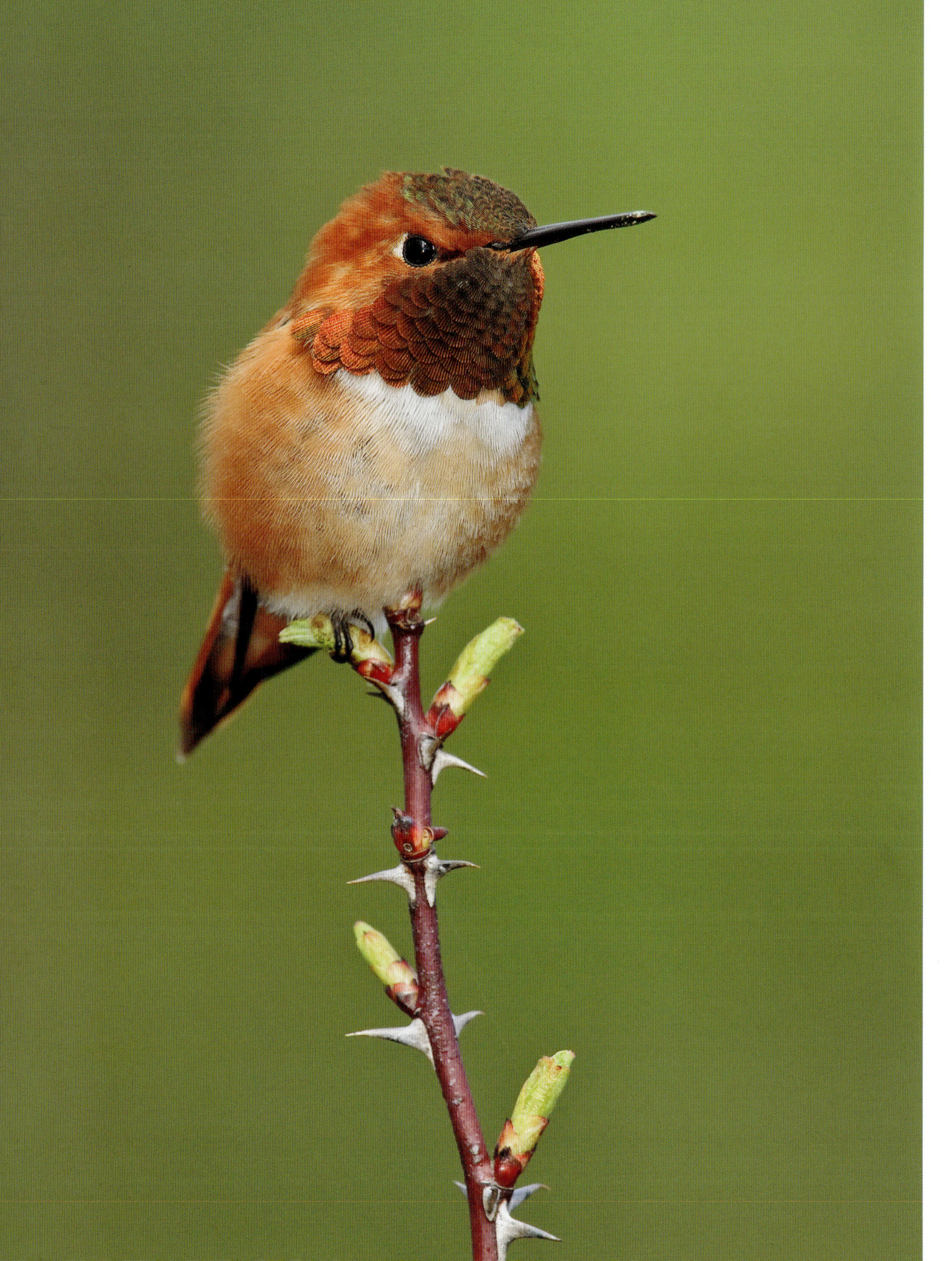

Rufous Hummingbirds often head to the mountains to take advantage of the late spring and the plentiful supply of flowers and nectar.

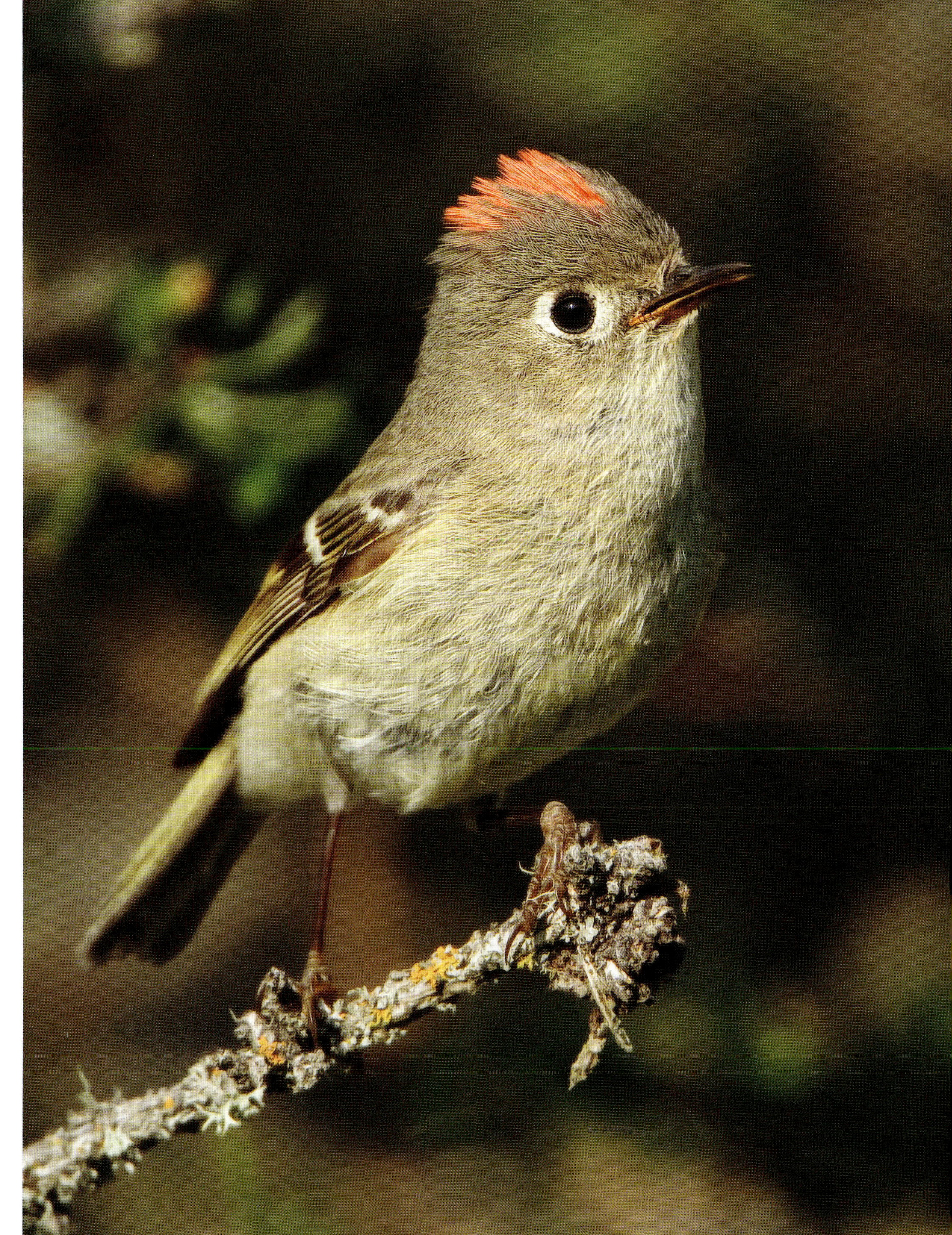

A Ruby-crowned Kinglet sings his exuberant song from an exposed perch.

Horned Larks nest in open areas and can often be found in alpine habitats throughout BC. This mother has several open mouths to feed, a duty she shares with their father.

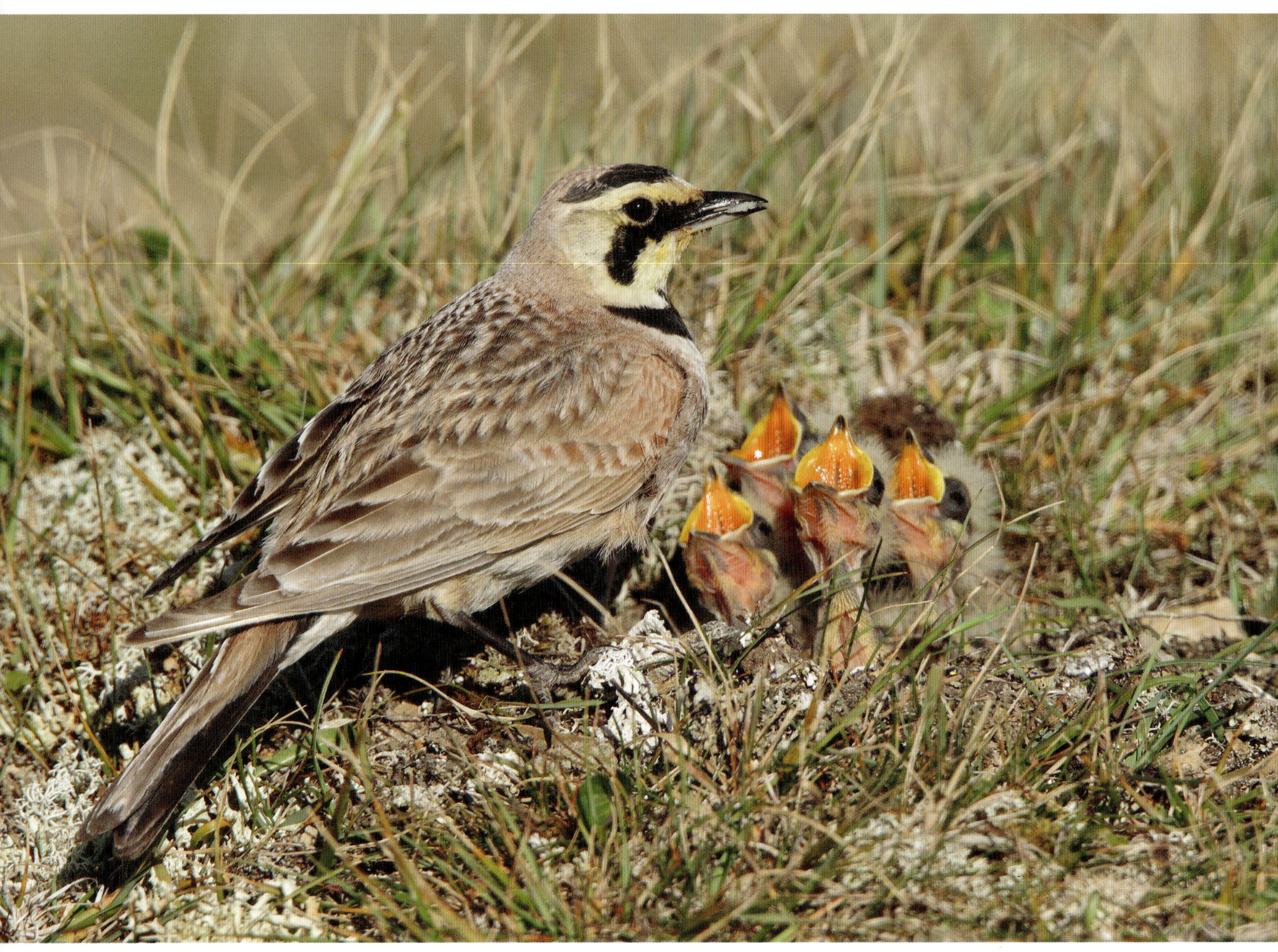

The blue bill and stiff tail give away the identity of this male Ruddy Duck.

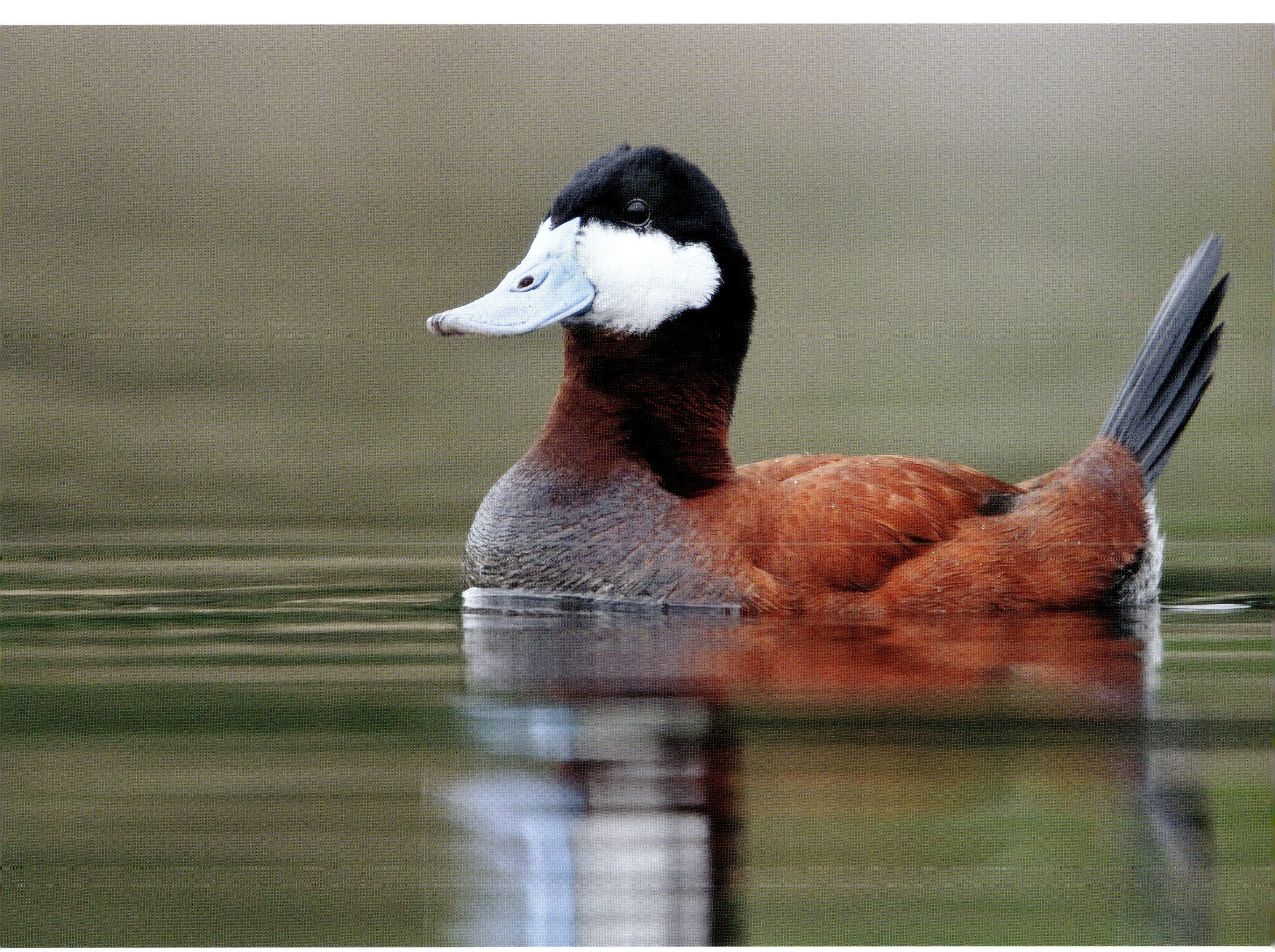

A common bird throughout Canada, the Gray Jay, or "Whisky Jack," is a confident and curious bird that will often approach hikers or campers for a close inspection.

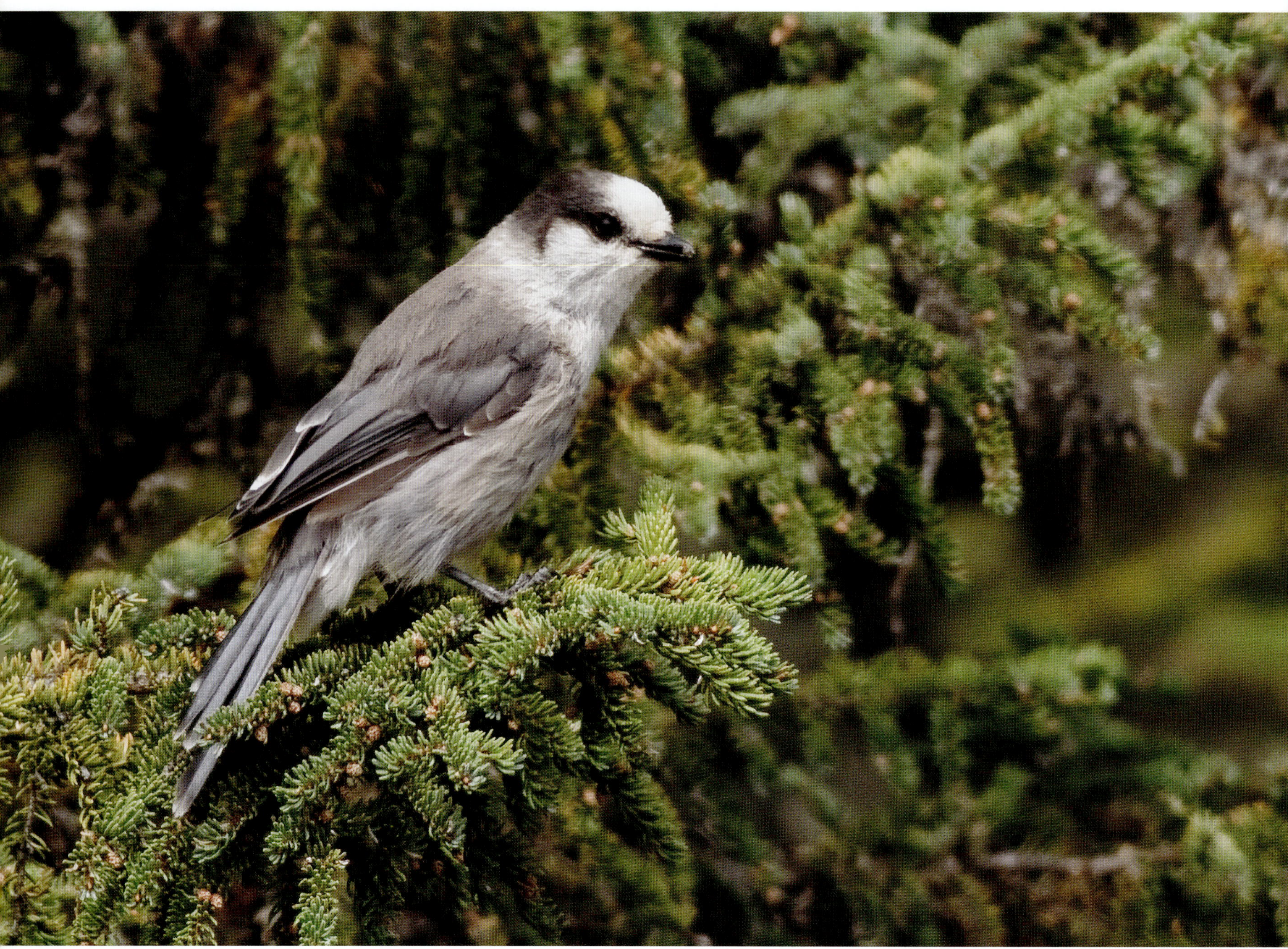

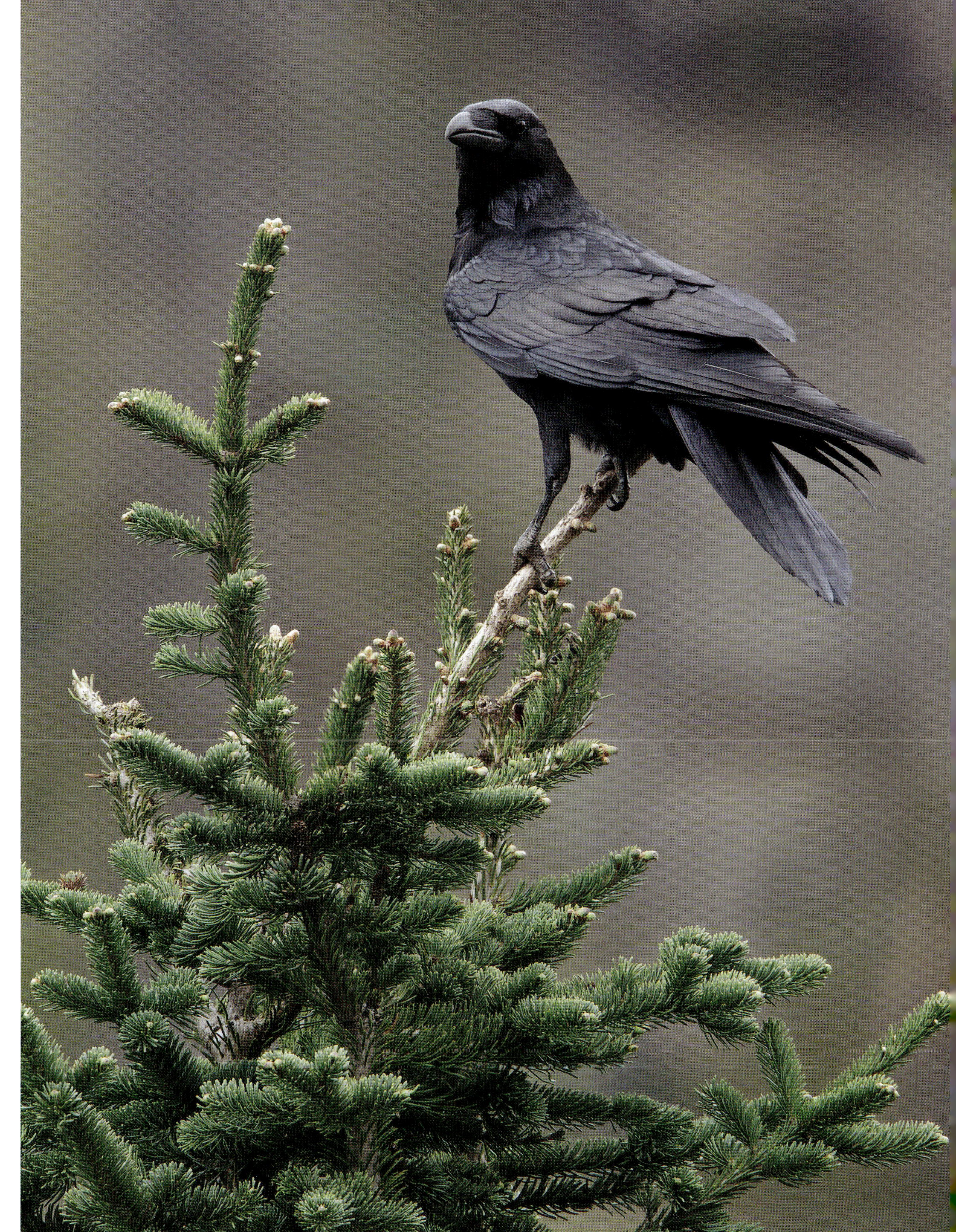

A Common Raven perches conspicuously on an open branch, surveying the surrounding landscape.

A Purple Finch perches to show off the stunning plumage for which it is named.

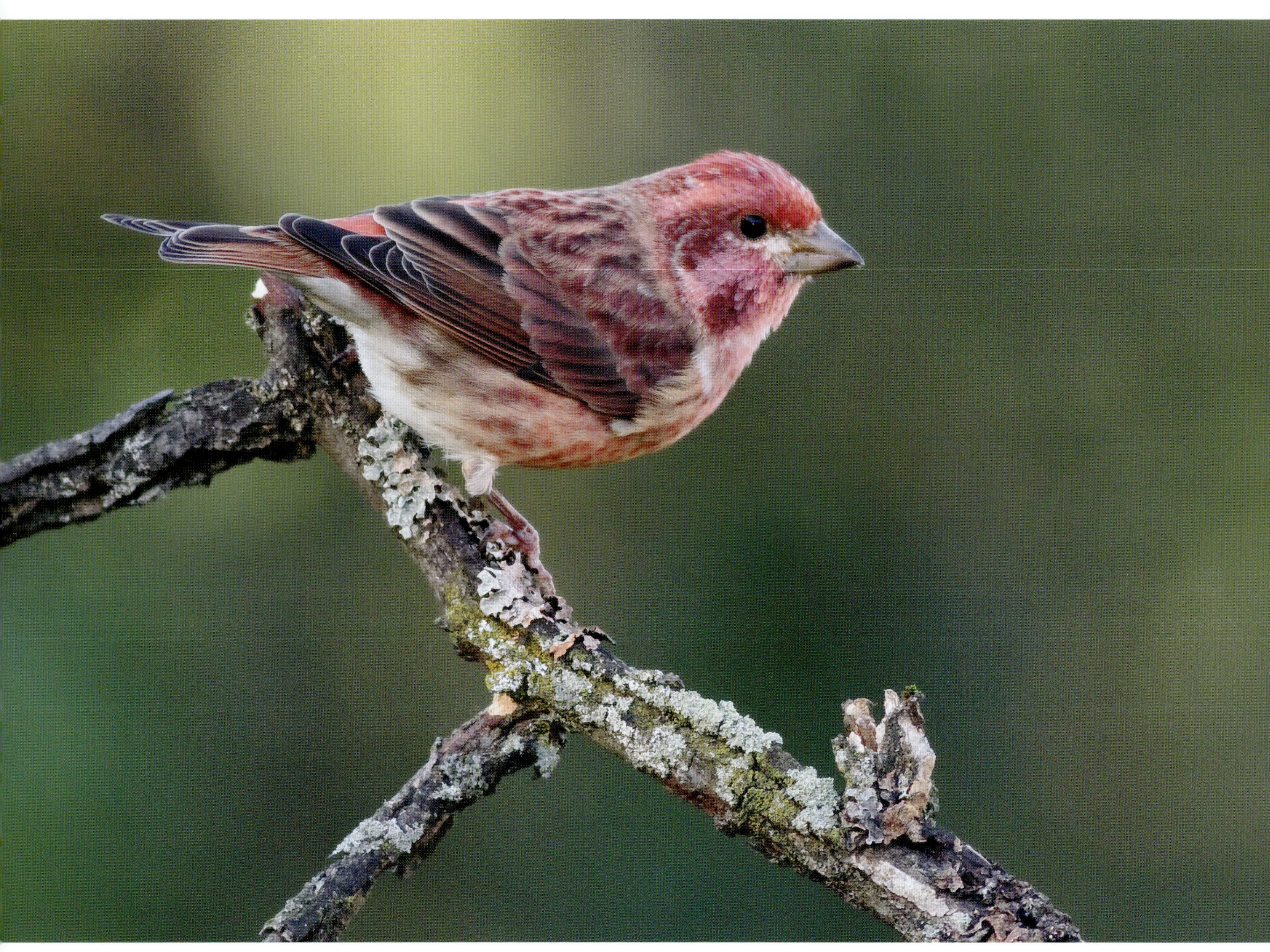

The Yellow-rumped Warbler is an adaptable species found in a variety of habitats across BC; the white throat of this male identifes him as the northern Myrtle subspecies.

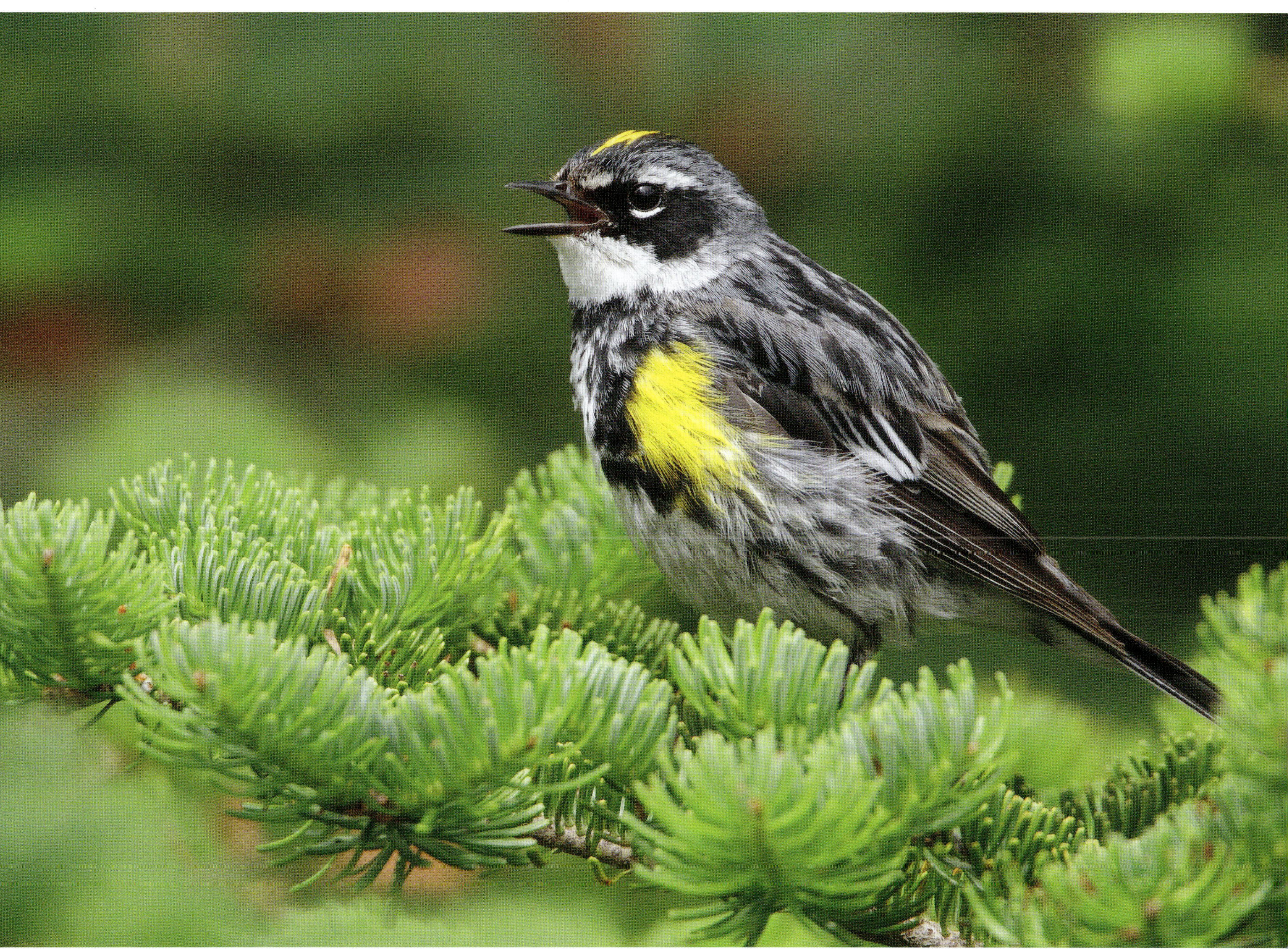

A male Ruffed Grouse puffs out his feathers and performs his drumming display.

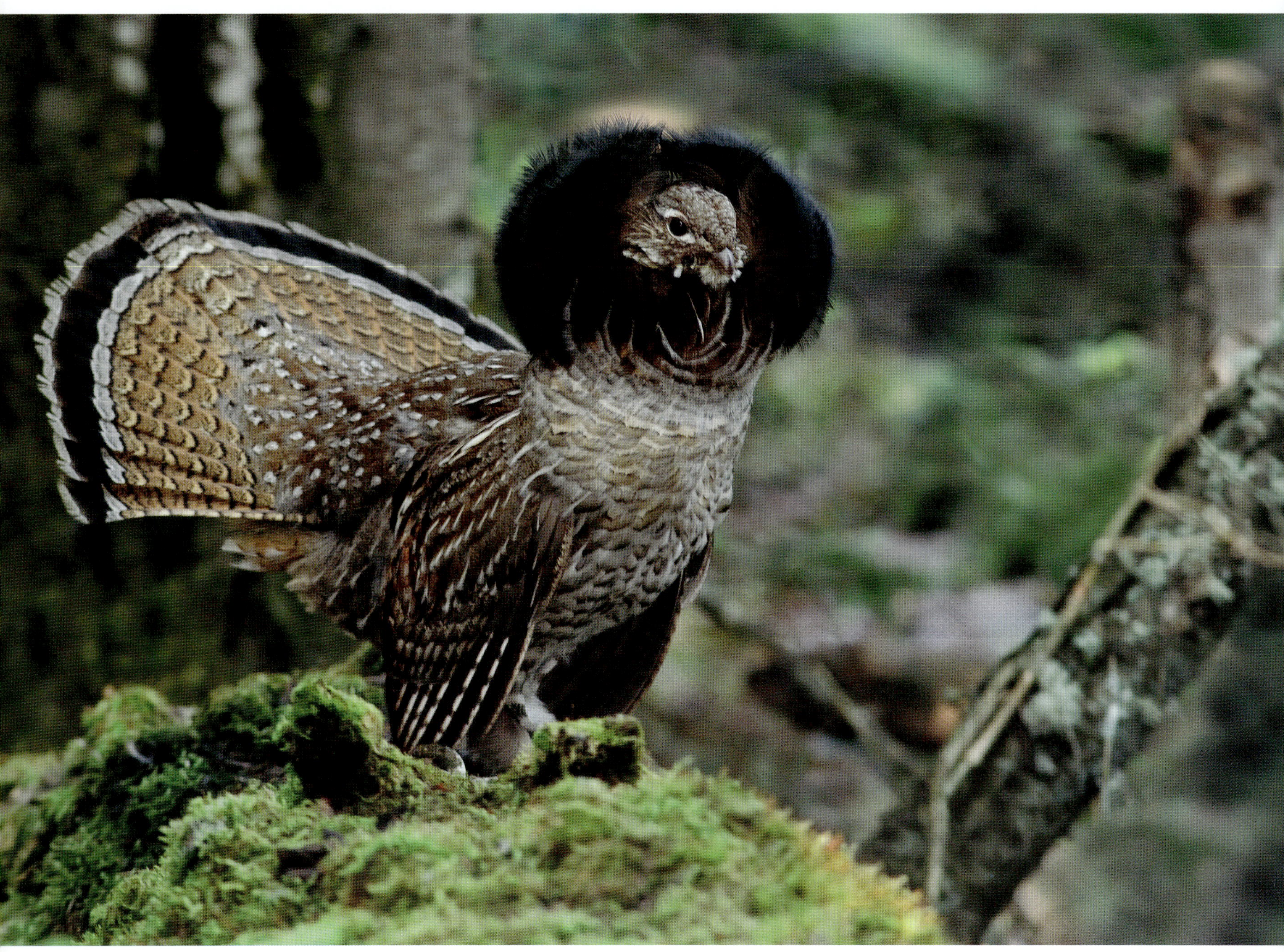

Eared Grebes form large and dense colonies on their nesting grounds during the spring and summer months.

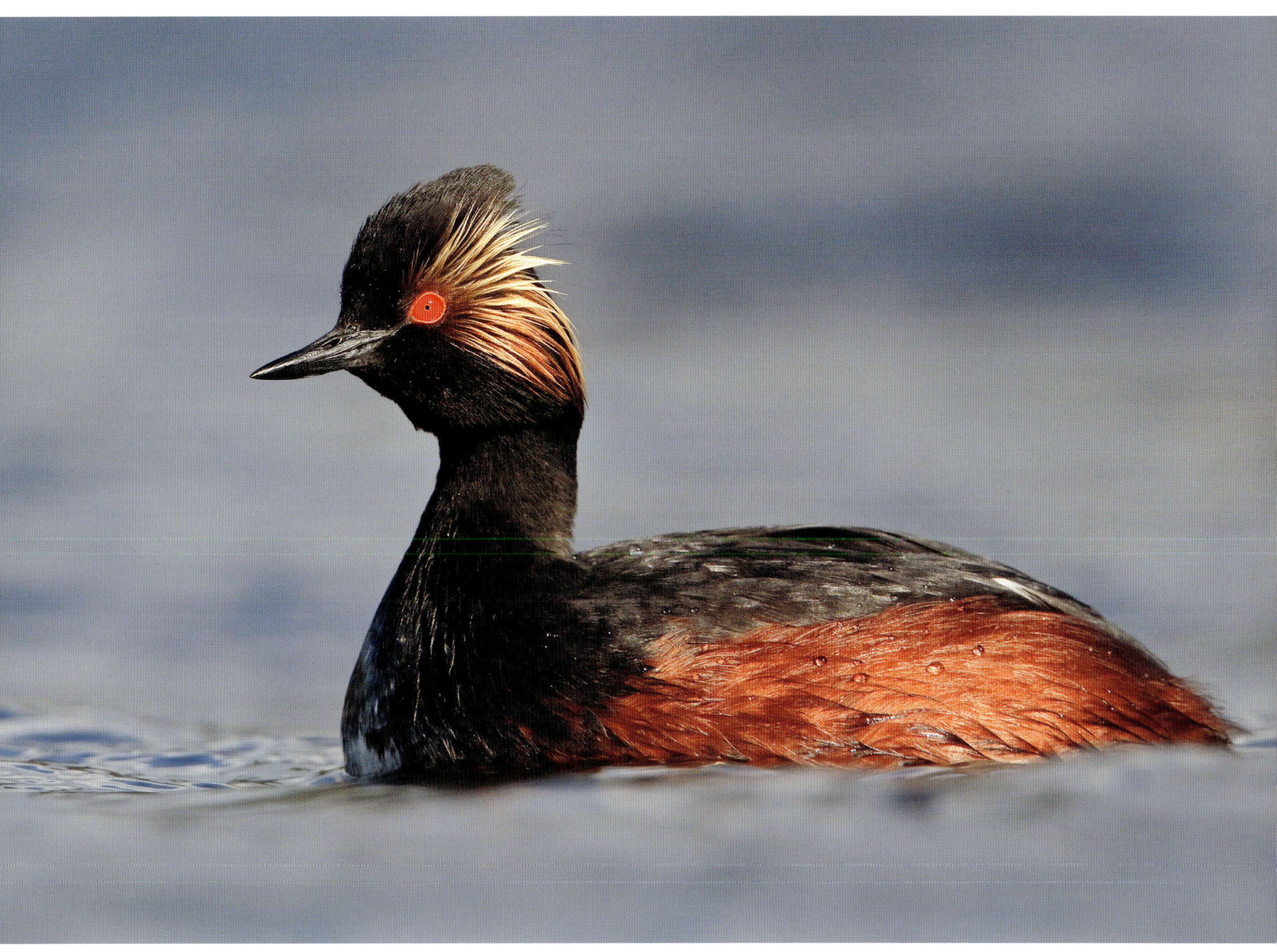

The Townsend's Solitaire is generally found in coniferous mountain forests.

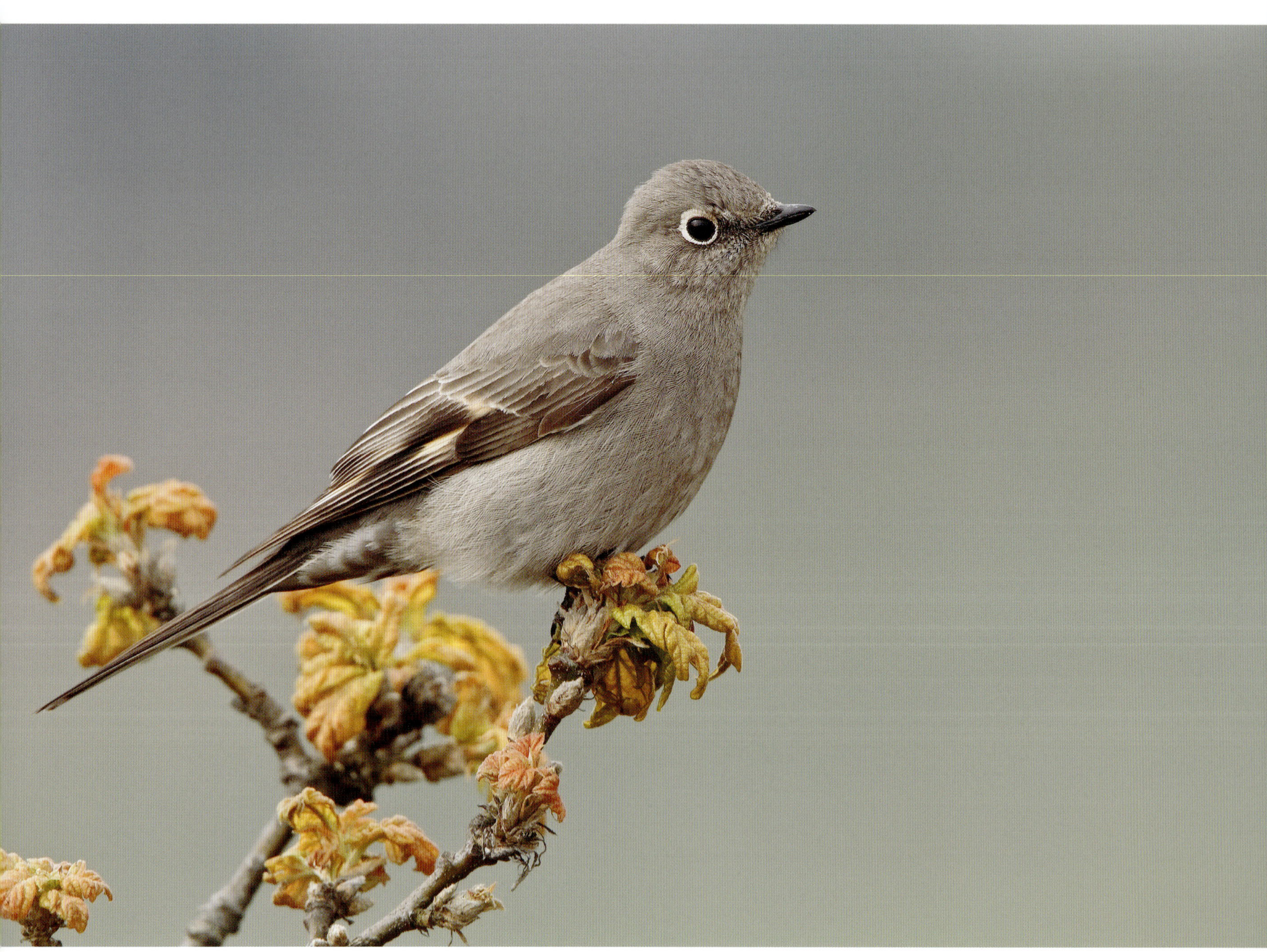

A female Sooty Grouse poses on an open branch, although these birds often stay close to the ground.

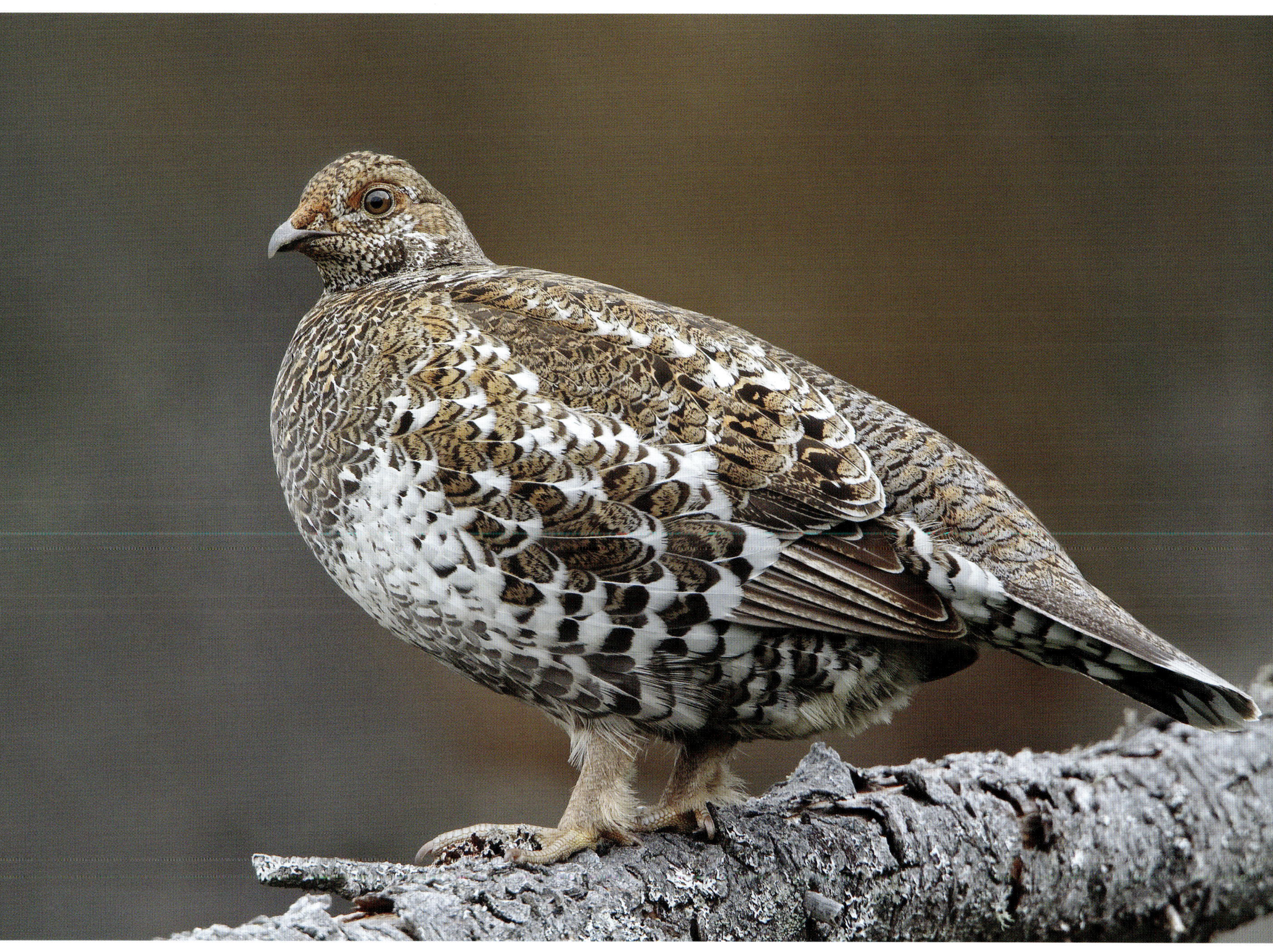

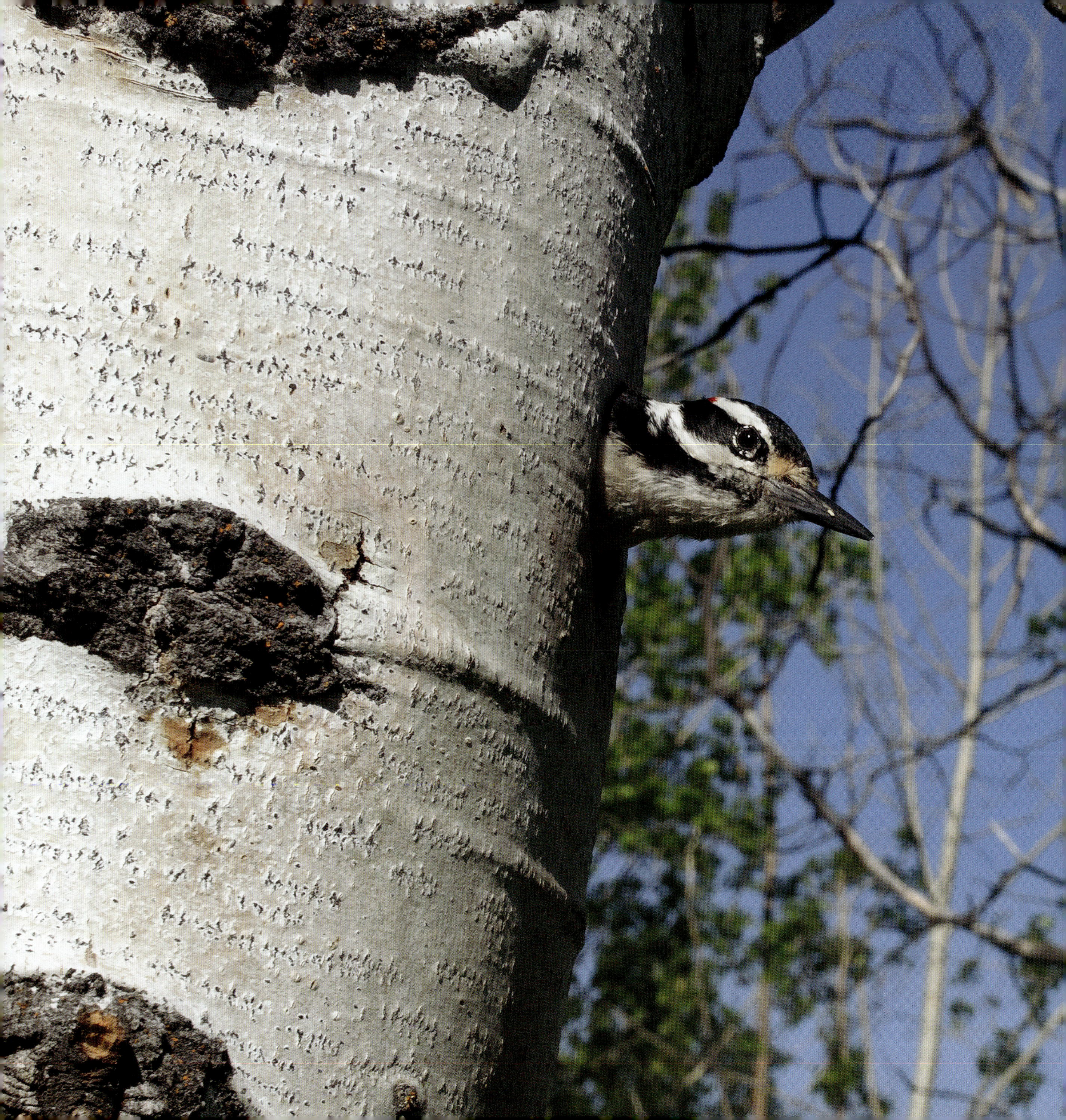

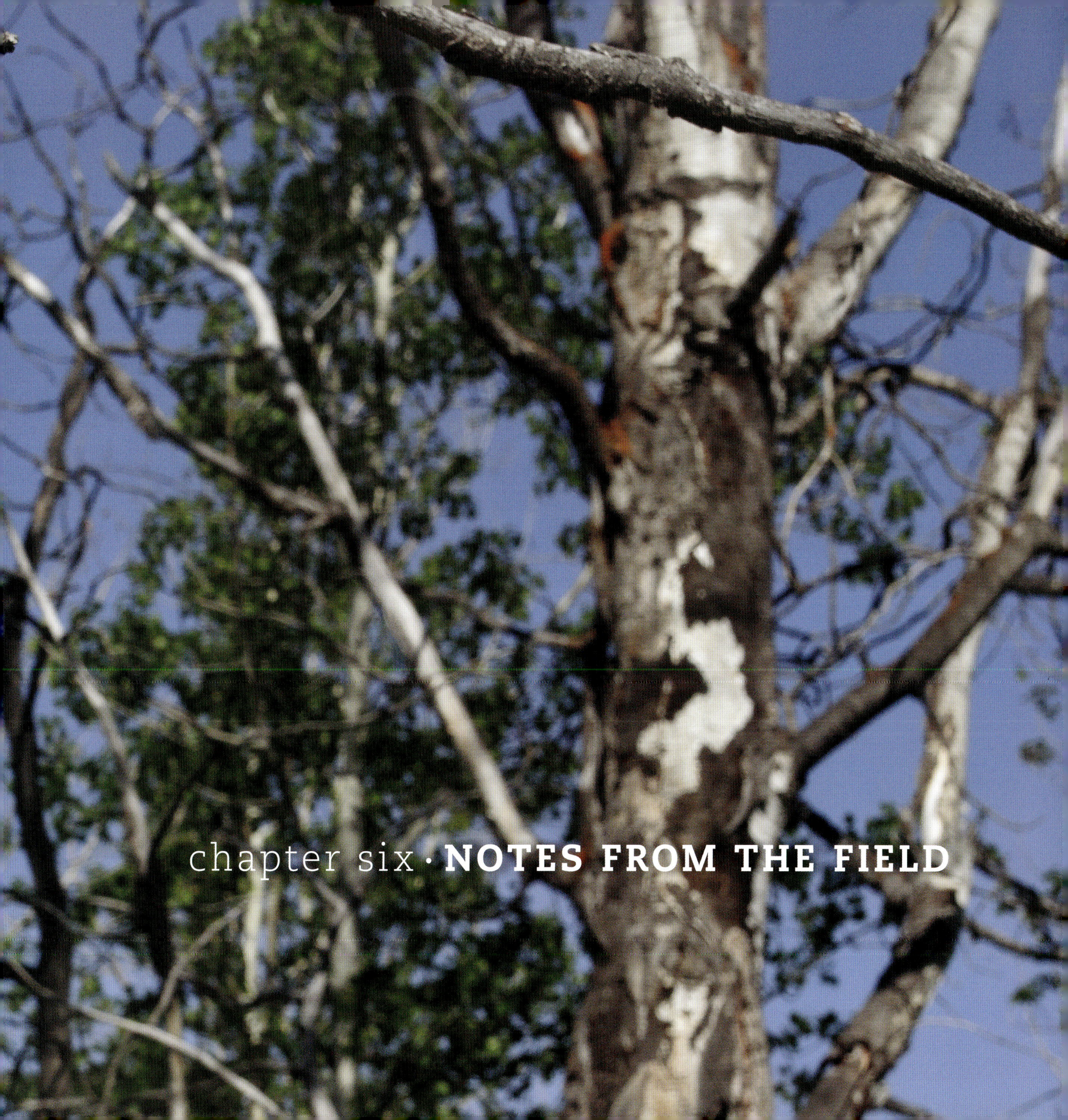

chapter six · NOTES FROM THE FIELD

I am extremely fortunate to have a career that allows me to spend so much of my time experiencing and enjoying the natural world. Being a professional wildlife photographer is a life that I dreamed about for a long time and now get to live. I love the excitement that comes with discovering the intimate details of birds' lives and the fact that no two days are ever the same. This chapter is intended to give a bit of a behind-the-scenes look at what it is like to be a bird photographer and what it takes to get "the shot." Being a successful wildlife photographer requires a lot of passion, knowledge, skill and determination all mixed in with a healthy dose of luck. You have to be obsessed with your subjects; for me, that has meant learning as much as possible about birds. I never imagined when I was younger that I would end up so fanatical about birds. I feel truly grateful to have found a passion in life that I thoroughly enjoy. Photography has turned from a hobby to a career that I love wholeheartedly, and for that I am very fortunate indeed.

THE TOOLS OF THE TRADE

It probably comes as no surprise that photographing birds requires heavy and expensive camera equipment. It is not uncommon for me to have more than 50 kilograms of equipment when travelling and chasing after birds. My standard kit generally includes two digital camera bodies, a variety of lenses from 17 to 500 millimetres, a very sturdy tripod and head, three or four flash units and a range of other accessories, depending on the specific birds that I am after. This may all sound like an incredible amount of equipment to lug around, and it is, but just imagine if we were still in the film era and also had to carry a few extra suitcases just for film. Now that would be difficult!

Each year digital cameras get better and better. We gain megapixels, lose noise and are able to push the limits of what is possible when it comes to bird photography. At the end of the day, however, all it really comes down to is a camera and a lens. You certainly don't need to have the latest and greatest camera equipment to capture a stunning photo.

LEARNING HOW TO FIND THE BIRDS

You can have all the fancy equipment you like, but to be a successful bird photographer, you must be a knowledgeable birder. Being able to confidently identify various species on sight is only the first step. The truth is, the most important tool any bird photographer has is not a camera or lens, but ears. Once a photographer moves past the conspicuous birds that are relatively easy to find, the game becomes decidedly more difficult.

I can remember the first time I was in the field with someone who really knew their calls. It was an eye-opening—and ear-opening—experience, to say the least. My birding companion and I were in southern Ontario in mid-May—the peak of spring migration. Beautiful and exciting birds were everywhere. There were so many species migrating through the area that it was hard to know where to look. The common birds were abundant. It seemed like every bird I pointed my lens or binoculars at was either a Yellow or Yellow-rumped Warbler. Meanwhile, my more experienced birdwatching friend was picking out new species left, right and centre. A Black-throated Green Warbler here, a Blackburnian Warbler there. He was spotting so many more species than I was, I knew I had to be doing something wrong. That was when he explained to me that he was birding not with his eyes but with his ears. He had tuned his ears to the subtle differences in the birdsongs and was able to tune out the Yellow-rumped Warblers and find the real prize birds. This was a complete revelation to me; I knew that in order to improve my photography, I would have to learn the birds' calls.

It wasn't hard to acquire a CD collection of birdsongs and sounds of North America. I started listening to some of the birds of my area, and in no time I could identify several species. Before long, learning these calls became a fun and challenging new hobby, and I was listening to them on my iPod and in my car. Once a friend borrowed my car for the weekend and was less than impressed with my musical tastes when he discovered I had left my birdsong CD in the car stereo. As crazy as I seemed to some friends, I was learning the birdsongs and this was translating into better photographs. I was not to be deterred.

Before long I found that birds had not only replaced my favourite CDs, but had also found a prominent place in my library. As my

A Tennessee Warbler sings from its territory in northern BC.

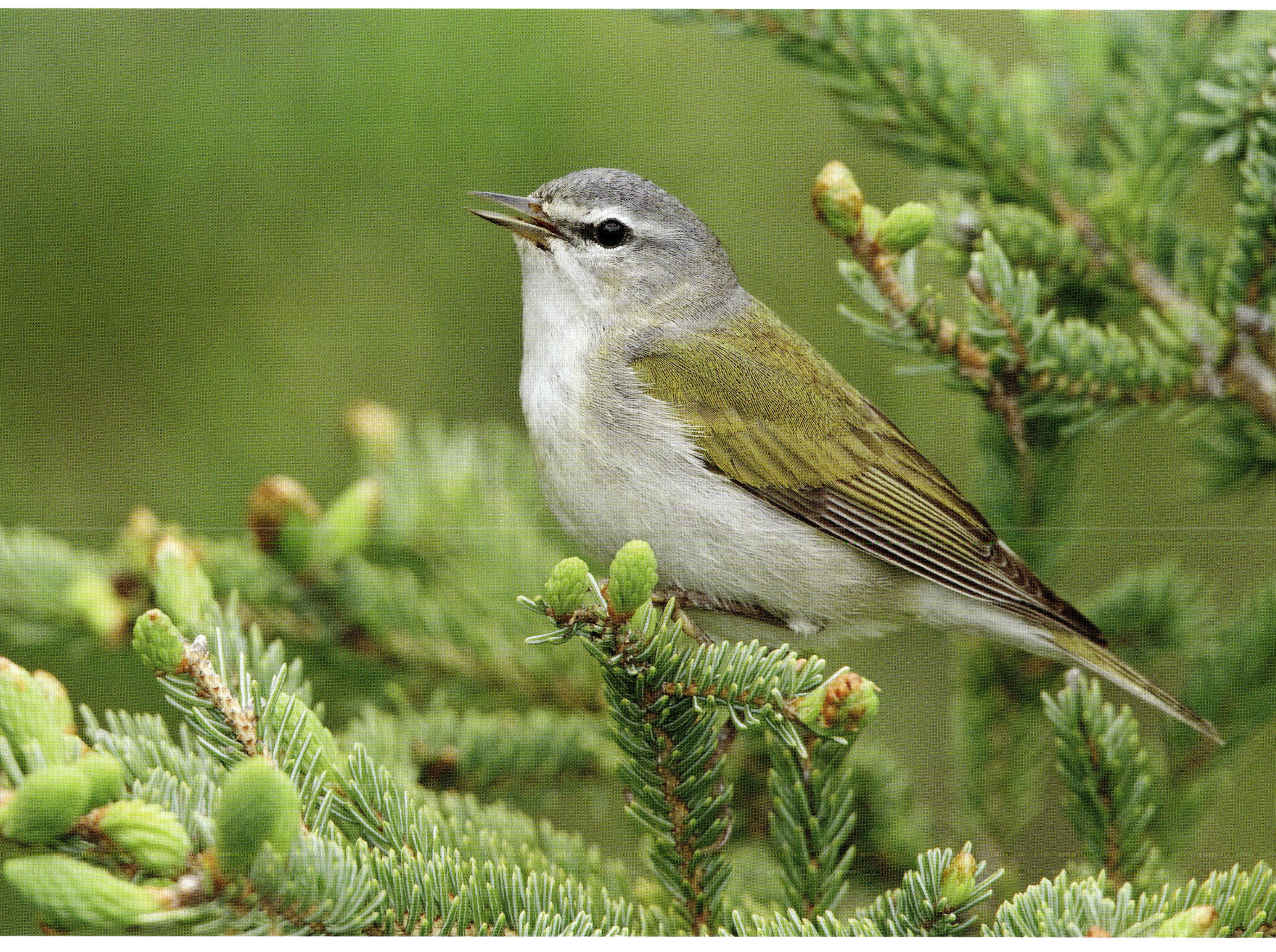

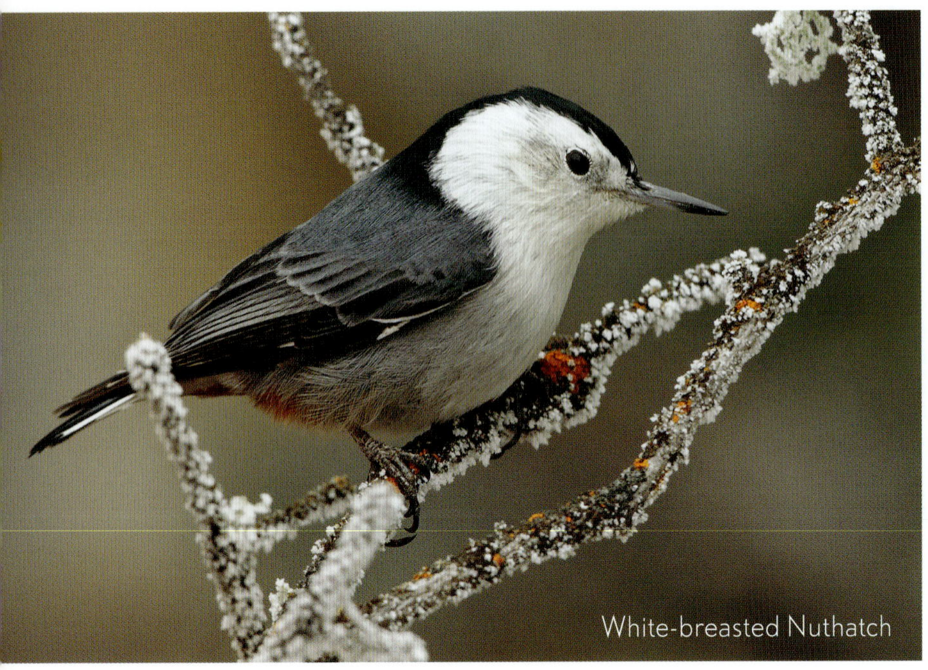
White-breasted Nuthatch

bookshelves filled with field guide after field guide, and bird books found a permanent home on my bedside table, it became clear that I was obsessed. My interest in birds was a healthy obsession, but an obsession nonetheless.

The books revealed fascinating tidbits of information about the daily lives of birds—things that I had no idea about, like the incredible migrations that many birds make, how many songbirds return to the same breeding territory year after year, and that there were so many different species that lived so close to my home. As interesting as these facts were simply to learn, I also knew that this information could be used in the field to improve my odds of capturing great photos.

Solid identification skills, familiarity with bird calls, knowledge of bird behaviour and countless hours in the field observing how birds lead their daily lives all improve the odds of predicting what the bird might do next. The sum of all these parts allows the photographer to know where to be to catch the shot, but, needless to say, nothing is ever certain in nature. Taking a great bird photograph ultimately comes down to many factors coming together, including luck.

GETTING "THE SHOT"

I often have the photo I am hoping to create of a particular bird in mind days, weeks or even months before I actually take it. I believe that visualizing what it is you hope to capture in advance is of utmost importance. Of course, just because I know what I am hoping to create does not mean capturing it is going to be easy. Getting the shot often requires scouting out locations and waiting for perfect conditions. Photographing birds (or any wildlife) is always a dynamic process. There are so many factors involved, and each constantly changes in relation to the others; the photographer who is unable to react is simply left wondering what went wrong.

When it comes to birds, one of the greatest skills is anticipating what the bird might do next, which does come with knowledge and experience. Being aware of your surroundings is of paramount importance. For example, imagine if you were out in the woods and spotted a Brown Creeper working its way up a tree in search of a meal. You try to get your lens on it, but, before you know it, it has moved up too high and around the back side of the tree. Taking a step back, you see it has vacated its original tree and flown to a new one, where it has again begun systematically searching for food, starting from the bottom and working its way up. In this case, the proactive thing to do would not be to chase the bird on its existing tree, but rather, anticipate that it will likely continue moving in the direction it is going, and then set yourself near the next tree it is likely to visit. The difference between being proactive and reactive in the field often is the difference between getting the shot you had dreamed of and going home empty-handed.

When a bird does cooperate and do as you expect, the technical aspects of capturing a good photo are generally quite straightforward. I often tell people that in order to create beautiful images of birds on a consistent basis, it is important to understand the many elements that combine to make a good photo. These include light, exposure, sharpness, composition, perch, background and pose. These components are not absolute rules that must be followed in every image, but understanding these elements will inevitably lead to better bird images.

Photography is all about light. Understanding that light has quality, direction and intensity, and knowing how to harness these factors, is essential for any bird photographer. Great photographs can be taken in direct sunlight, shade or under cloudy skies. Learning about light and how to work with, instead of against it, is a crucial element of bird photography.

In many cases, working in direct, low-angle light is the easiest option. The camera is able to create balanced exposures that have rich contrast and warm colours. When such quality light is not available, the photographer must decide whether or not it is still possible to create a great image. Sometimes exposures can be made that avoid the natural light and instead rely upon using artificial flash. Other times the "poor" light can be used to the photographer's advantage by trying for an artistic image. Sometimes, despite a photographer's best efforts, the conditions are simply not workable and a photographer has to know when to throw in the towel and try again another day.

Successful bird images must be properly exposed so that they do not look too light or too dark. If too much light reaches the film or digital media, the image will have white areas lacking detail. Similarly, too little light results in a very dark image lacking detail. Creating a correct exposure essentially boils down to controlling the amount of light that reaches the film or digital sensor. Cameras control this through the interworkings of three factors: the duration that the shutter is open (shutter speed), the size of the opening in the lens (aperture) and the sensitivity of the film (ISO speed). The best way to ensure proper exposure is to learn to read your camera's histogram and make adjustments through exposure compensation (adding or subtracting light from the way the camera meters a scene).

Most bird photographers are, with good reason, fanatical about how sharp their images are. This is because sharp and crisp bird images (especially around the eye) are much more intimate, professional and natural-looking. Although there are situations in which a photo can be beautiful and artistic-looking without being in focus, most successful images require the subject to be sharp. The sharpness of an image is dependent upon the photographer using good equipment, proper technique and support, adequate shutter speed to freeze any movement, and, most of all, accurate focus on the subject itself.

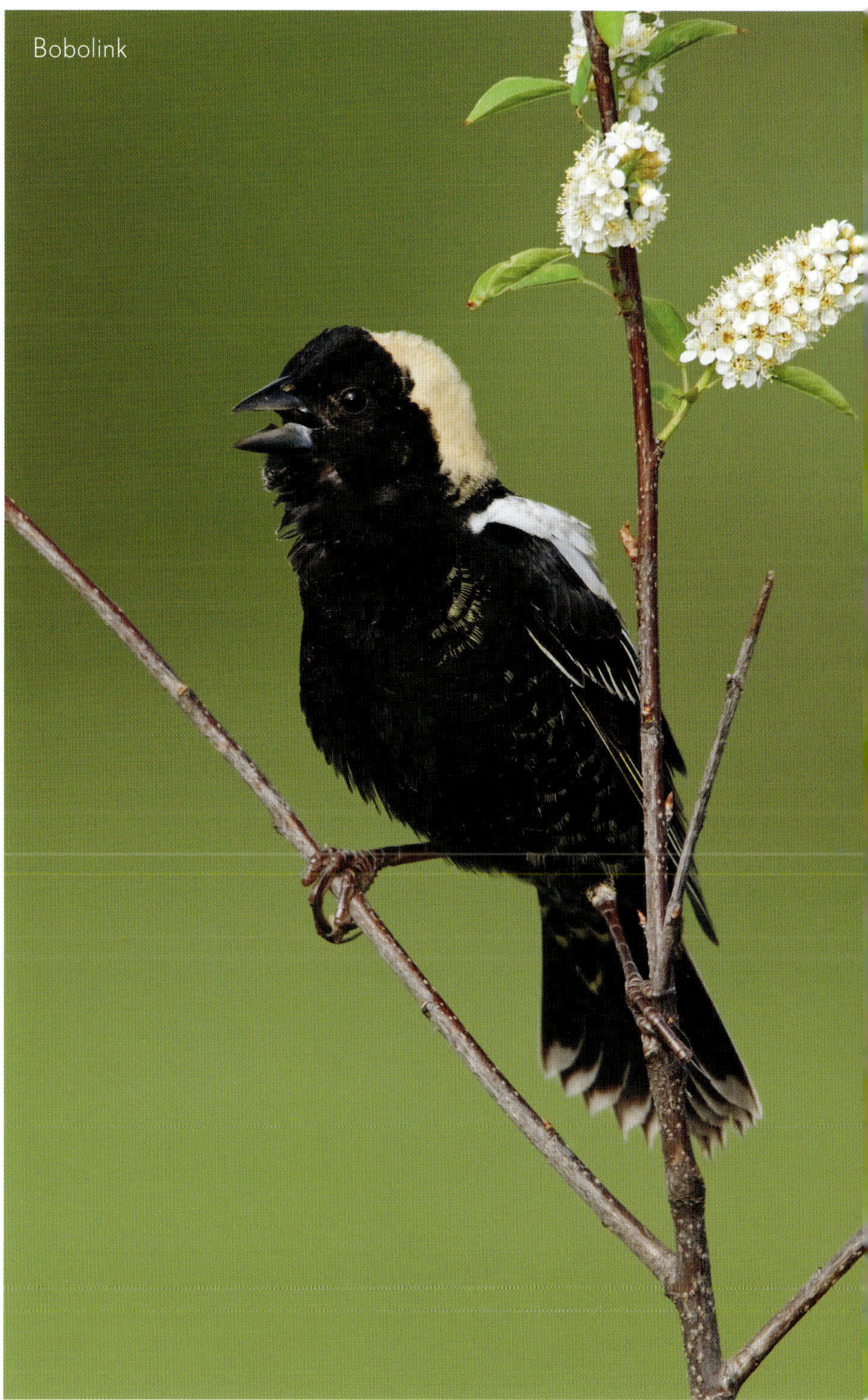
Bobolink

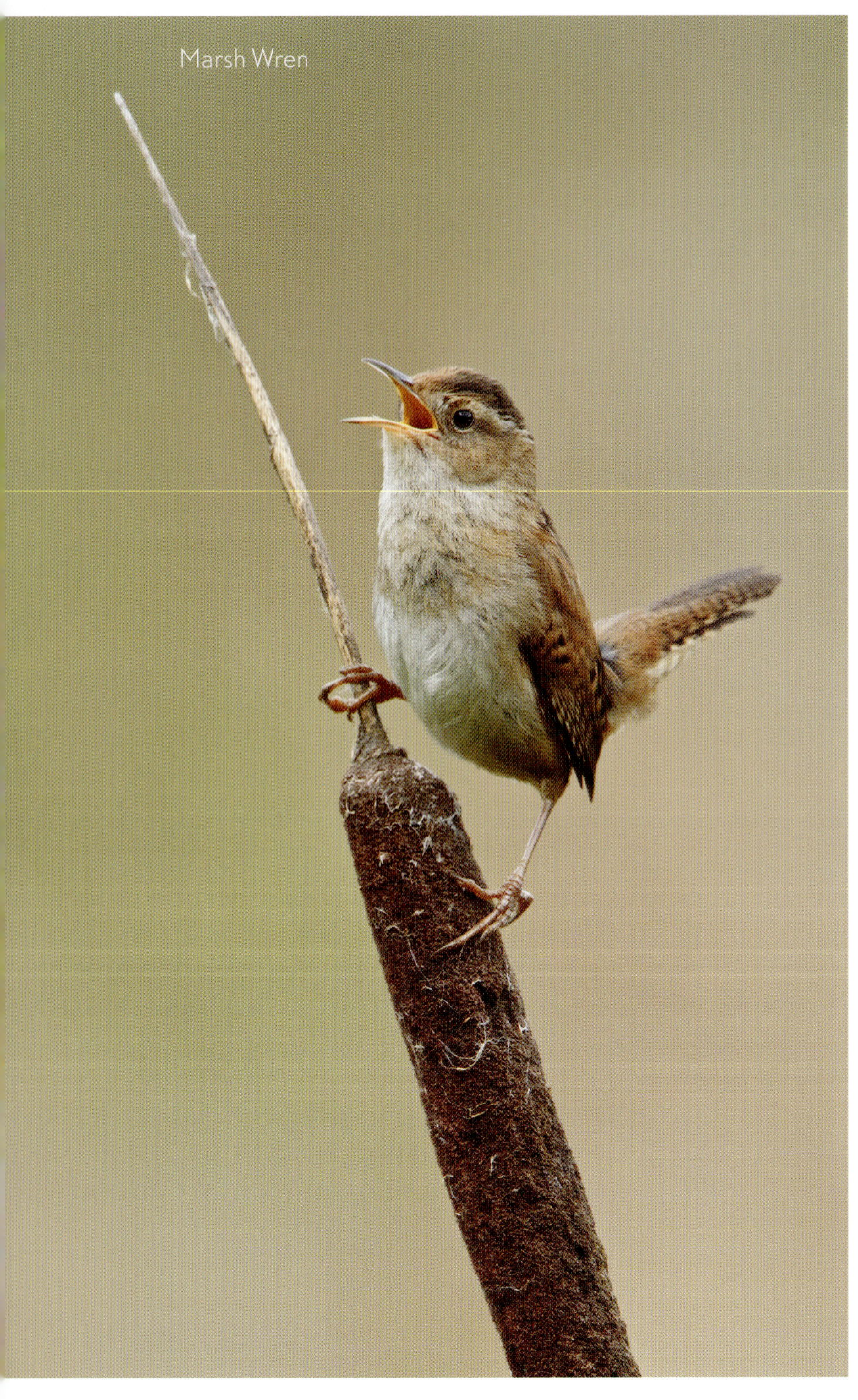
Marsh Wren

In addition to being properly exposed and sharp, an image must also be well composed. This generally refers to the balance of how the elements within the frame are arranged (bird, perch and background elements). Infinite possibilities exist, however, starting with standard compositional guidelines. The rule of thirds and ensuring that there is more room in front of the bird than behind it are good starting points.

Imagine an image of your bird that is properly exposed, well lit and sharp as a tack. Now imagine that this image shows the bird perched on a chain-link fence or hydro wire. Chances are that no matter how good an image is, it will not be successful unless the bird is perched on a natural-looking and appropriately sized perch. The perch should be considered as an important part of the image—perhaps even as important as the subject itself. It should give clues into the type of habitat where the bird lives and add interest to the overall image.

What many bird photographers often overlook is the backdrop upon which they capture their images. Otherwise superb photographs can be ruined by busy backgrounds or distracting elements in the frame. By creating distance between the subject and the background, bird photographers can produce images with backgrounds that are pleasantly out of focus and that highlight the bird rather than distract from it.

Even if all of the other elements are in place, a successful photograph cannot be created if the bird is looking away from the camera. Eye contact draws the viewer into the image and is essential for a great photo. Any number of poses can be pleasing. Some species like nuthatches even have characteristic poses that they often present. In general, the most desirable poses are those that have good eye contact and where the bird is turning its head slightly toward the camera.

All that being said, there is no one recipe that can be followed when it comes to creating beautiful images of birds. In fact, the most sensational images are often those that surprise us or show us something we have never seen before. Nevertheless, these elements can be used as a guide to help us create consistently stunning images of birds in their natural environment. When all of these factors come together, especially for a difficult and highly sought species, the photographer feels a tremendous sense of accomplishment. I often feel like jumping up and down or doing a back flip (if only I could). Usually, though, I simply say an audible "thank you" to the bird and then move on so that it can go about its day. There is no need to linger; I will have the photo to remember the special moment we have shared for years to come.

BEAUTIFUL PLACES

Perhaps the best thing about being a professional wildlife photographer is that my job takes me to some of the most beautiful places throughout Canada. I find trying to photograph a bird often slows me down so I can appreciate my surroundings in a more complete and satisfying way. While observing a bird and trying to figure out its patterns, I can take note of the fresh new leaves emerging from the trees, the way the spiderwebs glisten in the early morning light or how the smell of spring lingers on the gentle breeze. Because I slow down to photograph the birds, I find that despite my otherwise atrocious memory, I can look back at a photo captured years ago and recall with vivid detail the events of the day and the special details of that place. We Canadians are so incredibly lucky to have such a vast country where it is relatively easy to find solitude in a beautiful place of our own.

One of my favourite places I visited while collecting the images for this book was an off-the-beaten-path place in the southern Interior. It was mid-May—the most exciting time to photograph birds in Canada. With a full tank of gas in my Subaru and a copy of a back-roads map book at my side, I was in the mood for exploring. One of the birds I really wanted to photograph was the Williamson's Sapsucker—a specialty of the southern Interior. I decided the best plan was to drive some of the back roads and look for what seemed to be appropriate habitat for the sapsucker. Eventually I stumbled upon a spot that looked like it had potential and set up camp for the night. The next morning I awoke to find perfect conditions for photography. Already the dawn chorus was well under way and, though the sun was not yet up, I could tell that it was going to be a fantastic day. What had attracted me to this particular site was the abundance of poplar trees, in which sapsuckers love to build nests, and the number of dead trees due to the Spruce Budworm outbreak, which are great feeding places for the sapsucker. With lots of potential nest sites, this surely would be a good place to search. Little did I know just how good it would be. Before the day was through, I had found and photographed not only my coveted Williamson's Sapsucker, but also the Red-naped Sapsucker, Northern Flicker, Hairy Woodpecker and Pileated Woodpecker. It was an incredible day, and I look forward to returning to the place that the scribbles on my map book call "Woodpecker Land."

Another one of my favourite memories came on Vancouver Island. One morning I found myself climbing down a lush ravine into a gorgeous mountain stream. As I got closer to the water, I noticed a pair of Harlequin Ducks that were swimming around the

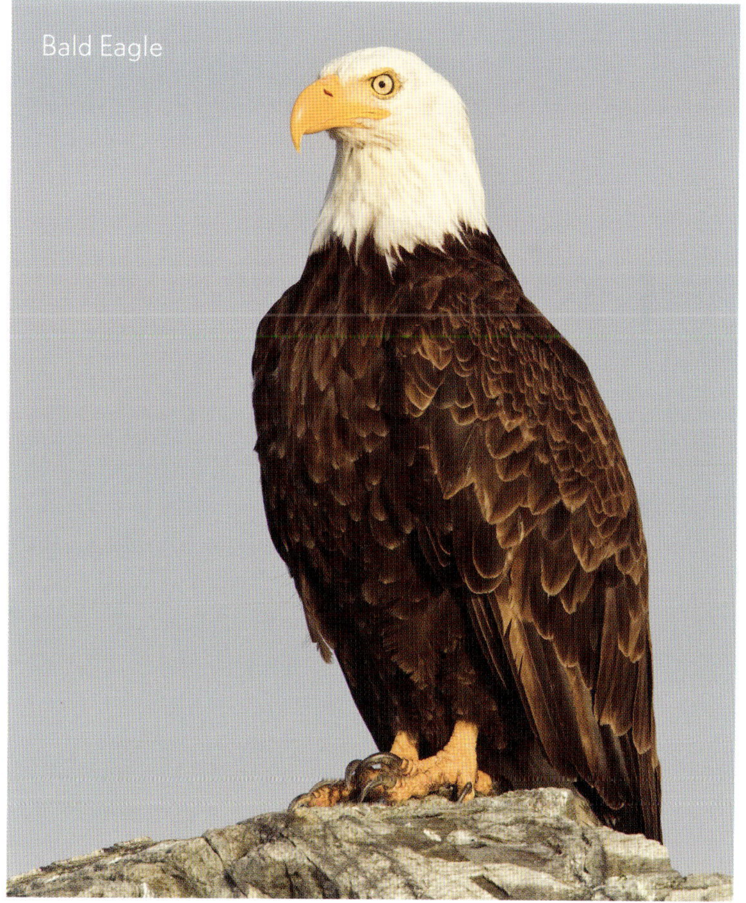
Bald Eagle

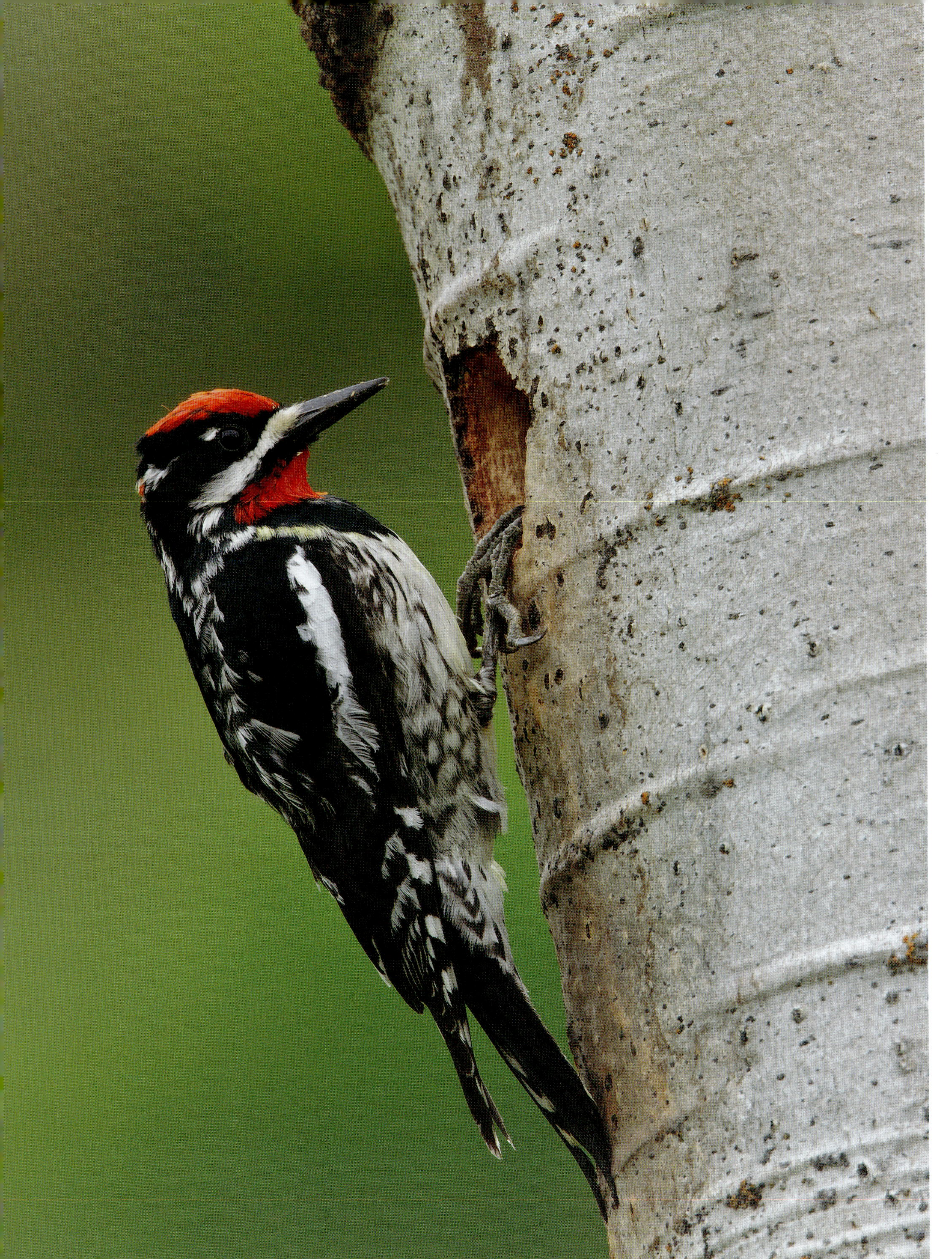

A Red-naped Sapsucker diligently excavates its nest cavity.

area. What made this encounter so special was that I was able to watch from above as the pair dove over and over again in search of food. I had seen Harlequin Ducks hundreds of times before, but this encounter was different. Whereas normally the birds disappear into the unseen aquatic realm when they dive for food, my vantage point and the crystal-clear water allowed me to see the birds swimming underwater.

CHALLENGING CONDITIONS

While being a wildlife photographer is certainly a dream job for many people, the reality is there are many frustrating moments that emerge while trying to photograph birds in the field. More often than not, things do not go as planned. Birds are shy and elusive creatures by nature, and this makes finding and photographing them a tremendous challenge. Often times you have to go to remote and strange places, wake up at inhumane times and spend significant amounts of time in uncomfortable conditions and positions. If you get the shot, all of these discomforts are easily forgotten and life is good. But when things don't go as planned and you go home empty-handed, the lingering memories of camping out for days in terrible weather with voracious mosquitoes can be a bitter pill to swallow. There have been many times when I've asked myself, "What the heck am I doing out here?"

When I think about creating the photo portfolio for this book, a few particular strange, scary and frustrating scenarios immediately come to mind. One came in June in the Okanagan Valley; I was desperately trying to photograph White-throated Swifts. In Canada these birds can only be found in the southern Interior of BC, where they live within the cracks of cliff faces. The obvious challenge when it comes to photographing White-throated Swifts is that they are among the fastest animals on the planet. After trying to photograph them from ground level, I quickly realized that my best intentions were futile. The birds were simply too small and too far away. I wanted eye-level shots of the birds so the photo would show these amazing creatures in a more intimate way. I knew that if I was going to get the shot I had in mind, I had no choice but to overcome my fear of heights and climb up the cliff face to a better vantage point.

And so up I went, one step at a time, being as careful as I could. Because I had my camera and lens in one hand, I only had one hand to help me climb; as I got higher, this started to make me sweat. Eventually I made my way to a nice spot from where I could safely stand and shoot. After 15 minutes of trying to get a usable frame, I knew that I had seriously underestimated the challenge. The problem was not just the speed of the birds (they can reach 320 kilometres per hour) but also the fact they frequently change directions. Keeping a bird in my viewfinder was almost impossible. Just as I thought I had one dialled in and was about to press the shutter button, it would disappear from view and I would have to start all over again. These White-throated Swifts were maddeningly difficult to photograph. I climbed back down the cliff without a single decent image.

As a wildlife photographer, you cannot simply give up if a challenging scenario presents itself. As hard as this shoot was on my nerves and patience, I knew it was theoretically possible to get a great image. I returned to the site the next morning to try my luck again. My arms were still sore from hand-holding my heavy lens the day before, and this did not help my shooting performance. As I climbed down the cliff later that day, the score stood two rounds for the swift and zero for me. I was learning, though. Each moment spent observing these birds gave me more information to work with and to develop a strategy to get the shot. Finally, on my third morning on that dodgy cliff face, all of the elements came together and I was able to get some shots of these elusive birds that I was really happy with.

Another great memory from my quest to photograph the birds of BC came one May day in Cranbrook. I was trying to photograph Eared Grebes and had found a wonderful spot. It was a clear and calm morning, and the sun was just about to clear the horizon. The conditions were absolutely perfect. My favourite way to photograph waterfowl is to actually get in the water so I can get very low-angle images of the birds. I put on my chest waders and hopped into the water. Spring may have arrived in BC, but you wouldn't know it by the water temperature. Once I got in the lake, I had to work my way through the reeds to get out to where the birds were. I was making some good progress and then—whoosh—I

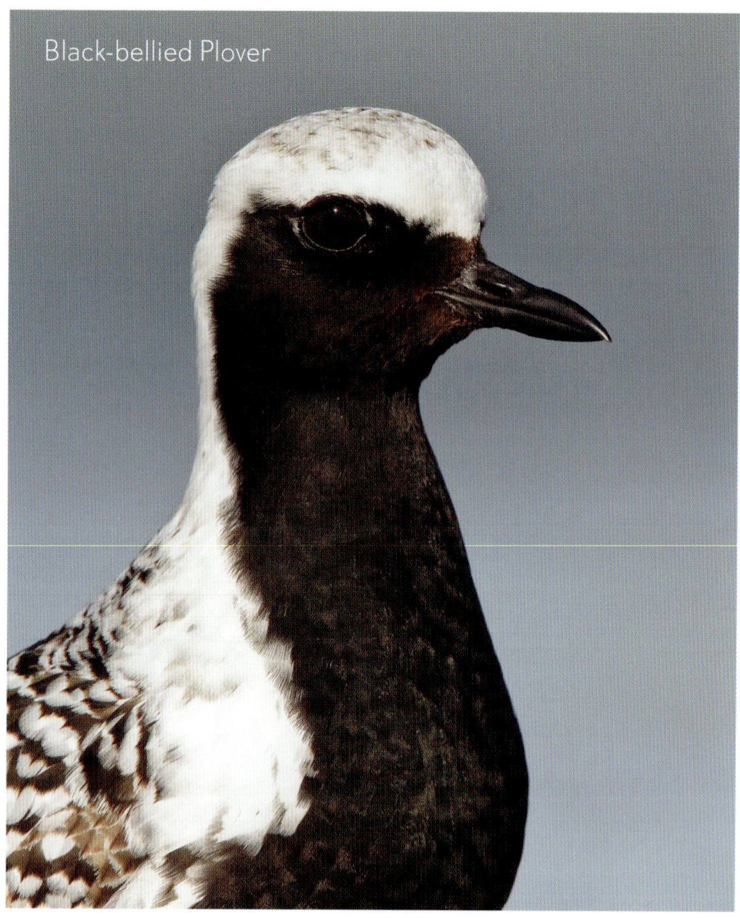
Black-bellied Plover

made one wrong step, and icy water came streaming in over the top of my waders. Not the way I was hoping to start my morning! Assessing the situation, I knew that if I wanted to take advantage of the early morning light and calm waters, there was no way I had time to get out of the water, back to my car, and then back to a good shooting position. I had no choice. For the next hour I stood there, chest-deep in freezing water that smelled like a swamp, with my teeth chattering and whole body shivering. Just as I was really beginning to question my decision to stay in the water, the grebes got used to me. As they became curious, they started to swim over and investigate. The conditions were perfect, and as I walked back to my car, sopping wet and near hypothermic, I knew I had nailed that shoot. I was a happy man.

Other challenges include spending 30 hours up on a sheer cliff face trying to get a decent flight image of a Peregrine Falcon; staying up late, night after night, trying to find owls; and getting lost in the woods more often then I would care to admit. These stories are not meant to sound like fickle complaints. After all, part of what I love about photographing birds is the challenge. Even though I often catch myself feeling frustrated about the weather or the uncooperative birds, I realize that, for me, even the worst day photographing birds in the field is still a pretty great day in the grand scheme of things. And eventually, I do find humour in the frustrating or strange scenarios I wind up in. At the end of the day, if I take one really nice image, I'm happy. Even if I do not manage to achieve this goal, I still enjoy the experience of exploring the beautiful places in this phenomenal place that we call British Columbia.

THE PARTING SHOT

I love being a wildlife photographer. I love the lifestyle, the time I get to spend in nature, the challenges, and the satisfaction that comes with capturing one-of-a-kind images of these fascinating and beautiful creatures. Perhaps what I love the most about being a bird photographer is the ability to share my passion and joy for birds and nature with my friends, family and others through my photos. Without these photos, it would be hard to share these moments of discovery, frustration and joy. No matter how much I enjoy being alone in nature, at the end of the day, these precious moments simply would not be as enjoyable if I could not share them with others.

Whether I am close to home searching for American Dippers and Red-breasted Sapsuckers in the temperate rainforest on Vancouver Island, or farther afield in the northern realms of the province walking through the spruce woods and trying to differentiate the songs of the various migratory songbirds, I love that this province has so much to offer a bird photographer. I honestly cannot think of anywhere else on Earth that I would rather live.

A male Townsend's Warbler perches on a Douglas Fir in the coastal forests of Vancouver Island.

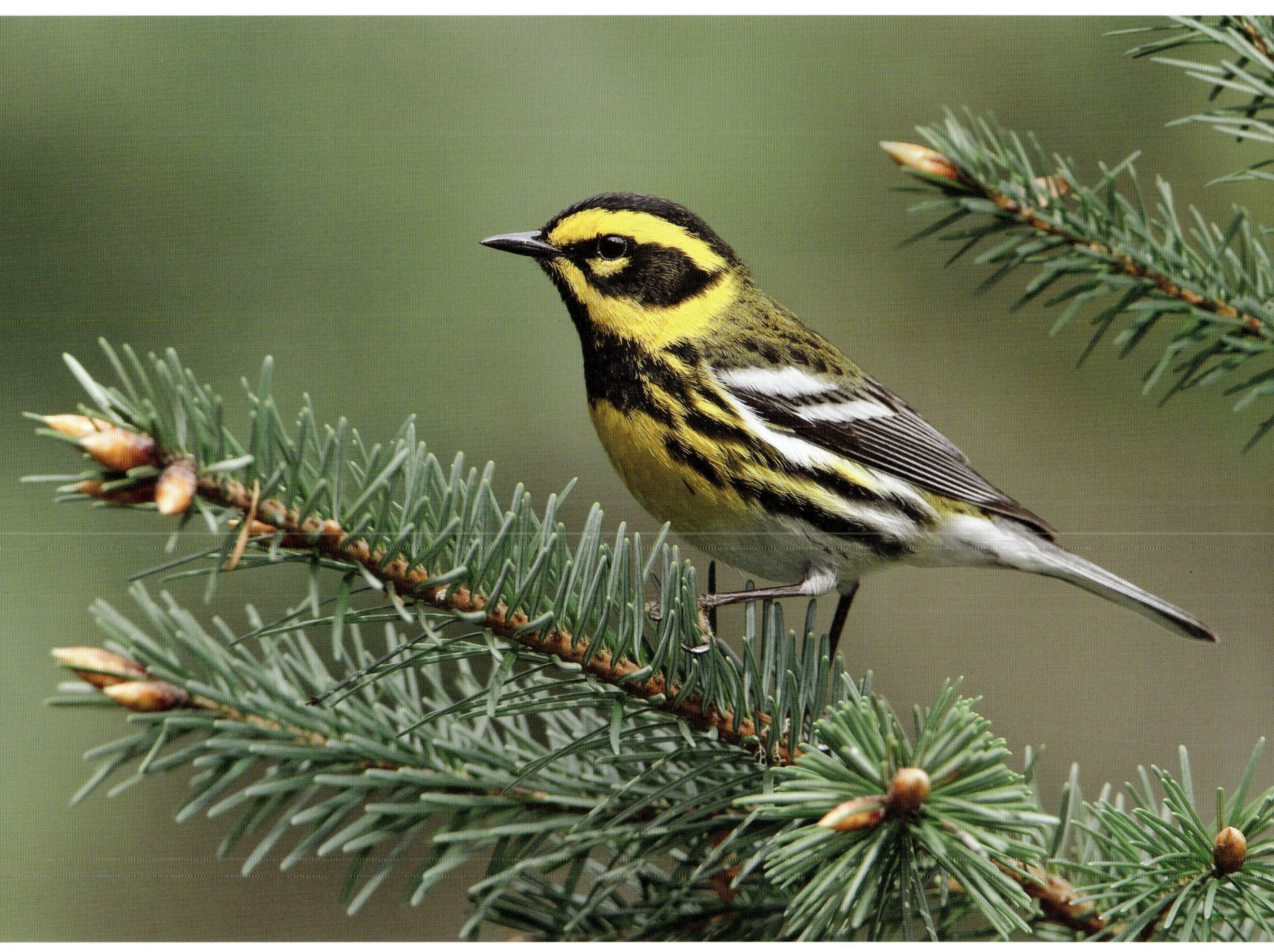

A Northern Pintail returns to the coastal waters of BC to spend the winter.

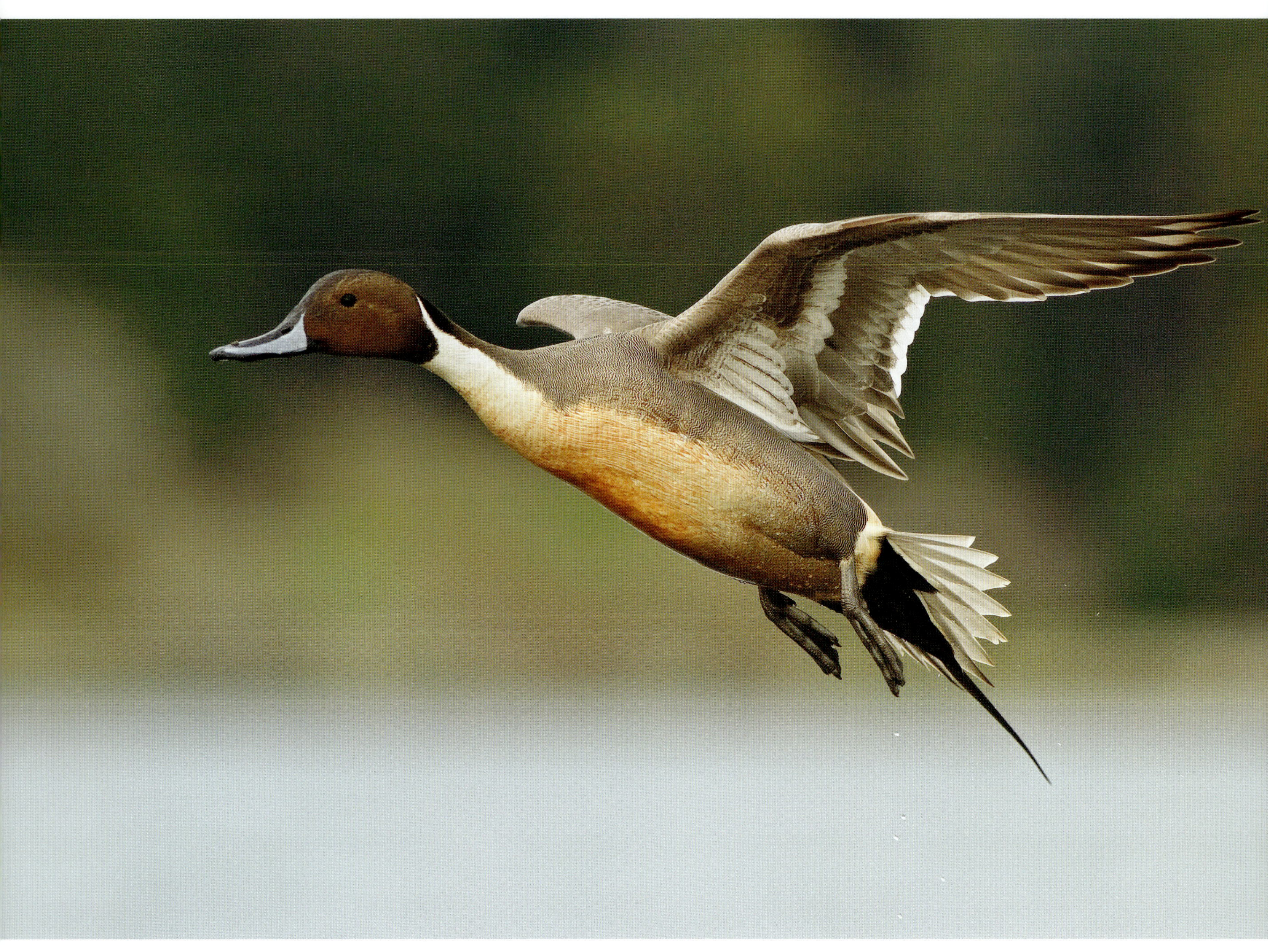

The Ring-necked Duck has a very subtle ring around its neck, usually only visible in direct sunlight.

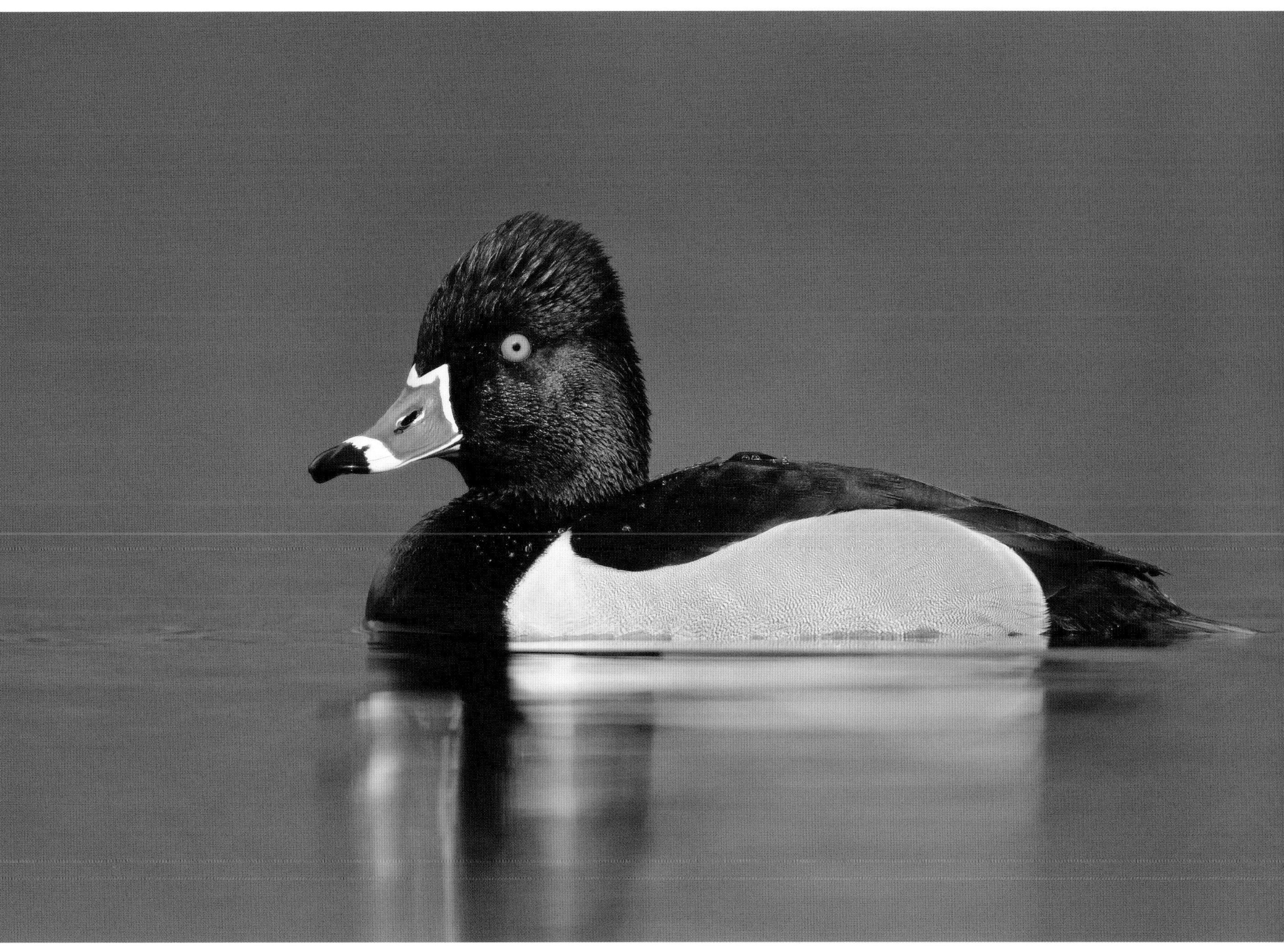

A Surfbird searches for its next meal along the coastline of BC.

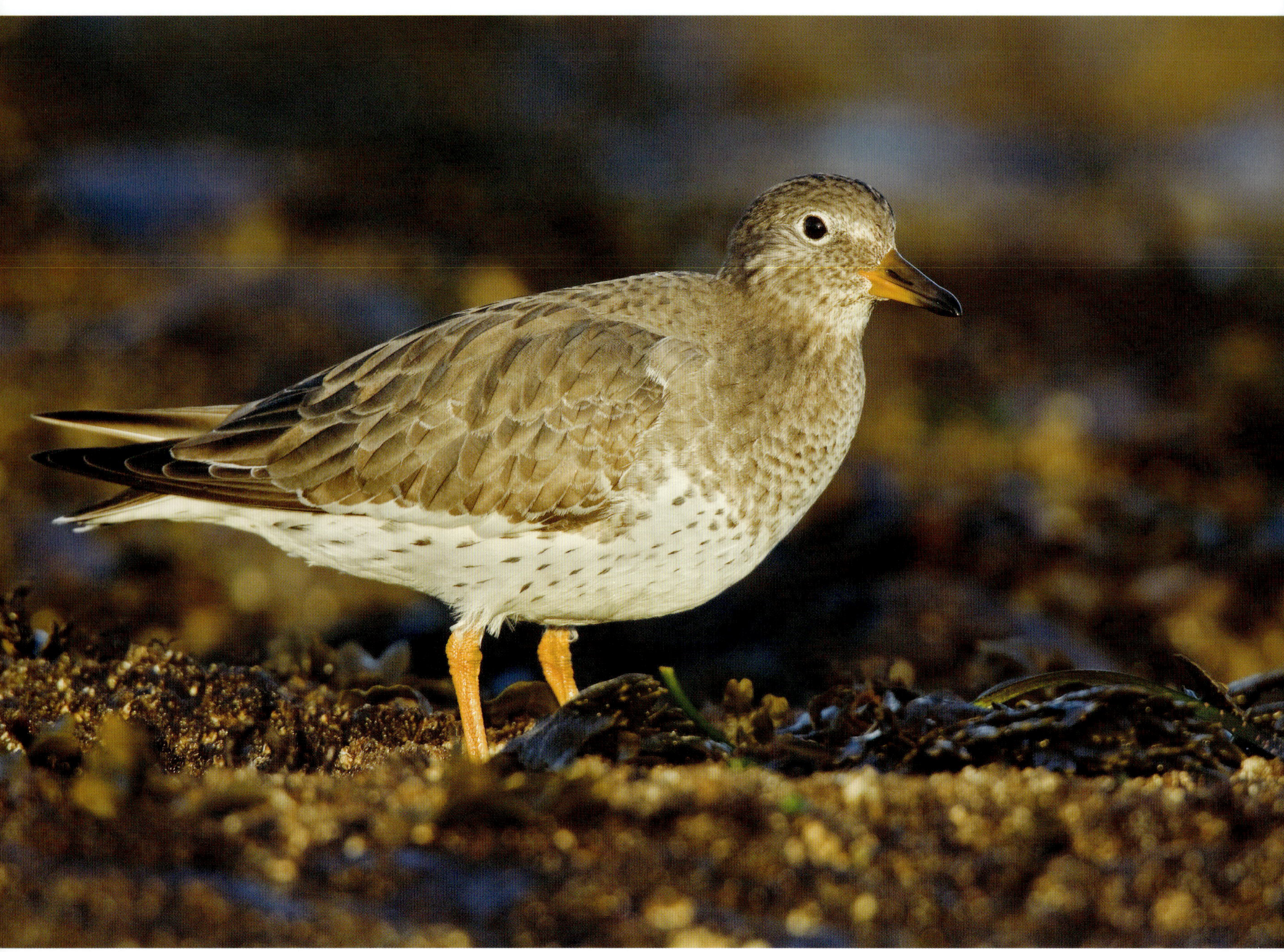

A speedy Bufflehead shows off its incredible colours as it flies past.

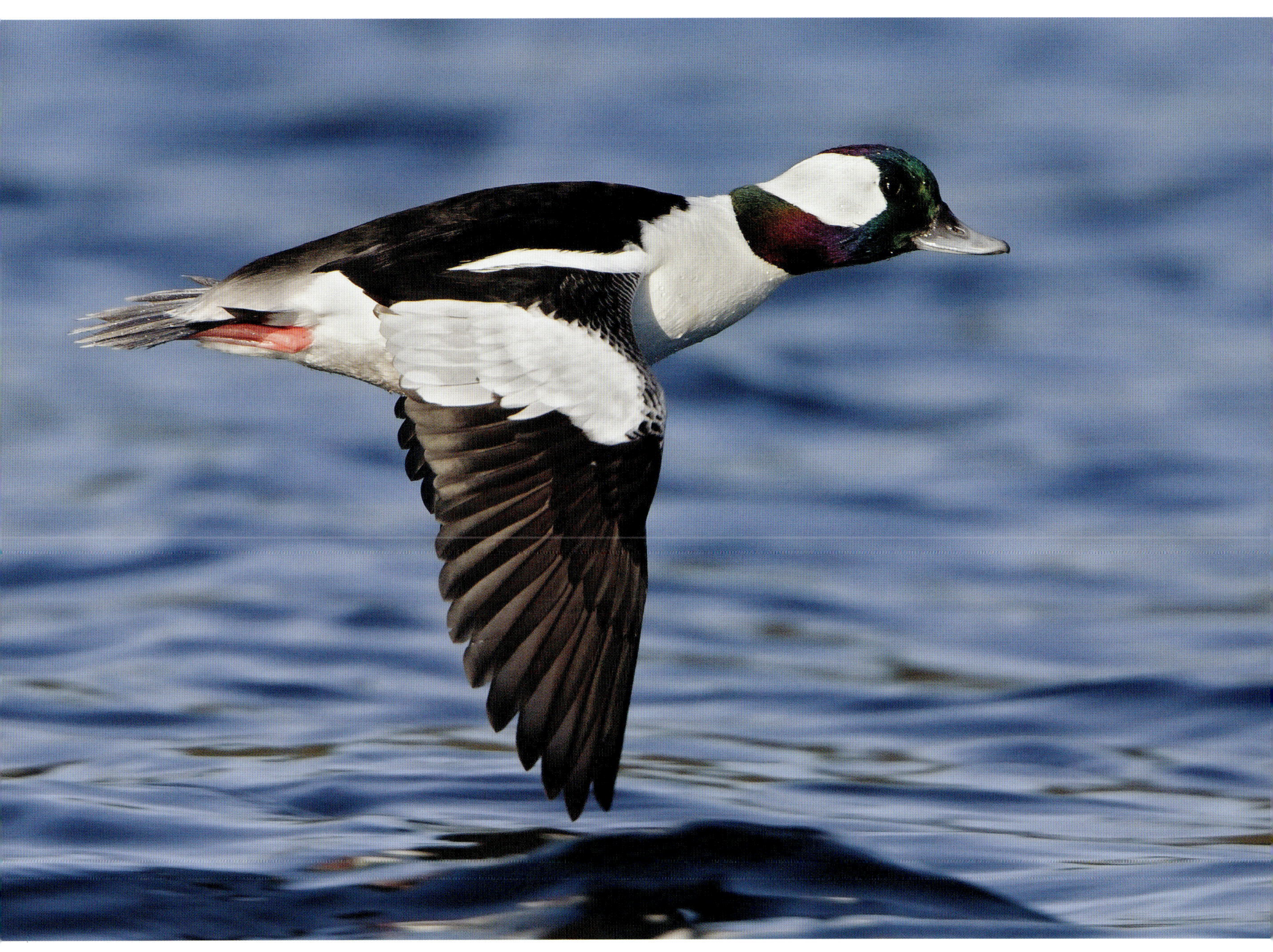

The Common Nighthawk is a master of camouflage and can easily blend in with its surrounding environment.

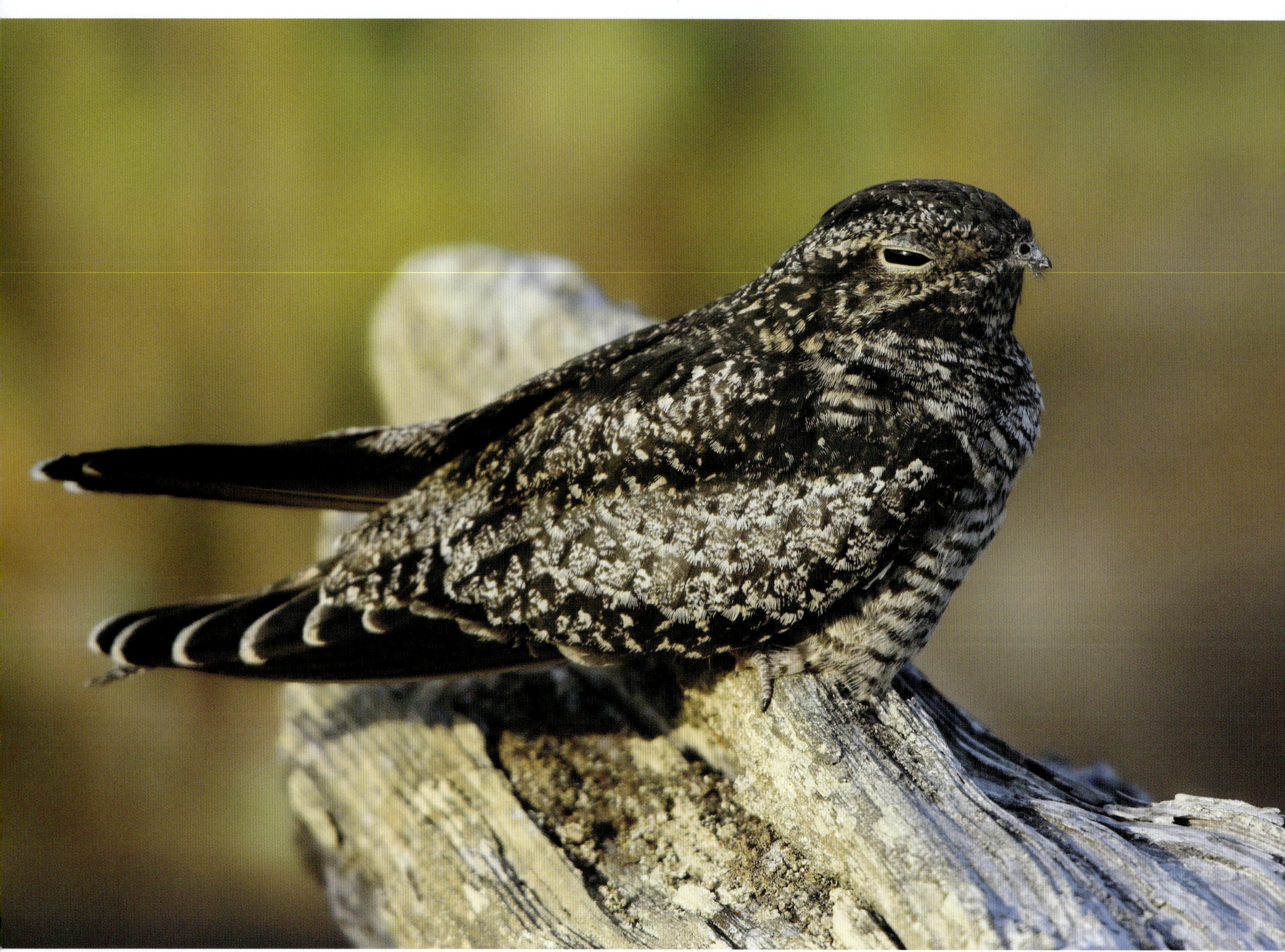

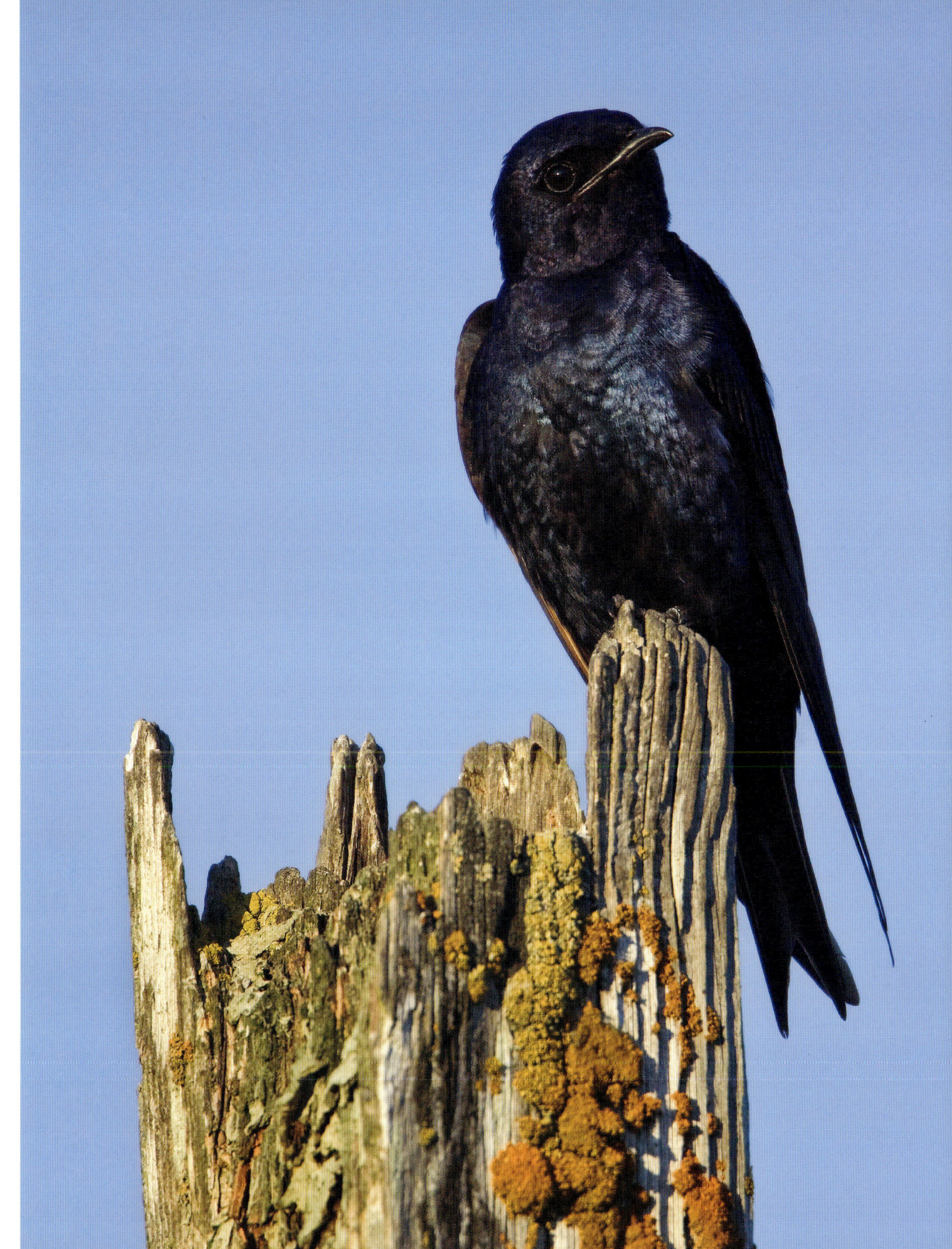

Purple Martins nest communally near bodies of water. They are true aerial masters and capable of snatching large insects from the surrounding skies.

Cliff Swallows nest in large colonies on cliffs or underneath bridges.

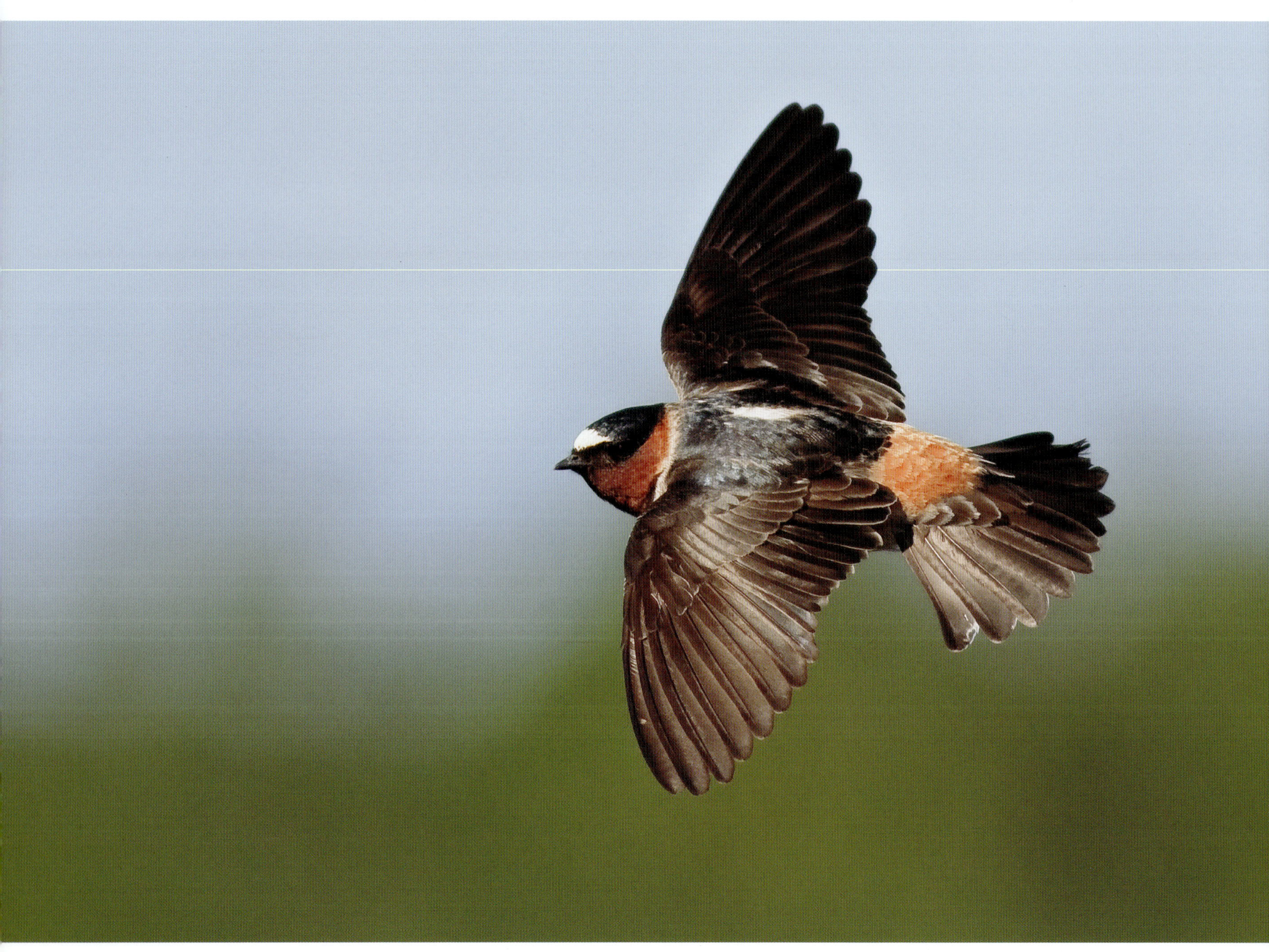

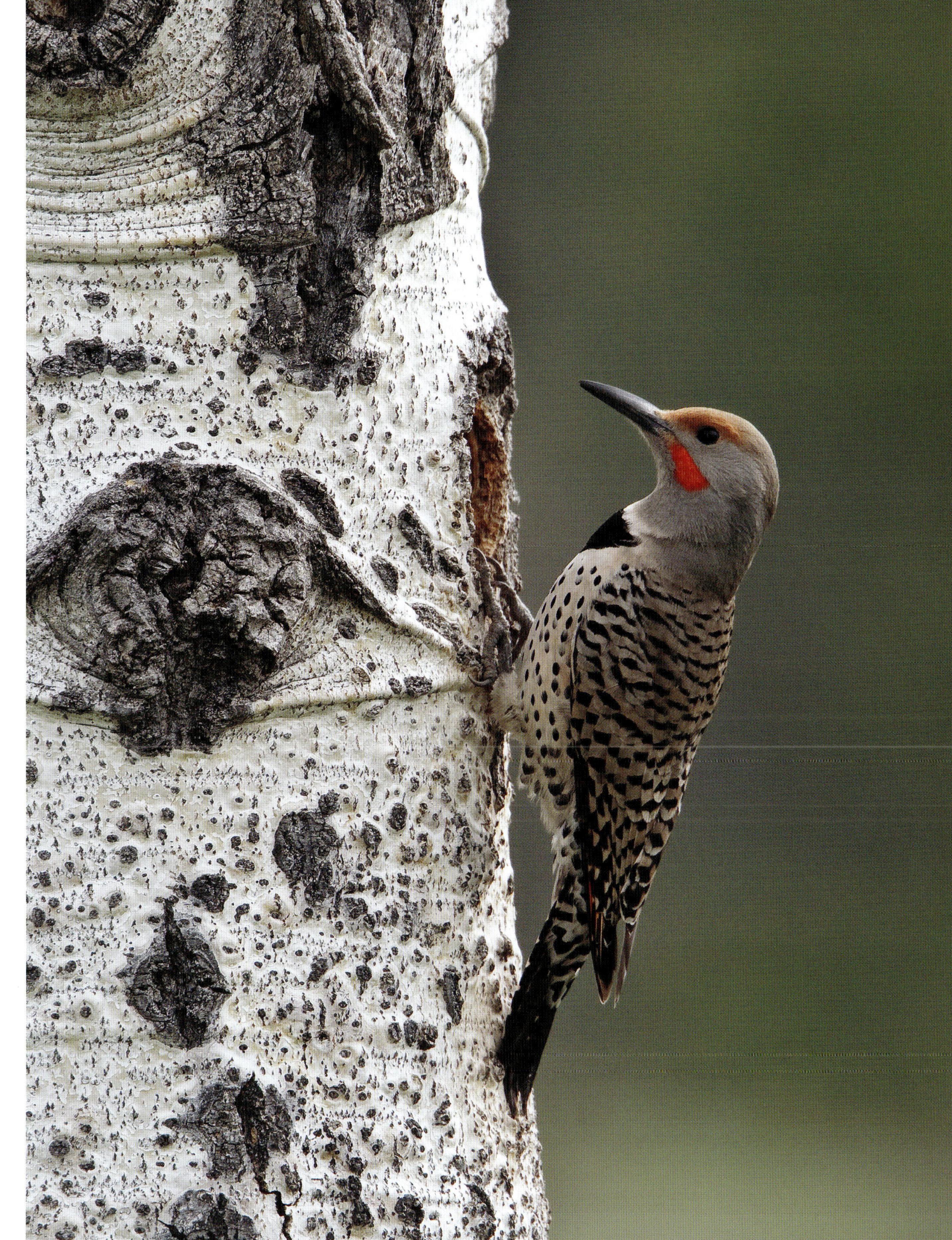

A Northern Flicker perches outside its nest cavity before disappearing inside.

The White-throated Swift is one of the fastest animals on the planet and very challenging to photograph.

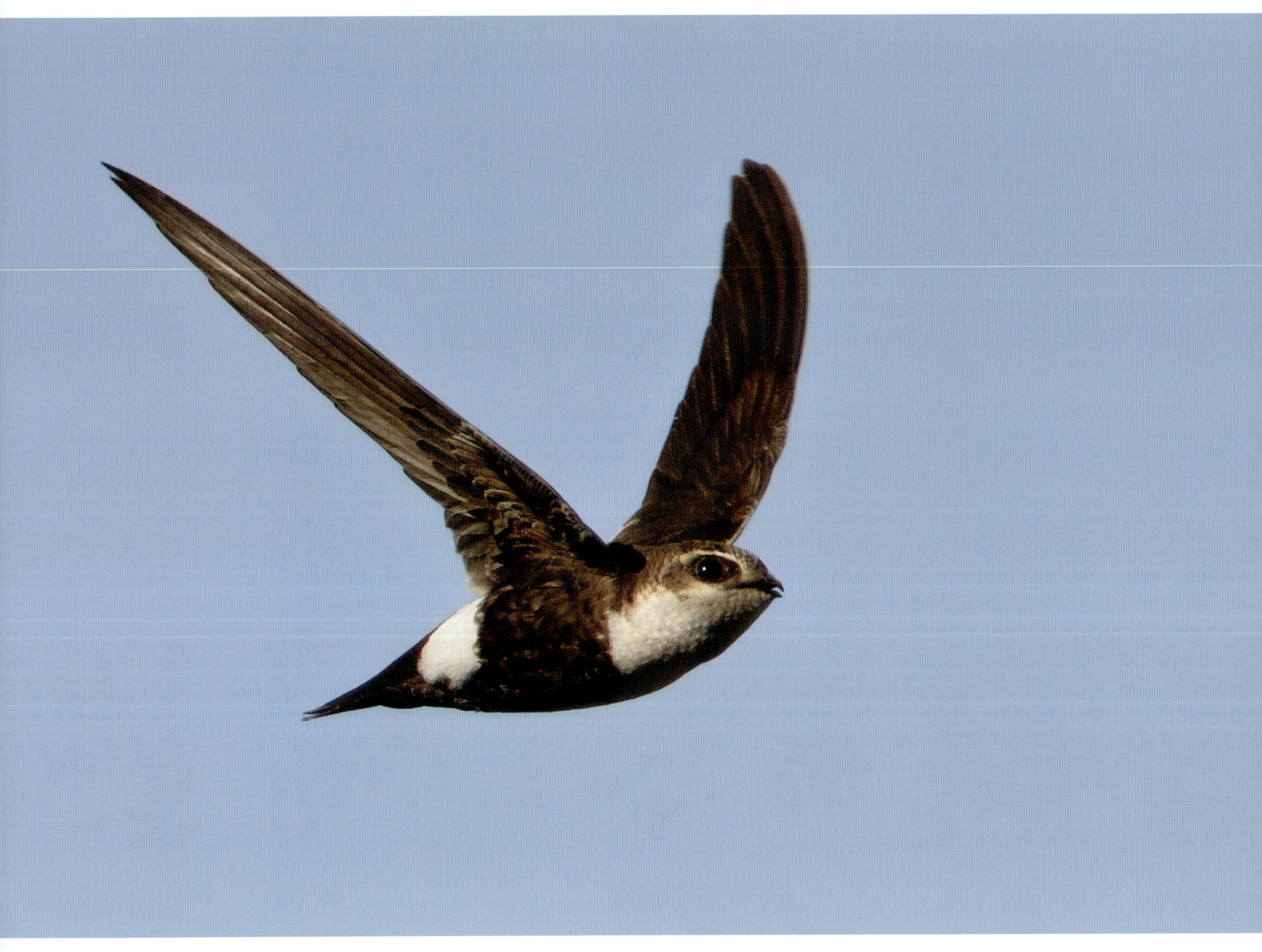

Formerly known as the Winter Wren, this species was distinguished as two different species. Birds west of the Rockies are now known as Pacific Wrens.

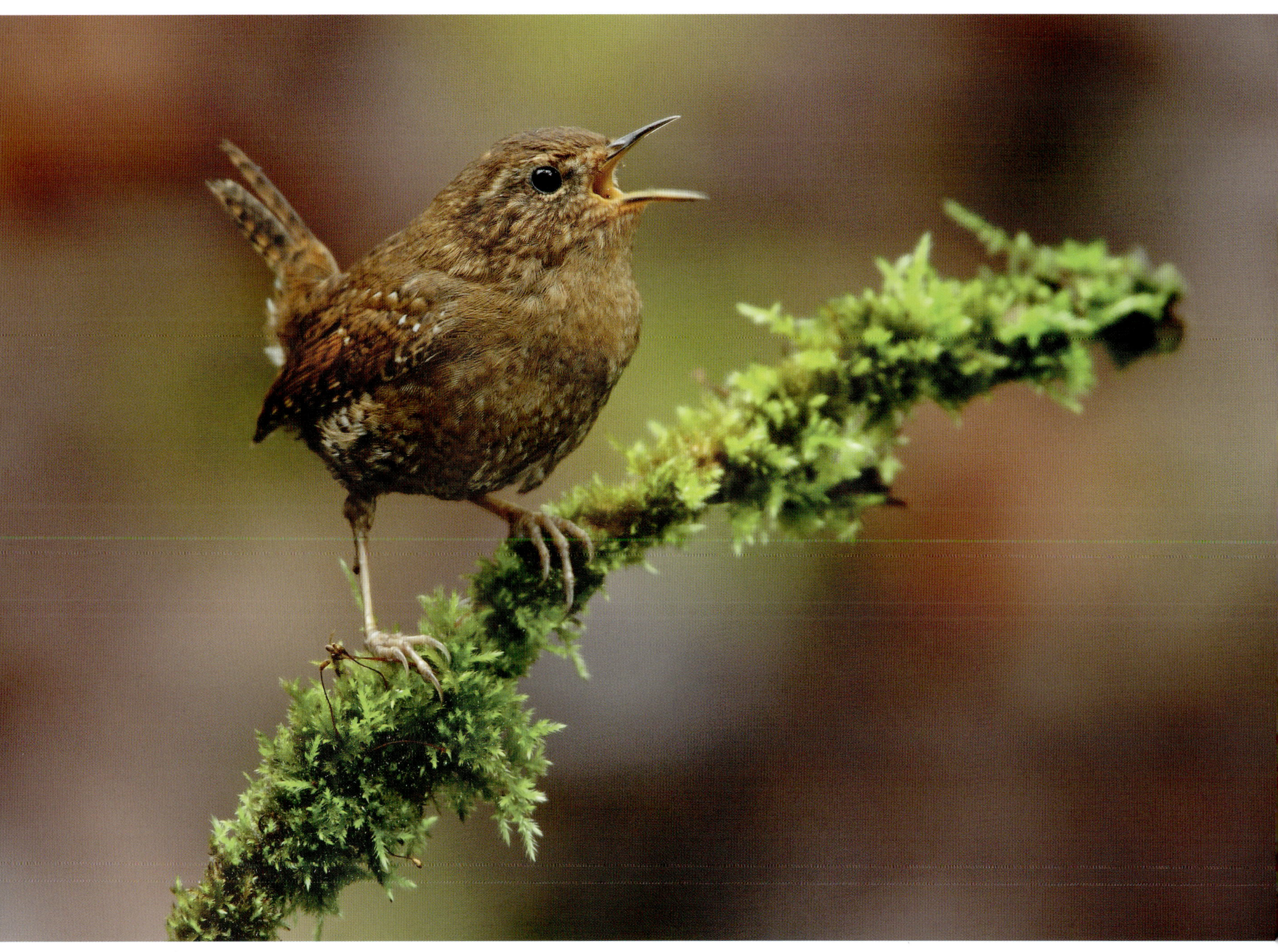

A common bird throughout North America, the Wilson's Snipe is most often observed in the air as it makes its winnowing, territorial flight sounds.

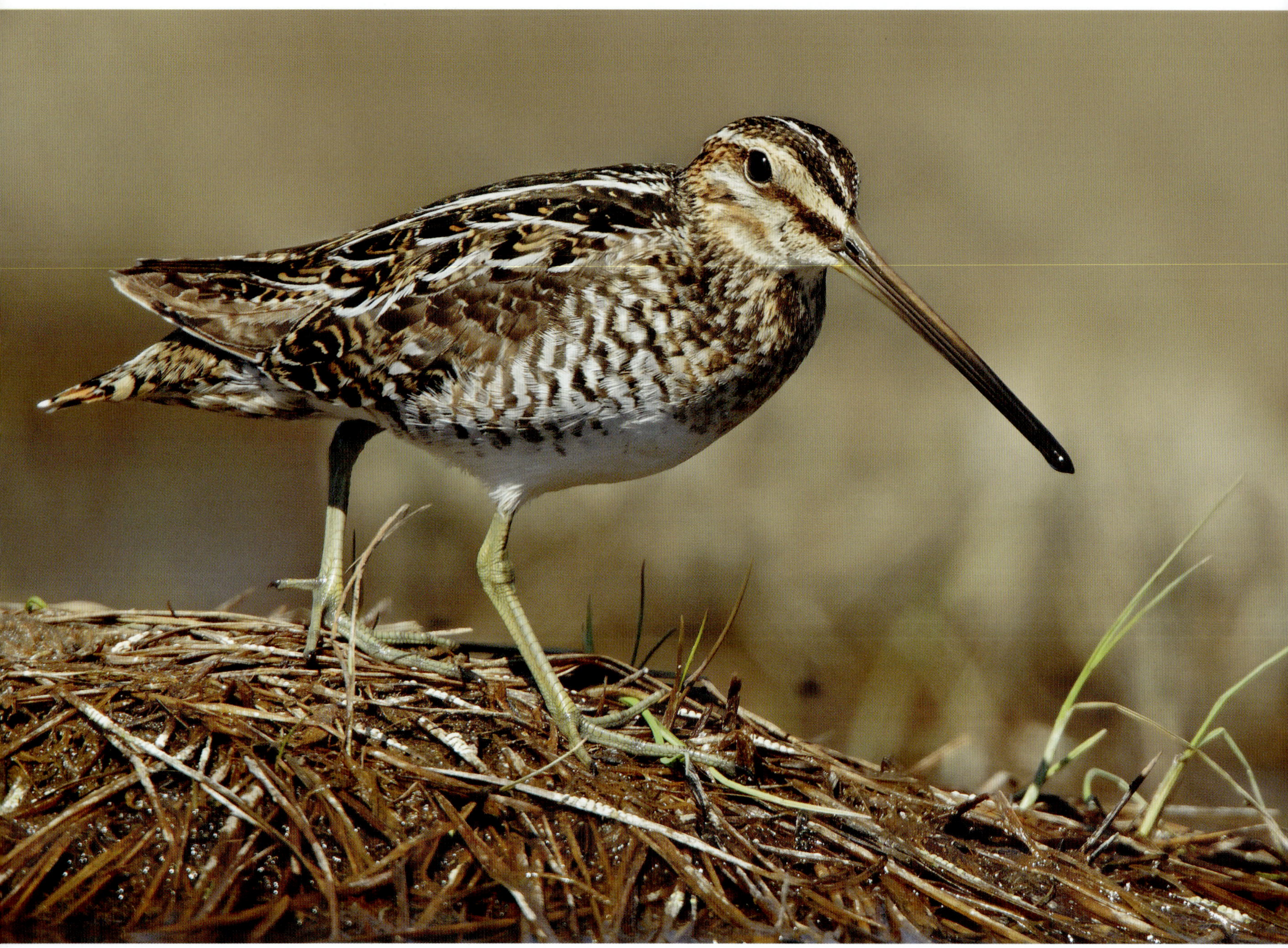

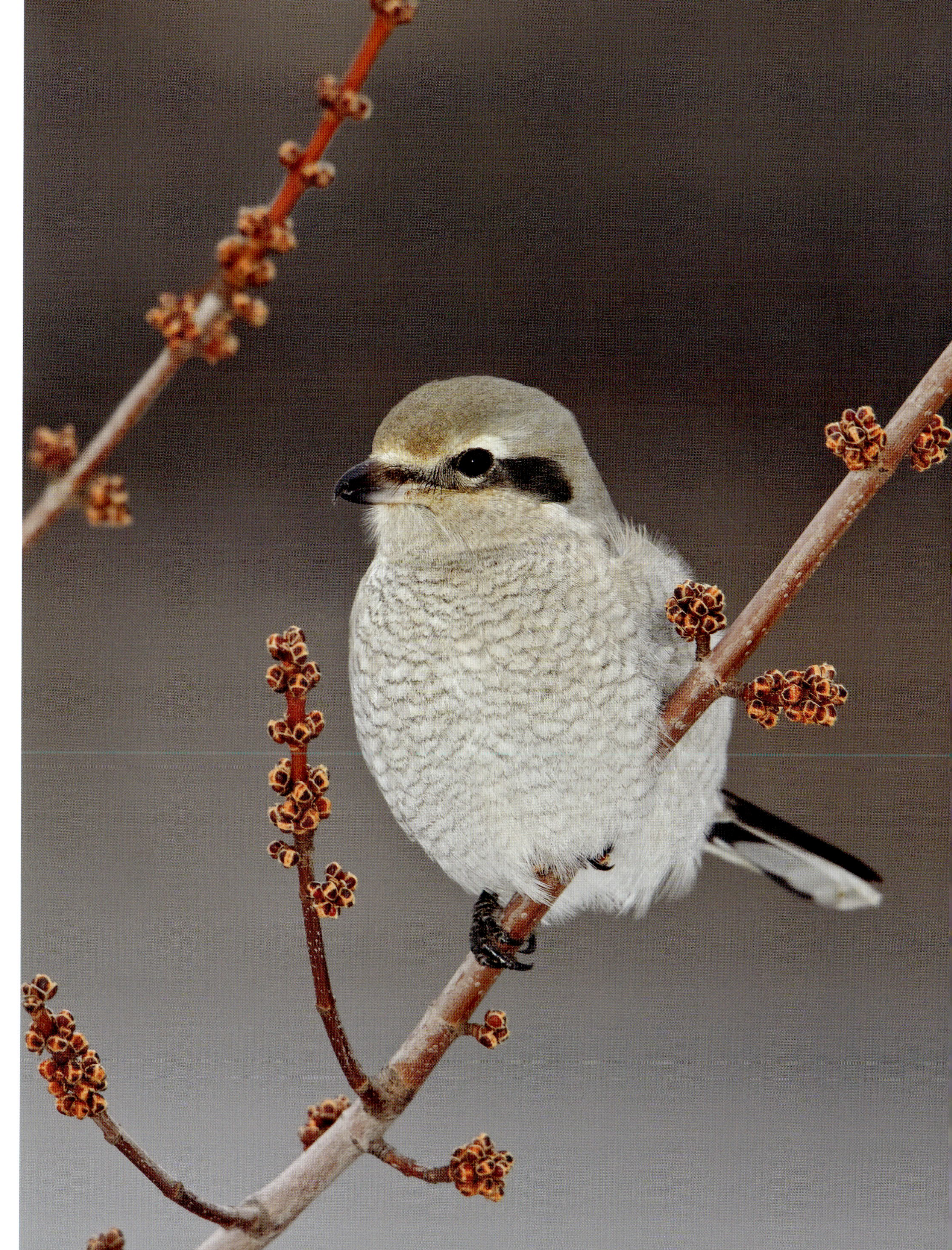

The Northern Shrike is often called the butcher bird for the way it impales prey on thorns or barbed wire while tearing it apart.

This Merlin prepares to feast on a Short-billed Dowitcher, which it captured during the fall migration.

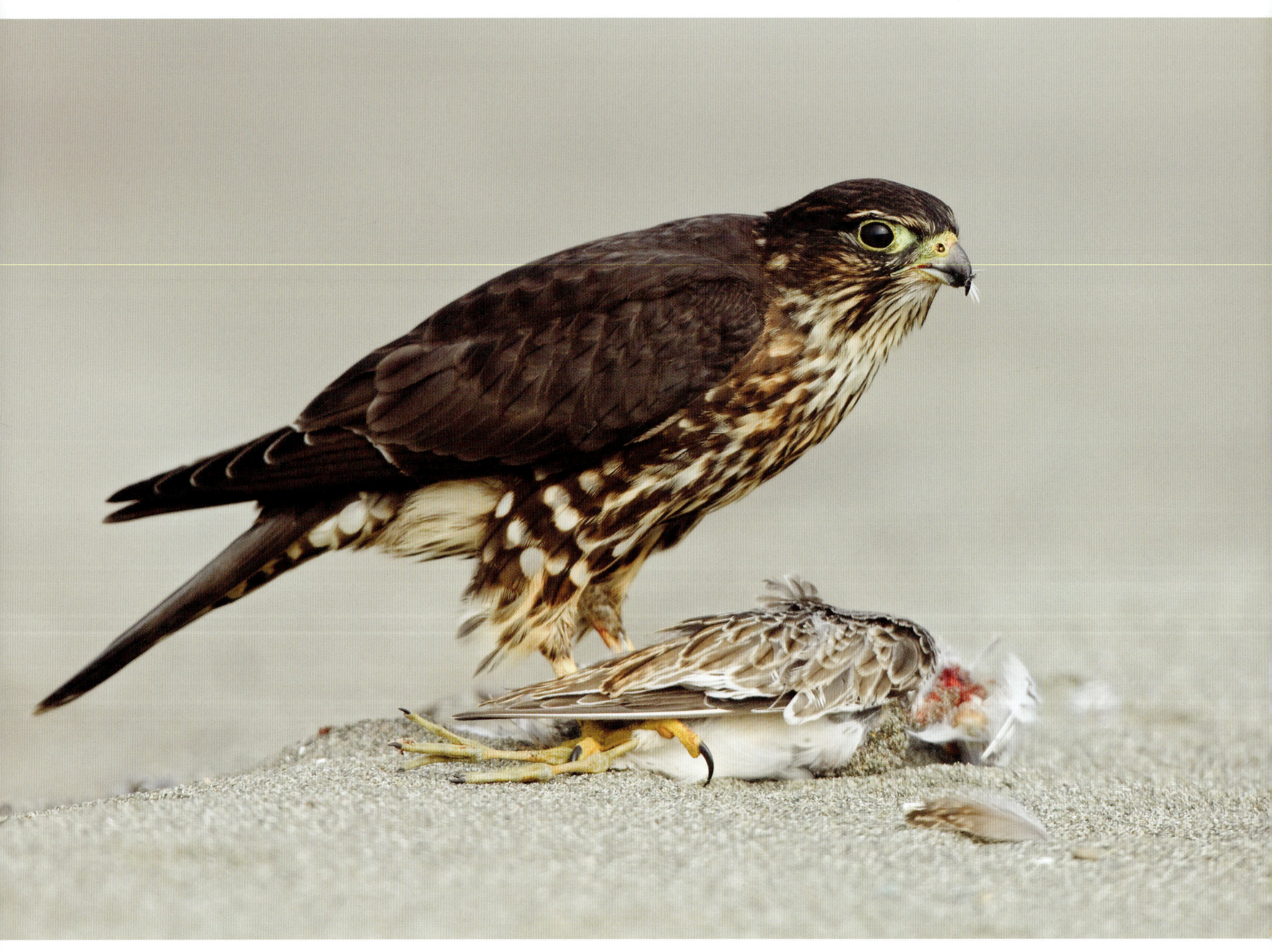

A male Common Goldeneye performs his mating display off the coast of Vancouver Island.

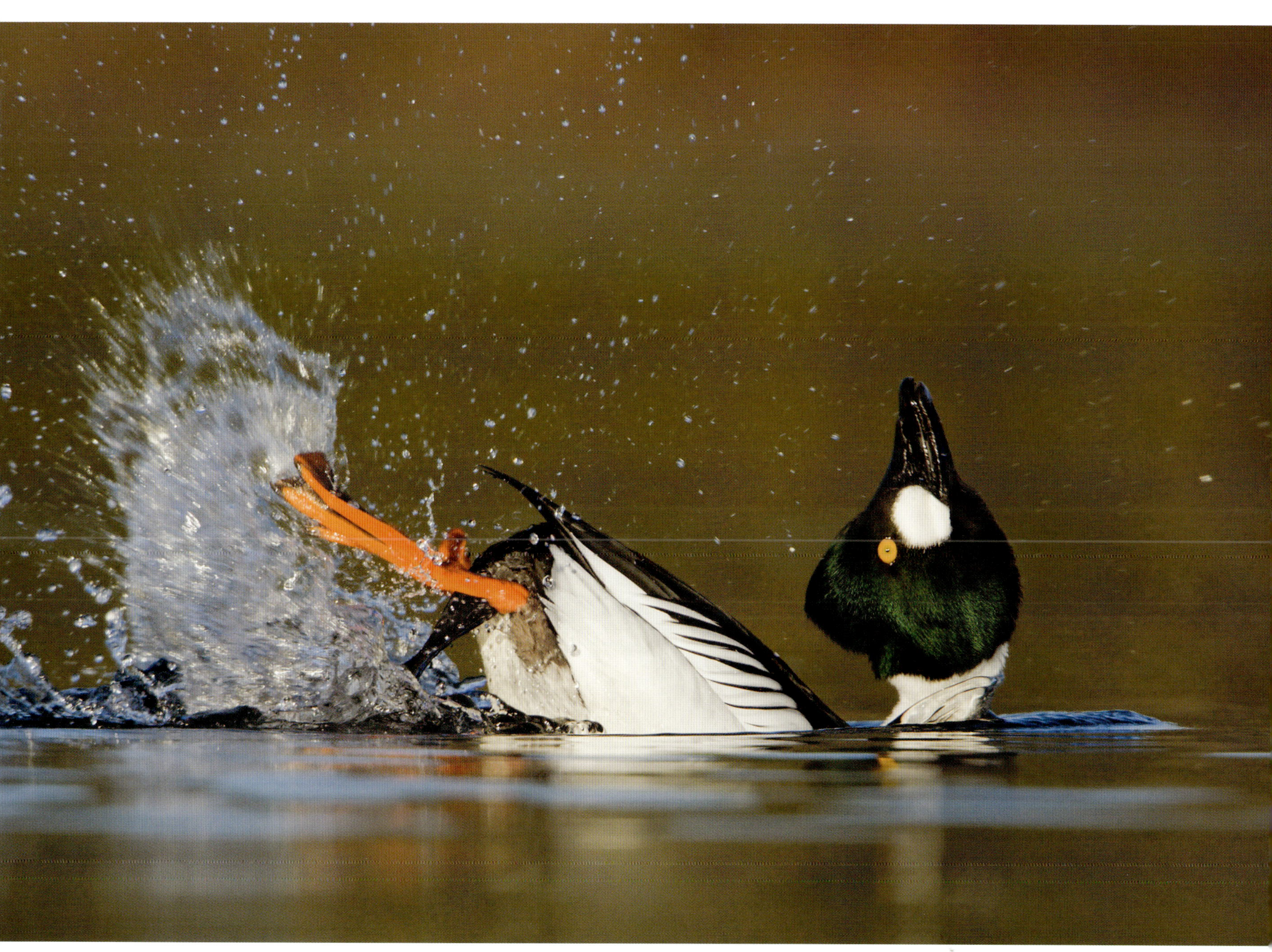

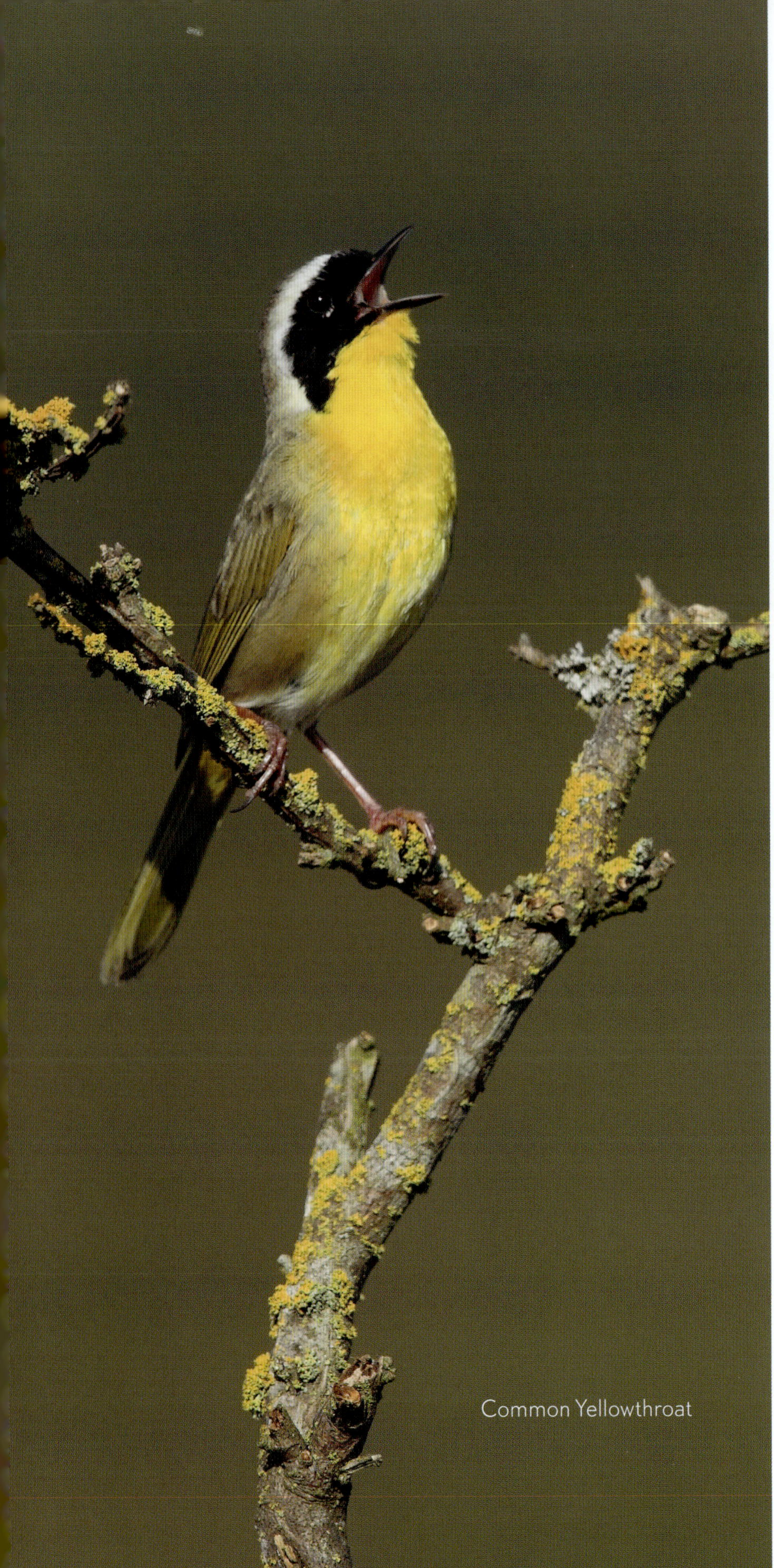
Common Yellowthroat

Acknowledgements

I am very grateful to a number of people who assisted me in the development of this book. In particular I would like to thank:

My parents, David and Shirley, and my brother, Owen, who have always supported me in my goals. I am very fortunate to have such a wonderful family.

All of the naturalists, birders, hikers and fellow photographers who have shared their knowledge and passion with me over the years. I would especially like to thank Dave and Winnie Wake, who helped introduce me to birds and gain an appreciation for them at a young age.

The talented photographers who contributed to this book. While I tried to capture all of the images for this book myself, there were a few photos that I had to ask for assistance. A big thank you to the following photographers:

- Alan Murphy (Tufted Puffin, p. 20 and Great Gray Owl, p. 94)
- Jared Hobbs (Short-eared Owl, p. 29, Sage Thrasher, p. 73 and Flammulated Owl, p. 79)
- Harold Stiver (Boreal Owl, p. 92)
- Matthew Studebaker (Golden-crowned Kinglet, p. 98)
- Jess Findlay (White-tailed Ptarmigan, p. 117)

My publisher, Heritage House, for the opportunity to produce this book and share my images of the birds of British Columbia. In particular, Rodger Touchie (publisher), Vivian Sinclair and Kate Scallion (editors) and Jacqui Thomas (designer) who directly made this book possible.